Women's Place
in the Academy

WOMEN'S PLACE IN THE ACADEMY

Transforming the
Liberal Arts Curriculum

Edited by

Marilyn R. Schuster and Susan R. Van Dyne

SMITH COLLEGE

ROWMAN & ALLANHELD
PUBLISHERS

ROWMAN & ALLANHELD

Published in the United States of America in 1985
by Rowman & Allanheld, Publishers
(a division of Littlefield, Adams & Company)
81 Adams Drive, Totowa, New Jersey 07512

Copyright © 1985 by Rowman & Allanheld

Library of Congress Cataloging in Publication Data
Main entry under title:

Women's place in the academy.

    Bibliography: p.
    1. Education, Humanistic—United States—Curricula—
Addresses, essays, lectures. 2. Women's studies—United
States—Addresses, essays, lectures. 3. Afro-Americans—
Study and teaching (Higher)—United States—Addresses,
essays, lectures. 4. Coeducation—United States—
Addresses, essays, lectures. 5. Attitude change—Addresses,
essays, lectures. 6. Sex discrimination in education
—United States—Addresses, essays, lectures. 7. Higher
education of women—United States—Addresses, essays,
lectures. I. Schuster, Marilyn R. II. Van Dyne, Susan R.
LC1011.W64 1985   375'.0088   84-27566
ISBN 0-8476-7407-X
ISBN 0-8476-7408-8 (pbk.)

85 86 87 / 10 9 8 7 6 5 4 3 2 1
Printed in the United States of America

Contents

Acknowledgments

We are grateful to each of our contributors for the willingness to analyze their institutions, their projects, their colleagues, their courses, and themselves. Their candor and critical self-appraisal testify to their resourcefulness and to their enduring effectiveness as change agents. We'd like to recognize those teachers, administrators, and librarians on each campus whose willingness to become students again makes curriculum transformation happen. Of course, the measure of our shared work is not only anthologies like this one, but the students on each of our campuses who tell us "the difference it makes."

Peggy McIntosh, Director of Faculty and Curriculum Development for the Wellesley College Center for Research on Women, has offered her support for curriculum transformation projects across the country by her participation and through matching funds for consultants. Her determination to engage teachers and institutions in the most comprehensive transformation is a constant spur to the imagination.

Without the encouragement of Martha Ackelsberg and the example of Betty Schmitz, our work would surely have gone more slowly and less well.

Support from the National Consulting Program of the Wellesley College Center for Research on Women contributed invaluable opportunities to test these insights in a variety of institutional settings. Support from the Smith Project on Women and Social Change gave us time to write.

I
Curriculum Transformation: Redefining the Core

1

Curricular Change for the Twenty-First Century: Why Women?

Marilyn R. Schuster and Susan R. Van Dyne

Coherence in the Liberal Arts: Complicating the Questions

The realities of American higher education in the eighties—federal and institutional budget cuts, retrenchment in services and personnel, a highly tenured faculty, a shrinking pool of college applicants, the changing expectations for education and careers of women and men students—have led to the urgent need for a precise definition of the meaning and purpose of the liberal arts. How can we maintain excellence in the liberal arts and prepare students effectively for their lives in the workplace? How can we structure a coherent curriculum after years with few or no "basic" requirements? How can we incorporate vast new areas of knowledge in the curriculum without creating an unwieldy or quickly dated course of studies?

For the first time in history, women represent the majority of the college population. More, a growing percentage of women undergraduates (nearly 20 percent in some institutions) are older returning students. By the year 2000, more than 30 percent of all students in America who may apply to college will be members of so-called "minority" ethnic groups. The challenge these students present to higher education to create a meaningful curriculum is clear.

The case studies collected here focus on institutions, programs, and teachers who have succeeded in designing and implementing new curricular plans that incorporate recent scholarship on women and non-white cultural groups and, in doing so, restore quality and responsibility at the core of the liberal arts curriculum. Further, they show how specific faculty development plans enable highly tenured faculties with little turnover to respond to new learning and to develop new classroom strategies—in short, to become more effective teachers for this new student population.

In the last twenty years more information has been gathered about women's experience than has ever been available. As is the growth of computer science, the explosion of research on women's experience is a revolutionary factor reshaping American education in the final two decades of the twentieth century. The adaptability of the computer to all areas of the curriculum and its transforming effect on what and how we learn are widely recognized by administrators. The need for computer literacy has already spurred faculty-retraining programs on nearly every campus and has been identified in many institutions' core education requirements. The impact of scholarship about women throughout all academic disciplines and on our pedagogy has been steadily growing and may have an even more profound effect than the computer revolution on how we understand human experience, how we organize knowledge, and how we teach our students. As a faculty member observed, "Trying to add material about women to a conventional course is like adding the fact that the world is round to a course based on the assumption that the world is flat."[1] Just as the impact of computer technology can no longer be confined to the math department, the understanding of women's experience in every culture cannot be restricted to separate women's studies courses but has become crucially important to every course in the liberal arts.

Research on women not only has created a new body of knowledge, but is reshaping our understanding of the traditional curriculum: periodization in history, genres in literature, the role of the "private" or "domestic" sphere in politics, and the choice, design, and interpretation of scientific research questions. And yet, by and large, most faculties are not professionally current in this important scholarship and so pass on an incomplete version of human history in their courses. The translation of this information and perspective into the classroom cannot be accomplished merely by good will. Sometimes teachers experience more difficulty and more psychological resistance to understanding women than to learning about computers. Computer literacy programs and writing-across-the-curriculum projects for faculty have demonstrated that institutions need to make long-term commitments to faculty education and to offer substantial incentives and collegial guidance so teachers may gain access to this scholarship and incorporate its insights in courses in every academic field.

The essays in this volume provide the essential theoretical framework and practical strategies for reconstructing a comprehensive liberal arts curriculum for the twenty-first century. The primary focus of each essay is "the difference it makes" to have women in the curriculum. Until recently, material about women's experience entered the curriculum primarily through women's studies courses. The explosion of scholarship on women in the last two decades has led informed administrators and experienced women's studies teachers to undertake transformation of courses throughout the curriculum. The multicultural, interdisciplinary perspective that feminist scholarship has produced in concert with black studies makes us impatient with a curriculum that is predominantly white, male, Western, and heterosexist in its assumptions. In the words of Peggy McIntosh, the study of women, informed by work in black and ethnic studies,

> makes visible many *men* who were not previously featured in the curriculum. In fact, about nine-tenths of the world's population suddenly becomes visible when one takes the emphasis off the public lives of white Western men . . . and includes those who, for reasons of sex, race, class, or national or religious background, were defined as lower-caste.[2]

The partnership of women's and black studies has made possible critiques of the organization of knowledge in the traditional curriculum, of the exercise of power in the classroom, and of the political structures of the institutions in which we operate.

THE CHALLENGE OF DEMOGRAPHIC TRENDS

Administrators are more likely than faculties to acknowledge that the core curriculum of the 1950s no longer adequately serves the student population we must educate for the twenty-first century. The characteristics of the youth cohort, or the pool of potential applicants among traditional-age students, are changing dramatically. By 1990, groups currently designated as minorities in the educational system will represent 30 percent of the youth cohort nationally. In Texas and California, 45 percent of the high school graduates will be members of minority groups in 1990; in New York, the estimate is 32 percent, in New Jersey 28 percent.[3] Educators already question the validity of the designation "minority" and recognize that the traditional curriculum must be altered significantly to attract these students and educate them responsibly.

At the same time, the numbers of traditional-age students have declined and business and the military are competing to provide education for the adult learner. Women, who will represent the largest group of older students returning to college, organize their adult lives in substantially different patterns than in the past. Census statistics have already recorded the demise of the traditional nuclear family: less than 20 percent of the American population make up households in which both parents and two children live together; only 7 percent live in traditional families in which the wife or mother does not work outside the home. In 1980, more than 50 percent of mothers with pre-school children had full or part-time employment. With the life expectancy for women approaching 78, most women can anticipate at least forty years of work in their adult years, even if they spend ten years exclusively in child-rearing. All these statistics demand that we better educate our women and men students for adult lives in a multicultural world in which work will not be a choice, but an economic necessity. Administrators are beginning to recognize that curriculum transformation offers a creative and comprehensive response to these demographic realities.

WOMEN'S STUDIES AND CURRICULUM TRANSFORMATION

Women's studies faculty need to look both inward and outward as we seek to make the curriculum more responsive to women's experience, as we address the intersections of race and class with gender, and as we imagine alternatives to the institutional structures that have excluded women and non-white cultures in the past. Perhaps the central paradox we face is that we are trying to fight the marginalization of women's experience (and issues of race, class, and sexuality) in the academy, and yet it is through our unwanted marginality that we have forged our basic strength. Our vantage point outside the conventional disciplines allows us to see differently and to see more. Few of us would want to reify our marginality, but we should not lose the vitality of the critical stance it provides.

If we are to make higher education more responsible to the students of the last two decades of the twentieth century, we need to reach more than the self-selected group of students who take our women's studies courses, who, by recognizing their needs and interests, are already partially transformed. Further, it seems intellectually irresponsible to allow an increasingly tenured faculty whose primary research will never be on women to continue teaching as though scholarship on women and an informing feminist perspective did not exist.

As the essays in Part I argue, and as all the essays in this anthology bear out, transformation of the academic disciplines and institutional power structures is far from a dilution of women's studies. Transformation does not mean assimilation of the scholarship most compatible with the traditional liberal arts at the expense of difficult issues, such as institutional misogyny, racism, and homophobia. The experience of the past decade and of emerging curriculum transformation projects has shown that effective transformation is impossible without a base of researchers and teachers whose primary concern is women; similarly, women's studies departments and programs become marginalized and risk having little effect on the experience of most students if they are not linked to curriculum transformation projects.

INVISIBLE PARADIGMS

Women's studies has enabled us to see in all areas what we've come to call the "invisible paradigms" of the academic system and the larger cultural context that marginalize or trivialize the lives of all women, the lives of blacks and of ethnic minorities, and those outside the dominant class or culture. Invisible paradigms are the skeletons in the closet of even the most liberal institution or, to use another image to make the invisible visible, the infrastructure of our academic system. For us, the invisible paradigms are the internalized assumptions, the network of unspoken agreements, the implicit contracts that all participants in the process of higher education have agreed to, usually unconsciously, to bring about learning. This infrastructure has worked so long and supported the commerce of higher education so effectively that we no longer see it, notice its presence or, most important, name it for the determining force that it is. Not surprisingly, these invisible paradigms are organized around power (who has it and how we are allowed access to it) and around values (among available choices, what is important and what is best).

Inevitably, invisible paradigms are related to ideology. The more coherent an ideology, the less visible are these paradigms to those who perpetuate them. Because a feminist transformation of the curriculum is often opposed on the grounds that it is ideological, a definition of this often-volatile term is appropriate here. To us it is helpful to regard ideology as a dynamic system of values and priorities, conscious and unconscious, by which men and women organize their actions and expectations and explain their choices.[4] If the reigning ideology of higher education in the past has been pervasively male-defined, the practice and theory of black studies and women's studies proves that it is non-necessary, that other ideologies are possible. Florence Howe contrasts the types of political choices that education implies:

> In the broadest context of that word, teaching is a political act: some person is choosing, for whatever reasons, to teach a set of values, ideas, assumptions, and pieces of information, and in so doing, to omit other[s] . . . If all those choices form a pattern excluding half the human race, that is a political act one can hardly help noticing. . . . To include women with seriousness and vision, and with some attention to the perspective of women as a hitherto subordinate group, is simply another kind of political act.
>
> In a university whose goal is that abstraction called truth, no political act ought ideally to be excluded, if it might shed light on the ultimate goal. And the study of half the human race—the political act we call women's studies—cannot be excluded without obvious consequences to the search for truth.[5]

We've designed this anthology to bring to light as many of the invisible paradigms as possible. In Part I, Susan Kirschner, Jane Monnig Atkinson, and Elizabeth Arch examine the discrepancies between the stated intention of coeducation and the differential educational outcomes for women and men at Lewis and Clark College. They argue that a failure to attend to the gender imbalances in a coeducational curriculum, and to correct those that disadvantage women, means that women do not, in fact, have equal access to educational opportunities. Jeanine Elliott analyzes the historical change in definitions of an appropriate education for women as these have evolved at women's colleges like Stephens. By uncovering the links between educational models designed specifically for women and the range of adult roles considered appropriate in the society that an institution serves, she exposes the obstacles to a fully liberating woman-focused education and identifies strategies for overcoming them.

We believe that by naming these conventions we can begin to recognize that they have been historically constructed and are susceptible to change through conscious effort. Thomas Kuhn and Frederic Jameson have forefronted the presence of paradigms in all our organizations of knowledge.[6] Jameson argues that the history of knowledge is the history of paradigms: as these paradigms age we become aware of their limitations. While a paradigm is young, it functions primarily as a window, bringing realms of new data into view that were previously invisible. As the paradigm ages, we tinker with the lens, trying to correct for the distortions its use entails. In its dotage, a paradigm functions as a mirror; we must face our own presence and involvement in the perspective we have chosen to frame experience. This self-reflexive, final stage in the life of a paradigm prompts a search for new frameworks to organize perception and interpretation. The last twenty years of scholarship on women have brought us to one of the moments when a fundamental paradigm shift must occur.

Identifying the conventions that structure education is the first step toward transformation. We've used the term *transformation* to emphasize that the kinds of curriculum change these essays envision is a paradigm shift of profound dimensions. Other contributors have chosen other terms that are meaningful in their contexts. Margaret Andersen recommends recovering the helpful meanings of the term *integration* developed in the history of the civil rights movement and the evolution of black studies. Thus the integration of material about women and non-white cultural groups would involve multiple strategies for gaining recognition and validation within the traditional curriculum, while maintaining the identity and integrity of this knowledge. Johnnella Butler uses the term *generative process* to stress that a multicultural curriculum is not based on static coexistence but on change that affects all participants. The authors from Wheaton and Lewis and Clark identify their goals as "gender-balancing" their curricula to suggest the advantages that come to both women and men students from a fuller and fairer representation of human experience.

We have identified women-focused study as the proving ground for the most valuable lessons of the last two decades. Through research and teaching that focuses on women we have amassed an unassailable body of scholarship about women in increasingly diverse cultural contexts, have refined strategies for empowering the woman learner, and have developed an analysis of how the structure of education is embedded within other cultural systems; and so we have come to understand the ways that culture may reproduce itself in our syllabi and in our classrooms. In each of these areas, women-focused study has highlighted the importance of gender as a cultural construction (we have preferred to refer to gender throughout these essays rather than to sex). We want to be explicit that these lessons are more valuable the more we learn about all women, and the more careful we become about respecting differences among women rather than asserting commonalities that may prove false. It's important to note that our diverse cultures construct the experience of women differently.

We have tried to be mindful of difference throughout the anthology. In the first section, "Redefining the Core," two essays examine the relationships between women's studies and black studies, because we believe both are central to any definition of curriculum transformation. We all need to be constantly aware of the complexity of gender as a category of analysis, not merely of white women's studies, nor of exclusive attention to middle-class, heterosexual women. We need to be clear that race and class are not merely adjuncts, liberal afterthoughts to a concern for gender, but the essential means for understanding the diversity of women's experience and the experience of other subordinate groups.

These distinctions are important to us, but of course we are not alone in making them. We want to credit all our colleagues involved in the collaborative production of this new knowledge. We've included the experiences of small private institutions and large public universities from each region of the United States, case studies of women's colleges and schools committed to coeducation, the examples of transformed courses in literature, philosophy, social sciences, communications, and biology, and the experience of women and men teachers and of mixed-gender teams. We're glad to be able to include a number of collaboratively written essays; like our own, these represent working partnerships gratefully acknowledged. Characteristically, none of the contributors claims private ownership of these ideas, but each has agreed generously to analyze what others might learn from these individual case histories.

Strategies for Renewal

Our analysis begins with conceptual models for institutional change, compares proven mechanisms for faculty development programs, and ends with the crucible of the classroom. In each area, change has been made possible by the development of specific strategies that will make the curriculum more responsive to students who are female and/or who belong to cultures designated as minorities in the American educational system. The focus and the means for achieving change shift with each strategy: (a) non-sexist, non-racist, non-elitist; (b) sex-equity or affirmative action; and (c) gender, race, and class as categories of analysis. These strategies not only recognize the needs, expectations, and ambitions of the current student population, but also represent the multicultural world in which our students will live and work after they graduate.

The first strategy to evolve was an effort to correct for existing bias. Reviews of the language and images of textbooks, and of teachers' presentation of material, revealed that our educational materials and our teaching habits persistently excluded or trivialized women, and men and women outside the dominant race, class, or culture. This strategy is critical for raising consciousness; as a first step, the concern to become *non-sexist, non-racist, non-elitist* devotes primary attention to monitoring and deleting material that explicitly or implicitly demeans any group and to alerting faculty to possible bias in interactions with students. But to rest satisfied with this strategy alone ignores the possibility that a superficial improvement in unacceptable language or attitudes may camouflage a deeper, unspoken misogyny or racism that may operate in the classroom.

The next strategy attempts to produce *sex-equity or affirmative action* in course materials by adding a representative number of women figures, or a sampling of racial and cultural diversity, to the syllabus. This strategy may, unfortunately, be short-sighted, if a "representative number" from these groups is defined as an approximate ratio to their presence in the current student population. Teachers might more fruitfully ask themselves, does my syllabus recognize that half of human experience has been women's and that the majority of the world's population is not white?

The most transformative strategy employs *gender, race, and class as categories of analysis.* Along with a change in the actual figures on the syllabus, this strategy introduces a shift in the perspective or lens through which we see them. We ask new questions about the course materials and about ourselves as interpreters: How might the variables of gender, race, and class influence the experience, perception, or analysis of each of the items on the syllabus?

Throughout the discussion of the process of curriculum change in these essays, our effort is to demonstrate how each of the three strategies is relevant and necessary to achieve long-term personal and institutional change.

Notes

1.   Janice Monk of the University of Arizona and SIROW, in an unpublished paper.

2.   Peggy McIntosh, of the Wellesley College Center for Research on Women, "The Study of Women: Implications for Reconstructing the Liberal Arts Disciplines," *The Forum for Liberal Education* 4, no. 1 (October 1981): 3 (italics added).

3.   These statistics are reported by Harold L. Hodgkinson in "Guess Who's Coming to College: Your Students in 1990," a report to the National Institute of Independent Colleges and Universities, January 1983. The full report is available for $5.00 from NIICU and was excerpted in *Academe* (March-April 1983): 13–20.

4.   We are indebted to Mary Poovey's definition of ideology in *"Persuasion* and the Powers of Love," in *The Representation of Women in Fiction,* selected papers from the English Institute, 1981, eds. Carolyn Heilbrun and Margaret Higonnet (Baltimore: Johns Hopkins University Press, 1983), p. 178, note 2.

5.   Florence Howe, keynote address to the Wingspread Conference on "Liberal Education and the New Scholarship on Women," October 1982, reprinted as "Feminist Scholarship: The Extent of the Revolution," *Change* (Spring 1982): 20.

6.   See Thomas Kuhn, *The Structure of Scientific Revolutions* (Chicago: University of Chicago Press, 1962), p. 28; and Frederic Jameson, *The Prison House of Language* (Princeton: Princeton University Press, 1972), p. 29.

2

Stages of Curriculum Transformation

Marilyn R. Schuster and Susan R. Van Dyne

If we've learned anything in the last five years' efforts to transform the curriculum to include the experience of women and subordinate cultural groups, it is that we are engaged in a long-term process. While our goals are clear—to be inclusive, to see and respect differences, to recognize political motives in the structures of our knowledge—the results, in terms of concrete products, are still unfinished. The descriptions we offer colleagues are as much hortatory statements of what we must strive for as they are demonstrations of what we have accomplished. Nonetheless, because of the monumental body of scholarship on women that has accumulated in almost every discipline, our vision of a representative curriculum is no longer merely a negative definition of what we must overcome—sexist, racist, or class bias, exclusively patriarchal values, and female students who are invisible in the classroom.

In gaining commitment to these goals from administrators and teachers, we need to counter their impatience for the finished product, their understandably urgent demand for the transformed syllabus, the fully integrated textbook, the inclusive general education requirements, the truly liberal core curriculum. The shape and substance of these products become clearer the more we understand about the process itself. The curriculum, like education, is not static, and our eagerness to have closure, to touch actual products, should not make us forget that because knowledge is historical we will need to revise the curriculum continually.

We first describe the process of undertaking curriculum change because we have learned in our consulting work that individual teachers, planning groups, and institutions may move through the process faster, with less chance of being derailed, if they can anticipate the potential sticking points. While no description or theoretical account can substitute for actual engagement in the task, an intellectual overview can be a key strategy to help those participating in the change process to identify sources of resistance in others and in themselves.

Charting the Change Process

We produce something more dramatic than a ripple effect when we introduce women as subjects of study on a syllabus, when we take seriously the needs and authority of women students, and when we undertake the faculty development necessary to do both successfully. Outlining the evolution of curriculum change efforts reveals many parallels with the directions of the last twenty years of scholarship on women; the insights from that research have altered the content of many academic disciplines. Accumulation of this new data, in turn, generates new questions about the nature of women's experience and that of other groups not currently represented in the traditional syllabus. Because of the important landmarks in that scholarship, and because of the examples of curriculum change projects across the country, we can begin to identify the interactions between research questions and classroom practice that stimulate the transformation of the curriculum.

Our description suggests that teachers move through a sequence of stages, trying a variety of strategies to represent women and minorities adequately in their courses.[1] Yet these stages have fluid boundaries, and individuals may not experience them as a strictly linear progression. It is also unlikely that different groups of teachers within a single institution will move through the same stages at the same time. By organizing the description as a series of stages we illustrate that a range of phenomena are often associated; that raising a particular set of questions leads to similar kinds of curricular outcomes. Even more important, the more the commitments that lead teachers to ask these questions are understood, the more can continued growth among our colleagues be encouraged.

Table 2.1 highlights the major characteristics of the six stages of the change process. Included for each stage are the operative perspective for seeing women's experience, the questions raised about women in order to reconstruct the syllabus, the incentives that motivate faculty and govern their intellectual inquiry and teaching, the means or strategies they use to represent women on the syllabus, and the curricular outcomes, including the types of courses typically generated and the changes in the student's role in her education. In analyzing the sources of resistance to change at each level, we've focused on the obstacles for the teacher and for the student. Our observations are derived from listening to teachers involved in faculty development projects and to those who drop out or refuse to join them.

Stage 1: Invisible Women

In the curriculum of some institutions, the absence of women is simply not noticed. Although this phenomenon was much more common in the 1950s, it is hardly rare today. In fact, it may be the most harmful outcome of the recent push for curricular "coherence" that has moved many faculties in the mid-80s to reinstate a central core of required courses as the heart of a liberal education. To the extent that their search for coherence is nostalgic, faculties may simply reproduce the old orders and alleged civilities of their own undergraduate education rather than undertake a revision of the curriculum that would reflect the state of current knowledge.

A curriculum in which the experiences of women and of nonwhite cultures are entirely absent is not, of course, perceived as regressive or exclusionary by its supporters. Teachers arrested at this stage often claim the existence of indisputable "standards of excellence" and their moral, as well as intellectual, responsibility to maintain them. Excellence, in their definition, implies greatness; and their expectation is that we will all know and recognize

Table 2.1 Stages of Curriculum Change

STAGES	QUESTIONS	INCENTIVES	MEANS	OUTCOME
1. Invisible women	Who are the truly great thinkers/actors in history?	Maintaining "standards of excellence"	Back to basics	* Pre-1960s exclusionary core curriculum * Student as "vessel"
2. Search for missing women	Who are the great women, the female Shakespeares, Napoleons, Darwins?	Affirmative action/compensatory	Add to existing data within conventional paradigms	* "Exceptional" women on male syllabus * Student's needs recognized
3. Women as disadvantaged, subordinate group	Why are there so few women leaders? Why are women's roles devalued?	Anger/Social justice	Protest existing paradigms but within perspective of dominant group	* "Images of women" courses * "Women in politics" * Women's Studies begins * Links with ethnic, cross-cultural studies
4. Women studied on own terms	What was/is women's experience? What are differences among women? (attention to race, class, cultural difference)	Intellectual	Outside existing paradigms; develop insider's perspective	* Women-focused courses * Interdisciplinary courses * Student values own experience
5. Women as challenge to disciplines	How valid are current definitions of historical periods, greatness, norms for behavior? How must our questions change to account for women's experience, diversity, difference?	Epistemology	Testing the paradigms Gender as category of analysis	* Beginnings of integration * Theory courses * Student collaborates in learning
6. Transformed, "balanced" curriculum	How can women's and men's experience be understood together? How do class and race intersect with gender?	Inclusive vision of human experience based on difference and diversity, not sameness and generalization	Transform the paradigms	* Reconceptualized, inclusive core * Transformed introductory courses * Empowering of student

greatness when we are exposed to it. The questions posed at this stage in structuring a syllabus focus on the incomparable individual: "Who are the truly great thinkers, or writers, or actors in history?" Such criteria acknowledge no relativity in these judgments, nor any ideological context surrounding them.

If these values are reminiscent of Matthew Arnold and his father, their most recent incarnation in the American educational system was also influenced by the specific historical and social circumstances following World War II. The core curriculum most of us grew up on, Rhoda Dorsey reminds us, was designed for the predominantly male population returning to college on the G.I. bill.[2] What was regarded as essential knowledge was substantially shaped by both the producers and primary consumers of that education—the influx of fresh male Ph.D.'s who began teaching, even at women's colleges, in the 1950s, and the return of male students in great numbers to the college classroom.

Certainty and simplicity explain the popularity, in current debates, of plans to return to what is, in effect, an exclusionary definition of essential knowledge. The rallying cry "back to basics" rejects the last two decades of curriculum change as frivolous. Proponents of the old core would dismiss as confusing fragmentation the proliferation of women's studies and the diversification of ethnic and cultural studies, and would disparage student-centered learning as a misguided notion of "relevance." Serious students, they maintain, need sterner stuff, which they usually equate with the subjects, and often the very books, they themselves studied twenty or forty years ago. This definition distrusts education as process, and prefers fixed principles of value and judgment and supposedly timeless products.

It is not surprising that teachers who want to provide the "truly great" or "the best that has been thought and known" tend to conceive of their students as waiting vessels. Although the female (or male) student's passivity in this kind of curriculum is often very real, the professor does not imagine himself as exercising power in determining what is valued or regarded as "best," and would probably never admit or even understand that his choices on the syllabus or in the classroom are political or gendered. More likely, he sees himself as the vehicle for transmitting knowledge he imagines to be immutable and apolitical. Many male professors do not notice the absence of women; when a system of priorities, a set of values, or a syllabus serves a group's interests, or at least does not constrain them, members of that group find it very difficult to become aware of the inadequacies of these designs. The number of female professors who still see no inequity or omissions in the male-defined curriculum is even more startling, and serves to underscore dramatically how thoroughly women students may be deceived in believing these values are congruent with their interests.

How can this stage, in which the experience of women is omitted from the definition of essential knowledge, now be maintained or returned to, after twenty years of scholarship on women, the growth of women's studies programs, and the steadily rising proportion of women students in every classroom throughout higher education? It is ironic that women students themselves may unwittingly collude in its perpetuation. When no representation of women's experience appears in the curriculum, a woman student is encouraged to believe the "generic man" includes her. With no basis for comparison, she may erroneously assume that male-derived definitions of "the good, the true, and the beautiful" actually describe her own experience. Student resistance to this male-centered curriculum is surprisingly low; the profound reaction to its omissions occurs, for women, only after graduation.

Stage 2: Search for the Missing Women

Because most colleges pride themselves on a liberal learning environment as much as on their mission to conserve wisdom, committed teachers in Stage 1 raise questions about adding women to the curriculum because they become aware of the needs of women students. The conviction that a woman student needs role models may prompt the teacher to begin a search for the women missing from the curriculum. It is interesting that the number of bright women students who must be present in the classroom to prompt this question is disproportionately large compared to the number who are, even then, believed to constitute an adequate representation on the syllabus.

The search for women figures good enough to be included on the syllabus may be well meaning, but risks being short-lived because of the way questions are raised at this stage: "Who are the great women, the female Shakespeares, Napoleons, Darwins?" The missing women are assumed to resemble the men already present in the traditional curriculum; the criteria by which greatness and excellence are defined remain unexamined. A few women turn up when the syllabus is revised with these expectations, but they exist in isolation from each other, apparent anomalies within their gender.

Those "women worthies" who appear are usually actors in the public sphere—queens, martyrs, suffragists, female novelists with male pseudonyms—women whose outstanding characteristic is their similarity to men. Adding these women to the existing order on the syllabus provides students with the distorted view that women have participated only occasionally in the production of history or culture, or expressed themselves only eccentrically in their writing or behavior. The courses that emerge at this stage of attempted curriculum transformation show women's experience as the "special case" of the larger topic, which is still considered ungendered.

The fair-minded faculty member whose search for worthwhile women to study is guided by resemblances to the established male examples may find less than he had hoped. Most women's histories, recovered in such a search, will not measure up to the preeminent male model: as writers, their production will seem minor in form or scope; as political activists, their participation in the sweep of history will appear sporadic; as representatives of a culture, their significance will seem subordinate or muted; as biological or moral beings, they will appear derivative or flawed. It is important to notice that the "minor status" of most women, considered from this perspective in the change process, is attributed to an individual fault or inadequacy, a personal inability to achieve prominence, genius, or "universal" value. "If only Emily Dickinson had written longer poems, or Jane Austen broader novels; if only that reformer could have championed more than her specifically female causes" are the reasons we hear at this stage for not devoting more days of the semester to women's experience. In other words, the more women's experience and production have differed from men's, the less it will seem worth including in a survey of knowledge structured by male norms.

The very differences that could illuminate the study of both genders bar the admission of all but a few women to the traditional syllabus. The motivation of teachers at this stage is usually a liberal desire for equity within the status quo. Faculty members may become stuck here for some of the same reasons they find it difficult to do affirmative action hiring. All other things being equal, if a teacher must decide whether to choose a familiar male figure or to introduce a new female figure who may be equally relevant or important to the topic on the syllabus, it is less trouble to choose the man. The context of the established syllabus, like the context of the established department, makes it extremely unlikely that the token woman will seem equal to the same things or equal in the same way. Here the danger of regression is serious. To return to the familiar may seem less problematic, they may say, than to include "minor figures just to have some women." A teacher may experience an apparent conflict between his intellectual responsibility to teach the best or most important material in his field and his moral responsibility to include a representative number of women and minorities on the syllabus.

Stage 3: Women as a Subordinate Group

How can teachers overcome this anxiety? The solution, demonstrated in the scholarship about women in every discipline, has been to look beyond the individual and to begin a structural analysis of the experience of women and non-white cultural groups. The type of questions raised by faculty members at this stage shifts dramatically from the terms initially available in the structure of conventional syllabi. Instead of looking only at outcomes (actions, production, or expression) of individual women, the typical questions that move teachers into the next stage of the curriculum change process look for causes: "Why are there so few women leaders? Why are women's traditional roles (or forms of expression) devalued?"

These questions are often provoked by the frustrating search for the missing women. Rather than opting out of the transformation endeavor because of the initially disappointing results, concerned faculty members find themselves moved by extraacademic concerns. Women teachers raise such questions for their women and men students to enable them to seek social justice. Women and men teachers also begin redefining their intellectual responsibility. Rather than a narrowly defined responsibility to a disciplinary canon of great works or great acts, they broaden their inquiry to the historical and cultural context as the means for understanding the results they found at Stage 2. Such a comprehensive understanding of what constitutes their legitimate subject matter is liberating, yet it may create new sources of anxiety. As teachers begin a program of interdisciplinary reading and teaching, they often question their ability to judge work in fields outside their own specialty.

Both teachers and students often report that they feel angry discussing the new questions of Stage 3. The classroom heats up because the material introduced about women begins to reveal the "invisible paradigms" on which the old syllabi rest. The multiple structures of the culture that define women as a disadvantaged or subordinate group begin to emerge. We can readily understand that women students in late adolescence regard as extremely unwelcome the news that their opportunities may be in any way limited; likewise, young male students are uncomfortable with the possibility that male-defined cultural values or systems are unfair. Because most young women and young men have relatively little experience in the adult work world,[3] and because both groups are relatively unconscious of their gender socialization, they are skeptical of a structural analysis that suggests their behavior is either constrained (female) or culpable (male).

Student resistance to courses that focus on a structural analysis of gender asymmetry is quite high. Students, rather than faculty, are more likely to take flight at this stage in the change process. For women students especially, the temptation is great to disassociate themselves from the disadvantages they perceive as defining women as a group. As protection, they may cling to a faith in an "individual solution," the belief that their own merit or worth will be sufficient to overcome the disability of gender. Another reaction may be that such a picture of social reality may be historically true but irrelevant to their own future. Contemporary women students, whether or not they represent a "post-feminist" generation, may believe that the equality of their aspirations will be matched by an equality of opportunities as a result of the women's movement. Instead of becoming mobilized to examine the remaining persistent and pervasive gender inequalities and to work to change them, as their teachers might have hoped, these students, both male and female, may deny that the problem exists.

Despite the difficulties of this stage, we cannot afford to forget the valuable truths about women's experience, relative to men's, that we learned here. The early years of women's studies generated many important courses that examined the representation of women's experience as a subordinate group that continue to be valuable for a transformed curriculum. In literature, these might study "images of women" in the novels of the established canon of male authors, and identify stereotypes such as the virgin and the whore, the earth mother and the castrating bitch. In the social sciences, these courses might examine gender roles in the family and society or differential participation in the paid labor force. A common denominator among these courses is that they were conceived in a spirit of protest against the gender arrangements that shaped women's experience to their disadvantage. Their insights have enabled us to see the paradigms that govern not only our social behavior, but the assignment of values, the criteria for judgment that lead to a male-dominated syllabus. The first wave of women's studies courses brought women as a group (rather than as isolated individuals) onto the syllabus, yet their most striking characteristic was their oppression.

Stage 4: Women Studied on Their Own Terms

Fortunately for us, the history of women's studies and of black studies offers proven strategies for overcoming both the anger and disbelief of Stage 3. Black studies gave women's studies another perspective that has made possible the kind of curriculum transformation we are currently envisioning. We have learned from black studies that slavery was the most salient feature of black experience only from the narrow perspective of the dominant group and in a North American context. To study black experience in its own terms it was necessary to step outside the paradigms of the dominant group or the framework of the androcentric, white, Western syllabus, and attempt to adopt an "insider's" perspective. What became visible was the range and diversity of black experience, including forms of resistance to oppression and various sources and strategies for exercising power. Rather than focusing on cultural subordination, the evolution of black studies demonstrated that the multicultural realities of black experience could be articulated on their own terms.

The second major movement in women's studies courses and in feminist scholarship, especially in the humanities and the social sciences, has been to delineate the character of women's experience as women themselves have expressed it. This stage is crucial to successful transformation of traditional courses because only through developing women-focused courses do we discover the data we need to draw a full picture of human experience. This stage takes as its premise the eye-opening declaration of Gerda Lerner that "to document the experience of women would mean documenting all of history: they have always been of it, in it, and making it. . . . half, at least, of the world's experience has been theirs, half of the world's work and much of its products."[4] Rather than disappointment, disbelief, or anger, the participants in this stage of the change process, teachers and students alike, experience a liberating intellectual excitement, a sense of expanding possibilities.

For teachers, whole new fields of inquiry are opened; new areas for research, publication, and professional renewal become available. The compelling motivation most frequently described by teachers who have entered this stage is a voracious intellectual appetite: "What was and is women's experience, known as a subject rather than object? What differences among women, such as race, class, and culture, have contributed to their identities?" This stage produces the careful cross-cultural comparisons that will complicate the questions we ask about the dimensions of women's experience and that will enable us to avoid inaccurate generalizations about "all women" derived from a limited sample. Attention to race and class also brings into view the experience of most men who had been absent from the syllabus. As Peggy McIntosh argues, the determination to recover the experience of subordinate groups will give us access not just to women but to "about nine-tenths of the world's population . . . who for reasons of sex, race, class, national or religious background, were defined as lower-caste."[5]

Women students are attracted to the new material and new perspective because this stage of curriculum development can provide informed access to their own experience, and the means for valuing what they have lived. When we develop courses that focus on the actual experience of ordinary women, we often find illuminating patterns that allow us to understand, for instance, the politics of domestic life, or the artistic characteristics of non-canonical forms, such as letters and journals, or of collective or folk forms, such as quilts. Just as a female student may be inspired by the example of the extraordinary woman, the "women worthies" studied in Stage 2, she learns to reflect more self-consciously on her own daily behavior and her choices for self-expression by studying the wealth of nontraditional materials made visible in Stage 4.

Stage 5: Women as a Challenge to the Disciplines

What we learn in Stage 4 is too important to keep to ourselves, or to study with only a limited group of self-selected students in women-focused courses. The accumulation of data gathered from the insider's perspective causes us to question in profound ways the frameworks that organize our traditional courses: "How valid are current definitions of historical periods, standards of greatness or excellence, norms for behavior? How must the organizing questions of each academic discipline change to account for the diversity of gender, race, and class?" Teachers who have spent some time developing women-focused courses or who have read extensively in the scholarship on women are the most likely to undertake the most thorough form of curriculum transformation: testing the paradigms that have conventionally organized knowledge on the syllabus to exclude or marginalize women and other subordinate groups. In personal terms, the move from women-focused study to transformation of the conventional curriculum is inevitable, because most of us as teachers inhabit both worlds and must necessarily question how what we learned by studying women bears on the other courses we teach.

In institutional terms, the movement from women's studies to integrating or transforming the core curriculum is rarely seen as a natural or necessarily welcome outgrowth. When faculty members

who have enjoyed a Stage 1 curriculum for most of their professional lives are asked the questions typical of Stage 5, they often
feel that not only their own credentials are in doubt, but the
worth and integrity of their academic disciplines. Perhaps
because questioning the paradigms we use to perceive, analyze,
and organize experience pointedly asks not only what we know
but how we came to know it, the intellectual investment on both
sides of the debate may be higher than at earlier points in the
process of change. Even those who are willing to admit the validity of the feminist critique of the disciplines—that periodization
in history does not mark the significant changes in women's
estates, that canons of great art and literature are derived from
and reinforce male practice as most valuable, that the scientific
method defines objectivity in androcentric rather than gender-
neutral terms—may resist the deconstruction of their own discipline.

Underneath the wide variety of expressions of resistance is a
residual fear of loss, a reluctance to give up what had seemed
most stable, efficient, authoritative, transcendent of contexts, and
free of ideological or personal values—in short, a fear that feminist criticism means a loss of subject matter and methodology with
no compensating gain. "If the current systems are flawed," we
often hear, "they at least serve us better than no system at all.
When feminists can offer us a workable alternative, then we'll
consider reconceiving the total design of the syllabus."

In 1980, Catharine Stimpson characterized the first five years of
scholarship in *Signs* as "the deconstruction of error" and
identified the next major task as "the reconstruction of theory."[6]
Yet the very tools that allowed us to document the errors have
already provided the strategies for an alternative construction of
the syllabus. To allay the fears of wholesale loss, and to demonstrate that feminist theory has moved beyond merely offering a
critique, those engaged in curriculum transformation need to be
explicit about the ways that gender as a category of analysis
enriches and illuminates traditional subjects, including the experience of elite white men. Using gender, race, and class as primary
categories of analysis will transform our perspective on familiar
data and concepts as well as reveal new material to be studied.

How is this possible? All the earlier stages of feminist analysis and curriculum change have highlighted the operation of gender as a principle for exclusion or subordination of material on the syllabus. If the conventional syllabus purported to be gender-neutral or gender-free, we now recognize that it is inevitably and pervasively gendered. Recognizing the gendered nature of all texts allows us to recuperate material that, in our earlier anger, seemed corrupt or false and to teach it in a new light. Having uncovered the error that most material on the conventional syllabus is derived from male experience yet is erroneously generalized to represent the human condition, we might, nonetheless, agree that these are helpful descriptions of what it means to be male and of a certain race and class at a certain moment in history. Stage 5 unequivocally means a loss of old certainties, but the gains are the recovery of meaningful historical and social context, the discovery of previously invisible dimensions of the old subjects, and access to instruments of analysis (gender, race, and class as significant variables) that expose strata of formerly suppressed material.

Stage 6: The Transformed Curriculum

What paradigms would make it possible to understand women's and men's experience together? What would a curriculum that offers an inclusive vision of human experience and that attends as carefully to difference and genuine pluralism as to sameness and generalization actually look like? Although we possess the tools of analysis that allow us to conceive of such an education, we can't, as yet, point to any institution that has entered the millenium and adopted such a curriculum. What would exist there would depend on the recognition that any paradigm is historical and that no one framework is likely to serve for all time. This stage promotes process rather than immutable products and fixed principles.

Our descriptions so far resemble an ideal frame of mind, a hypothetical state, more than they promise a syllabus we could distribute to classes next term. Perhaps the greatest danger at this stage is the impatience for a concrete product. Administrators and teachers who are persuaded that the curriculum could be improved by more equitable representation of gender, race and class, often underestimate the time it will take. Gerda Lerner has suggested that if patriarchy has held sway for more than 2000 years, we should not be surprised if, in a discipline like history, it takes several dozen women scholars, fully funded for the length of most grants, even to imagine the categories that would have to change to bring this curriculum into being.[7]

While the goal of a Stage 6 curriculum is often readily assented to, the means may seem too costly or cumbersome. Many well-meaning college presidents and deans wish to move directly from Stage 1 to Stage 6 with no allocation of resources nor enduring, clear commitment to women-focused study. They are tempted to believe that the promised land can be attained without passing through the difficult terrain of women's studies. Some curriculum change projects risk foundering because good intentions, especially of administrators who want to sponsor programs that will be perceived as apolitical, are substituted for the expertise developed by those who have taught and contributed to the scholarship on women. It would be an intellectual mistake of monumental proportions to believe that we can do without or bypass women-focused study in the name of the greater good of the transformed or "gender-balanced" curriculum. The vital work of Stage 4, studying women on their own terms, generates the transformative questions that stimulate the change process as well as provide the data and alternative paradigms that inform the whole continuum of curriculum transformation we have described.

We'd like to propose some of the elements that would characterize a transformed course. We've intentionally included the teacher's and student's relationship to the changed subject matter and to each other as crucial ingredients. A transformed course would

- be self-conscious about **methodology** and use gender as a category of analysis, no matter what is on the syllabus (even if all males);
- present changed content in a **changed context** and be aware that all knowledge is historical and socially constructed, not immutable;

- develop an **interdisciplinary perspective,** to make visible the language of discourse, assumptions of a field, and analytical methods by contrast with other fields;
- pay meaningful attention to intersections of **race, class, and cultural differences within gender,** and avoid universalizing beyond data;
- study new subjects in their **own terms,** not merely as other, alien, non-normative, and non-Western, and encourage a true **pluralism;**
- **test paradigms** rather than merely "add on" women figures or issues, and incorporate analysis of gender, race, and class by a thorough reorganization of available knowledge;
- make student's experience and **learning process** part of the explicit content of the course thereby reaffirming the transcendent goals of the course; and
- recognize that, because **culture reproduces itself in the classroom,** the more conscious we are of this phenomenon, the more likely we are to turn it to our advantage in teaching the transformed course.

Notes

1. We are indebted, in developing our description of the stages of curriculum transformation, to the work of Gerda Lerner, who detailed the new questions raised by the study of women's history in her 1975 essay "Placing Women in History: Definitions and Challenges," in *The Majority Finds Its Past: Placing Women in History* (New York: Oxford University Press, 1979), and to Peggy McIntosh, who analyzes the effect of a changing curriculum on women's lives in a moving narrative, *Interactive Phases of Curricular Re-Vision: A Feminist Perspective* (Working Paper No. 124, Wellesley College Center for Research on Women, 1983), and to Mary Kay Tetreault, Elizabeth Arch, and Susan Kirschner of Lewis and Clark College, whose scale of disciplinary change reflects interviews with participants in their 1981 faculty seminar, "Measuring the Impact of Faculty Development in Women's Studies" (unpublished paper presented at the conference of the National Women's Studies Association, Humboldt, Calif., 1982).

2. Goucher College president Rhoda Dorsey, in her remarks at the opening panel of college presidents at the Skidmore College Conference "Towards Equitable Education for Women and Men: Models from the Last Decade," 11 March 1983.

3. Of course, some students have always worked; students at public institutions are more likely than the privileged, mostly white population of elite schools to have experienced at first hand the gender inequalities in the workplace. Such experience may ready them for a feminist structural analysis, or only reinforce their sense that these pervasive inequalities are "natural."

4. Gerda Lerner, *The Female Experience: An American Documentary* (Indianapolis: Bobbs-Merrill, 1977), p. xxi.

5. Peggy McIntosh, "The Study of Women: Implications for Reconstructing the Liberal Arts Disciplines," *The Forum for Liberal Education* 4, no. 1 (October 1981): 3.

6. Catharine Stimpson, originally in a talk for the Smith College Project on Women and Social Change, Smith College, Northampton, Mass., 12 March 1980.

7. Gerda Lerner, in a comment at the Wingspread Conference "Liberal Education and the New Scholarship on Women: Issues and Constraints," sponsored by the Association of American Colleges, October 1981.

3

Reassessing Coeducation

Susan Kirschner,
Jane Monnig Atkinson, and
Elizabeth Arch

How Equal Is Coeducation?

Historically, coeducational colleges in America have assumed one of three forms.[1] Some have educated women and men in the same institution under separate curricula. Oberlin, the first coeducational college in the United States, established different curricula for its male and female students as early as the 1850s. Other colleges and universities followed Oberlin's example. Florence Howe cites an 1874 announcement by the president of Kansas State University that his institution offered "three streams for students to choose from: agriculture, mechanics, and women's."[2] A second pattern followed by some institutions has educated women and men in coordinate colleges; examples are Radcliffe and Harvard, Barnard and Columbia, and Spelman and Morehouse. But most coeducational schools today fall into a third category comprised of institutions that claim to offer an identical education to women and men within the same college and the same curriculum.

Lewis and Clark College is a small liberal arts college in the Pacific Northwest. From its beginnings in 1867 as Albany College, it has characterized itself as coeducational. What was meant by that term in those early years can be gleaned from this centennial history of the college:

> The student body numbered eighty-six, forty-three women and forty-three men. Albany always received women on equal terms with

men, never keeping them separate in academic work or making special rules for them, as in some neighboring colleges. Both were "scholars" or students, and often the scholastic records of the women were higher than those of the men. The only concession made to the women was that English might be substituted for higher mathematics.[3]

Thus, from the start Lewis and Clark fit the third model of coeducation, with the one significant exception. And over a century later, in 1981, Lewis and Clark still prided itself on being an institution that provided an equal education for both women and men within a single curriculum.

But a report to the college in 1982 entitled "The Issue of Gender in the Lewis and Clark Curriculum" suggested a different picture; in actuality more than one curriculum operated at the college. The report detailed how women and men were receiving different educations within what was considered a single curriculum, and were partaking of college experience in divergent ways. ("Curriculum" included the courses students elected, the majors they chose, their off-campus study and work opportunities, and the extracurricular activities that together represented their full undergraduate education.)

What had been the "only concession" of the 1860s was in effect being reproduced on a wider scale not by official dictate, but by student choices within the curriculum. Men were gravitating to the sciences, business administration, political science and economics, while women were concentrated in the humanities, the "softer" social sciences of psychology and sociology, and in one science, biology, which at Lewis and Clark is heavily weighted toward environmental studies. What is more, the International Programs, believed to be outstanding at the college, showed considerably more women than men availing themselves of opportunities for intercultural learning. By contrast, the executive ranks of student government were dominated by men. Thus, although Lewis and Clark in theory offered a single curriculum to all students, differential participation in the curriculum by gender raised important questions about whether we were realizing our mission to provide equal education to women and men. We argued that a truly liberal education should involve students in all areas of the curriculum in ways that replace apprehension with comprehension. And we asked whether the institution was doing enough to challenge students to examine their presuppositions, biases, and fears in certain areas. Given the patterns of course selection we found, the institution could in effect be systematically disadvantaging many of its women students as well as some of its men.

In her discussion of Oberlin College's formerly sex-segregated curriculum, Florence Howe explores the unstated links between education and the larger society:

> Oberlin was founded to train ministers on the frontier who could not afford the relatively expensive colleges on the East Coast. The women students were important to the domestic arrangements of this young community in the wilderness of Ohio; but they certainly were not going to be ministers. Why then were they studying? There had been a special curriculum designed for them, minus the Greek but with English Literature. . . . Why had they come? Why were they taught? It is a puzzling question until you consider that ministers on the frontier (or anywhere else, perhaps) need wives who are able to work with them.[4]

In other words, Oberlin provided the appropriate education for ministers' wives preparing "to be better mothers and . . . teachers of young children."[5]

At that time, what was appropriate in the preparation of men at Oberlin was not necessarily seen as appropriate for women. Not only were their studies different, but their participation within the intellectual community was constrained as well. For example, at commencements, women were not permitted to "orate" the written essays that they, like their male counterparts, were required to prepare: a male professor read their essays for them. Even when that rule was changed in the 1850s, they could only read their essays, not "orate" like the men.[6] And just as the formal curriculum was bifurcated by gender, so extracurricular activity also channeled women and men in different paths. All students worked at Oberlin, both to support themselves and to keep the institutional costs down. But women had no classes on Mondays, because "Mondays were laundry days, and women washed, ironed and mended the men's clothes."[7] They also cleaned men's rooms and waited on them at meals.[8]

The Oberlin curriculum represented a nineteenth-century effort to prepare women for a particular and limited social niche. It also channeled women and men into different courses that reinforced the nineteenth-century split between the public and domestic spheres. From that time on, liberal feminists, including Lucy Stone (an Oberlin graduate), sought to remove the barriers restricting women to domestic roles and to promote equal educational opportunities. For years this meant granting women access to the same curriculum as men in either coeducational or separate women's institutions. But could it be that a coeducational curriculum in the 1980s unintentionally contains a tacit and unacknowledged women's curriculum that functions to limit women in ways similar to Oberlin in the 1850s? The Lewis and Clark 1982 report revealed that this might well be the case and proposed a feminist alternative for what coeducation within a single curriculum could be.

An alternative approach to rethinking contemporary coeducation—one that we advocate—is to offer women and men equal access to the same curriculum, and at the same time to ensure that the curriculum is not limited to male-defined values and concerns. In other words, it is necessary not only to encourage women to participate fully in the curriculum with men, but also to rethink the curriculum in light of both men's and women's experience and perspectives. Feminists have been working toward this end at Lewis and Clark. This essay describes our efforts to date and devotes special attention to the strategies we applied to this endeavor.

Redefining Coeducation

WHERE ARE THE WOMEN?

Prior to 1981, Lewis and Clark gave precious little attention to women, women's studies, or feminist concerns. The general policy statements of the institution mentioned neither women nor gender, nor did the institutional reports prepared for accreditation purposes five years earlier. There was no women's studies program; the affirmative action policy was weak (full-time women faculty hovered steadily under 20 percent); and only a handful of diverse courses on women was scattered through the curriculum. Although feminist faculty and students occasionally worked together to plan lectures and symposia that aroused interest and enthusiasm, such efforts were sporadic. And while faculty and students both recognized the need for better organization to confront a variety of issues—from sexual harassment to affirmative action, maternity leave, and day care—they failed to sustain interest long enough to accomplish any lasting results. In short, prior to 1981 there had been no effective challenge to the institution's complacent neglect of women's issues.

The first obstacle to be overcome, then, was institutional lethargy. The catalyst for doing so was a faculty seminar on women's studies held at the college in the summer of 1981. A National Endowment for the Humanities grant to the college supported faculty development to increase expertise in cross-disciplinary and cross-cultural approaches that were to form the basis of a new program in general education. Coincidentally, a visit to the campus by historian Gerda Lerner in the spring of 1980 had aroused considerable interest among members of the college community, including Irene Hecht and David Savage, both historians and associate deans of faculty. Savage was also in charge of the NEH grant. As a result of Lerner's visit and encouragement from Hecht, Savage selected women's studies as the topic for the faculty development seminar to be held in 1981.

The seminar brought together women and men faculty who differed widely in academic rank, discipline, politics, and previous acquaintance with feminist scholarship. The seminar itself offered participants an intense month of reading, lectures, discussions, and course planning with four visiting scholars—Susan Contratto (psychology), Florence Howe (literature), Carolyn Lougee (history), and Michelle Rosaldo (anthropology)—and each other. Although faculty found "being a student again" difficult and the entire process exhausting, the seminar provided participants with an opportunity to immerse themselves in the materials and to work collectively with others. And since feminist scholarship suggests innumerable links to social issues, it is not surprising that the participants found the basis for a common commitment to changing both the curriculum and the wider institutional context in which it operated.

Some members of the seminar focused on an immediate social agenda—to change the institution's performance on affirmative-action hiring or sexual harassment. Others found the intellectual issues of rethinking academic disciplines more compelling. At the end of the seminar, the group decided to meet in the fall to organize and begin working to effect curricular and institutional change. Developments since that time have stemmed directly from the commitments and actions of this group.

INSTITUTIONAL CONSCIOUSNESS-RAISING

The initial problem was how to gain serious institutional attention to feminist issues. A potential solution came in the form of a long-range planning process initiated by a new college president to reexamine institutional goals and priorities. Galvanized by promising opportunities for change, our diverse assortment of seminar participants, aided by some new feminists on the faculty, put aside political and personal differences to work together as an effective lobbying group. To the surprise of all, we made significant strides in a relatively short span of time.

In preparation for a faculty retreat, the first step in the long-range planning process, the group met regularly to plan strategies for institutional "consciousness-raising." Strategies included adding articles on women's studies to the packets of reading distributed to faculty before the retreat; ensuring that one of the lobbyists was present in each small-group discussion during the retreat; and preparing those representatives to raise questions about the coeducational nature of the institution and its differential effects on women and men. Because of this careful planning, and perhaps because no other faculty interest group was as effectively organized, integrating women's studies into the curriculum emerged from the voting at the end of the retreat as a top institutional priority.

The consequences of this vote were far-ranging because it legitimated the issue and empowered what came to be known as the Women's Issues Group to press for institutional attention to gender issues. Although the faculty as a whole did not move immediately to transforming courses, increasing awareness improved the climate for learning, especially among women students. The president of the college established task forces on sexual harassment and affirmative action, both of which resulted in new institutional policies. Also, a highly successful annual women's studies symposium was inaugurated to bring feminist scholars to campus and to provide a forum for students and faculty to present work focused on women. And most significant for the process of curricular change, the acting dean of faculty, David Savage, commissioned two Women's Issues Group members, Susan Kirschner and Jane Atkinson, to prepare the 1982 report with recommendations for integrating the new scholarship on women into the curriculum.

Gender-Balancing the Curriculum

From the start, we defined our task in terms of gender issues, not women's issues. This focus derived in part from our theoretical predispositions[9] and in part from our recognition of the need for a strategy that might win over colleagues and students who might be threatened by the prospect of women-focused study. As faculty members grounded in the humanities, we searched for a term that could comfortably include our view that integrating the curriculum meant including works by and questions about women in the content of any course, as well as any different and yet-to-be-discovered approaches from other disciplines and departments.

In addition, initial evidence on differential use of the curriculum by women and men suggested that factors outside the curriculum might be just as important to consider as the curriculum itself. We needed an unthreatening term to designate our comprehensive concerns—one that could cover both the curricular integration of women's studies and an exploration of the curriculum, faculty, and students within a wider institutional perspective. With suitable apologies for awkwardness of phrase, we chose "gender-balancing the curriculum." To us the phrase "underscore[d] the fact that integrating the new scholarship on women involves a better understanding of both women and men, and the systems in which they participate"[10] and offered us sufficient flexibility to consider all factors (both internal and external to the institution) that might affect the ways in which male and female students approach and experience the curriculum. We also hoped the term might act as a strategy to free our audience from preconceived notions or biases about women's studies. (This tactic may have helped to win the report a fair hearing.)

Throughout our work we appealed to colleagues representing diverse ideological and methodological positions with the suggestion that attention to gender and to feminist scholarship (which we always phrased as "the new scholarship on women") could benefit them as both teachers and scholars. As part of our efforts to gauge the willingness of faculty members to undertake curriculum change, to broaden the base of our political support, and to disseminate information about scholarship on women, we conducted interviews with faculty members in nearly all the academic departments (missing a few only because it was summertime) with the announced goal of gathering information about personal and disciplinary perspectives on gender.

Our interviews were deliberately open-ended. We asked how gender issues were or might be incorporated into departmental courses, what differences our informants had noted in their teaching and advising of women and men, and how feminist scholarship had or had not made itself felt in their fields. Inquiries led to fascinating insights into everything from institutional history to sexual harassment. We felt at various times like institutional analysts, psychotherapists, and provocatrices. Most of our colleagues were receptive, at least on the surface, and some were downright enthusiastic. A few expressed skepticism and concern about the "feminization" of their disciplines. (It is interesting that this was a worry not in the sciences, but in some of the "harder" social sciences.) In general, our interviews seemed to generate good will and perhaps contributed to a sense of collaboration and "ownership" on the part of our informants, whose names were listed in an appendix to our report.

In addition to faculty, we interviewed a number of administrators. We did so because our intuition and our preliminary data suggested that the ways students use the curriculum were linked to more general experiences at the institution and in society. Thus we sought information about college admissions, financial aid, career planning and placement, counseling, residence halls, campus programs, international programs, and alumni/ae, as well as academic support provided by the library, writing and math skills centers. In each case, we asked informants for their perspectives on any differences they might note in the experience of women and men at the college.

We also collected statistical data from the administrative offices. Much of this concerned information on student majors and student participation in curricular and extracurricular activities. The difficulty we encountered in collecting statistics in a form that could be analyzed with sophistication and accuracy (a number of major institutional reports had not considered gender in their evaluations) was in itself an interesting finding. We strongly recommended that future planning for long-term institutional research include gender as one factor for analysis.

The interview materials and figures allowed us to demonstrate in the 1982 report that, in actuality, more than one curriculum was operating at the college. While in theory a single curriculum was in effect, a consistent pattern emerged to show that students might well experience the curriculum differently according to gender. The distribution of female and male graduates across the majors over a five-year period showed a significant weighting by gender. Some of our informants suggested that many students majored in particular fields not by active choice, but by default because of fears of deficiencies in quantitative or verbal skills. While we granted that cultural expectations within the family and in earlier schooling contributed greatly to the college patterns we found, one function of higher education has traditionally been to challenge the effects of unconscious socialization. We believed Lewis and Clark's obligation was to provide a truly liberal education that would engage students in all areas of the curriculum. How could we end this unconscious gender-segregation?

CROSS-GENDER COMPETENCE: RETHINKING COURSES

Given our original charge to recommend means for integrating the new scholarship on women into the curriculum, many of the faculty were surprised that our recommendations came down as heavily as they did on math and science literacy for women students. But it became apparent from the figures (including math proficiency scores for entering students) and from the interviews that the college was allowing large numbers of women and some men to graduate without the skills that would allow them to fulfill their aspirations. Significantly, equal numbers of female and male students visit the Career Planning and Placement Center, which suggests that both women and men are anticipating professional careers. Quantitative skills and computer literacy are fast becoming a *sine qua non* for most career tracks. Unless we intervened to promote students' belief that they had genuinely equal access to the full range of the college's resources, the institution was failing to educate adequately nearly half its population for the adult lives they planned.

The report offered a variety of suggestions regarding ways to promote math and science literacy, including integration of science and humanities in the college's required courses in general studies, exploration of new ways of teaching science and math, and greater emphasis on science as part of the liberal arts. In addition to integrative measures, the report proposed a variety of remedial measures, including expansion of the Math Skills Center and perhaps some compensatory non-credit courses offered on an experimental basis. In this section of the report, the interviews were crucial not only for identifying the problems, but for generating ideas for their solution.

As feminists, we felt somewhat uncomfortable focusing much of our report on female deficiencies in the areas of math and sciences. But the comparable disadvantage that some men face in language and writing skills was already offset at Lewis and Clark by a very effective Writing Center and by a "writing across the curriculum" approach to develop student abilities in writing. Evidence did suggest, however, that fewer men than women were developing proficiency in foreign languages, and that women, far more than men, participate in the fine international studies program available through the college. In this way, the report counterpointed male and female weaknesses and proposed that a truly gender-balanced curriculum would mitigate both these trends.

GENDER AND THE EDUCATIONAL CLIMATE:
RETHINKING INTERACTIONS

As well as focusing on curricular issues, the report considered a series of concerns loosely defined as "educational climate." Since the notion of gender-balancing had been formulated with reference to the need for understanding both women and men and the systems in which they participate, it followed that consideration of gender at Lewis and Clark should include discussion of the ways in which women and men students experience the institution differently. For example, while involvement in student activities is high for both sexes at Lewis and Clark, policy-making positions in student government are typically dominated by male students, despite conscious efforts by staff in the Dean of Students' division to encourage women to run for office. Since student affairs is an area in which male and female students can develop important skills of leadership and cooperation, we found it significant and troubling that this coeducational institution harbored a tendency to replicate rather than challenge the inequities of the wider society.

In another area, we reported on startlingly frank discussions with both male and female faculty members that revealed some of the subtle and not-so-subtle ways in which teachers' interactions with students can differentially shape students' experience of the institution. For example, several male teachers volunteered that they were in fact intimidated by women students. (When asked, several others concurred.) One male faculty member confessed that he preferred to avoid office meetings with women. Others noted that they enter easily into friendships with male students, but avoid forming such relationships with female students. Three informants, two men and one women, noted that they have been easier on women in their classes. By contrast, several women faculty claimed to push their women students harder because they felt that men get such motivation elsewhere. Clearly, such attitudes have educational and professional consequences. If, in fact, some male faculty members avoid encounters with women outside of class, women may be at a disadvantage in seeking academic advice from a predominantly male faculty. They may also be excluded from the kind of collegial relationship with their mentors that could help them professionally. And if professors hold back in challenging women students, are those students adequately prepared for work in a competitive climate after graduation?

This part of the report was strategically designed to serve a consciousness-raising function. Contradictory and conflicting comments from both male and female faculty members were listed to give some sense of the variety and range of attitudes and kinds of interactions. To allay fears that a monolithic code of behavior was being demanded, we emphasized that there should be ample room for a variety of teaching and professional styles. But we stressed that whatever style particular teachers preferred, care should be taken to ensure that the choice not adversely affect either sex. Appended to the report was a copy of "The Classroom Climate: A Chilly One for Women?" prepared by Bernice Sandler.[11] While some faculty members found the documentation of the classroom climate tedious, others, including some who had never thought through the issues, declared the article helpful. For at least one male professor, who confessed to serious problems in dealing with women students, it proved to be an epiphany. Our treatment of relations between teachers and students seemed to generate support for the new task force studies of sexual harassment and affirmative action.

Gender and a Liberal Education—Maintaining Visibility

The summary of the report was designed to anticipate a charge that the gender imbalances we had discovered are rooted in society at large and that consequently little could be done at the college to change them. We stated that it is essential for an institution dedicated to critical inquiry and to coeducation to do more than passively reproduce existing social patterns. Women's studies, we suggested, presents a challenge to think creatively and well about the mission of a coeducational liberal arts college. In the final section we presented a list of recommendations for an institution seeking to be fully coeducational (appendix to this essay).

By drawing to the attention of the institution the gender-segregation of our curriculum and the utilization of our college resources, our report has undeniably influenced the institutional agenda. The importance of focusing on gender as the college moves to improve the quality of education and student life cannot be underestimated. Programs designed and implemented for "the general good" that refuse to acknowledge the potential differential outcomes for students by gender will fail to correct the problems we have identified.

Lewis and Clark's struggles with what have proven to be the more intractable issues could be very helpful to faculty and administrators elsewhere. The first of these—to establish closer integration of sciences and humanities—has been addressed in a preliminary way by a task force reviewing the college's general studies program, but with only peripheral attention to its gender implications. The second, having to do with improving quantitative and language skills, has also been addressed not specifically in terms of gender, but more generally in reconsideration of the college's graduation requirements. the third, a recommendation to establish a subcommittee of the curriculum committee to foster and support gender-balancing, has been included as part of the newly affirmed institutional mission, and therefore it will be one of several collegewide concerns to be assigned to constitutional committees for attention and implementation. Slowness of action on these three recommendations could serve as a healthy reminder of the enormity and difficulty of the task—and the tentative nature of our successes thus far.

In summary, the report served to promote the idea of gender-balancing the institution as a way of living up to its coeducational responsibilities. Gender-balancing, as it has taken shape in the report and in discussions among faculty and administrators, entails both infusing gender issues, wherever appropriate, into the liberal arts curriculum and giving serious attention to the educational experience of women and men. Much progress has been made: a number of faculty members, both male and female, treat gender issues in their courses; plans to redesign the college's core curriculum have included gender as a major concern; feminist faculty have been hired; a women-in-science group for students has been formed. In short, the integration of gender issues in the curriculum and classroom seems on track.

Nonetheless, the report was accepted too readily and discussed too little. "Gender-balancing" quickly became an institutional buzzword to denote an unmitigated good to which all members of the faculty and administration were presumed to be devoted. This aura of good will has endured, yet many faculty still give no attention or only token attention to issues of gender in their courses and have little heeded pedagogical suggestions about mitigating the chilly climate of their classrooms. In other words, the kinds of changes in curriculum, behavior, and attitude mandated on the institutional level need to be implemented on the individual level.

The continuing question, then, is how to translate and infuse the institutional commitment to gender-balanced education into the behavior of faculty and students so that the goal can actually be achieved. One key to our success to date has been administrative support for gender issues. But this support could backfire if administrative support is perceived as administrative pressure that violates the academic freedom of faculty to teach and act independent of institutional mandate. For this reason, the strategy we favor is to emphasize to colleagues in a positive way how thinking about gender issues can work to their benefit as scholars and teachers.

It remains our conviction that the best way to gain lasting results in this endeavor is for faculty members to be challenged by respected colleagues, or by exposure to feminist scholarship in their field, to examine the implications of gender in their own discipline. That is what occurred in the cases of Associate Deans Hecht and Savage and seminar participants, with significant institutional, professional, and personal results.

Feminist Scholarship and Gender-Balancing the Curriculum

At Lewis and Clark, a new development may well provoke that challenge for others, although it will no doubt strike some readers as a curious reversal of patterns elsewhere. Unlike many institutions, Lewis and Clark has never had a women's studies program. Instead, it has had isolated women's courses and growing faculty and administrative concern for gender issues. Now that gender-balancing has been adopted as an institutional goal, a group of concerned feminist faculty has drafted a plan for a Gender Studies Concentration with a director to coordinate curricular offerings on gender and to foster gender-balancing across the curriculum. On the one hand, this program should organize gender offerings in a coherent fashion to provide students with logical curricular sequences, and the opportunity for a more detailed and extensive examination of feminist scholarship. On the other hand, the program should provide a source of information, energy, and encouragement to the faculty to achieve the college's coeducational aspirations both in terms of curriculum and in terms of educational climate. In other words to succeed, a gender studies program must assist in sustaining both personal and institutional commitment to gender issues and provide enough intellectual excitement to persuade uninvolved faculty that others are "on to a good thing."

The recent history of feminist efforts at Lewis and Clark College has been presented here not as a model to be replicated everywhere, but as an example of how political efforts at a particular point in an institution's history have paid off. The Lewis and Clark case is unique in certain respects. Thanks to its sluggish response to feminism in the 1970s, it was ripe for gender issues in the 1980s. With no separate women's studies program, the way was clear for gender-balancing and gender studies proposals. Unlike many institutions, where feminist pressures come primarily from students and junior faculty, at Lewis and Clark the source of support has been "top down." the advantages of such a situation include financial and programmatic leverage for change. Some dangers include disaffection or even backlash from faculty and students, who may perceive themselves on the peripheries of these developments. Positive signs that these dangers may be waning include new student calls for joint faculty, staff, and student cooperation around women's issues, and the formation of at least two feminist support groups for men, including students and at least one faculty member, to explore what it means to be a man *and* a feminist. While some feminists may see this as cooptation, those of us who have espoused gender-balancing as our goal can only cheer.

The transparent implications of Oberlin College's institutional and curricular policies in its early years have provided an appropriate backdrop for considering modern curricular questions. By providing a clear view of the ways in which a school could prepare students to fit social expectations that we no longer accept, it revealed the limits of a curriculum used not as a key to the world of knowledge and insight, but as a track to a circumscribed way of life. The new scholarship on women and a truly coeducational education as we have defined it should free both women and men to explore their individual potential in the fullest and the most open way possible.

Notes

1. Thomas Woody, *A History of Women's Education in the United States,* vol. 2 (reprint ed., New York: Octagon Books, 1974), p. 224.

2. Florence Howe, "Three Missions of Higher Education for Women: Vocation, Freedom, Knowledge," *Liberal Education* 66 (Fall 1980): 285–97.

3. Martha Frances Montague, *Lewis and Clark College 1867–1967* (Portland, Ore.: Bindford and Mort, 1968), pp. 11–12.

4. Howe, "Three Missions," p. 289.

5. Ibid., p. 288.

6. Ibid., p. 290.

7. Ibid., p. 289.

8. Patricia Sexton, *Women in Education* (Bloomington, Ind.: Phi Delta Kappa, 1976), p. 47.

9. Compare Michelle Rosaldo, "The Use and Abuse of Anthropology," *Signs* 5 (1980): 389–417.

10. J.M. Atkinson and S. Kirschner, "The Issue of Gender in the Lewis and Clark Curriculum" (Portland, Ore.: Lewis and Clark College, 1982).

11. For the Project on the Status and Education of Women of the Association of American Colleges, 1982.

Appendix

**The Issue of Gender in the
Lewis and Clark Curriculum
1982 Report**

JANE ATKINSON AND SUSAN KIRSCHNER

Recommendations

If the institution resolves that gender-balancing the curriculum is an important and necessary step to take, it would be a mistake to leave the process to individual good will and happenstance. If the college is to pay more than lipservice to the issues raised in this report, the following steps might be in order.

1. Formation of a task force to consider gender issues at the institution.

2. Administrative coordination of efforts to gender-balance the curriculum.

3. Establishment of a subcommittee of the Curriculum Committee, to serve as a faculty resource for coordinating courses, syllabi, and faculty development projects in the area of gender studies.

4. A closer integration of the sciences and humanities at the college for the purpose of insuring that all students, regardless of sex, partake of a truly liberal education. Attention to quantitative and language skills should be a priority.

5. Integration of gender studies into the college's long-range faculty development planning. A college Grants Officer with expertise in a number of fields, including women's studies, would be a boon for all faculty wishing to undertake research and further training in any area.

6. Further collection development in women's studies as part of library planning.

7. Review and clarification of faculty affirmative action policy; education of faculty members to achieve greater consistency in applying affirmative action guidelines.

8. Inclusion of gender as a category when collecting and analyzing data on students, faculty, and staff. Gender-specific information is currently unevenly collected and difficult to retrieve. If and when an Office of Institutional Research is established, an on-going appraisal of gender-related concerns should be a priority.

9. Faculty considerations of the document of sexual harassment for the purpose of improving working relations among faculty, staff, and students.

4

Redefining Women's Education

Jeanine Elliott

Conflicting Models for Women's Education

The history of Stephens College reflects the changing and often conflicting definitions of women's education that have been articulated in American higher education since the founding of women's colleges and the establishment of coeducation more than one hundred fifty years ago. Two models for women's education dominated before the 1960s. One maintained that women should be educated to fit specific social roles through a curriculum that paid attention to women's experience as defined by the dominant cultural norms of the society which the college serves. The other assumed that women, whether in women's colleges or in coeducational institutions, should have access to the same education as men.

The first model takes women into account and, in fact, fashions an education specifically for women students, but serves to maintain a social structure in which women are subordinate. Lacking a feminist perspective that recognizes the differential in power between men and women in the culture at large, educators who adopted this definition of women's education sought to socialize women primarily for their traditional roles in society as educated wives and mothers. At the same time, however, these institutions were student-centered in their curriculum design and enabled women to grow within the roles available to them. Stephens College, for example, had a strong emphasis on community responsibility and personal integrity in both its academic and co-curricular programs between the mid-20s and the late '60s. As the woman student learned to function in her college and then in the larger community, she gained a sense of self-worth linked to her female identity and made connections with other women. This kind of knowledge was invaluable for the young, middle-class, white woman who was to spend her adult life in the highly structured communities of southern towns or as a corporate or military wife. But what value is there in educating the whole person and encouraging a self-worth that permits only limited access to society?

Proponents of the second model, arguing for the same curriculum as is taught in men's colleges, have tended to devalue women by ignoring women's experience and cultural production. To study what men have considered valuable or relevant is to overlook the work and knowledge that have been carried in the female culture. Whatever self-confidence is achieved by the woman student in mastering the terms defined by such a male curriculum is gained at the loss of the sense of rootedness and connection that comes from affirming others like herself. To learn to discount women either explicitly, through the study of misogynist literature, rhetoric, or method, or implicitly, through the invisibility of women in the curriculum, means that a student will devalue her own experience as a woman.

The first curriculum model recognizes that women are different from men, but assumes that to be different is to be subordinate, to be less than men. The second curriculum model assumes that women are equal and the same as men, but negates real difference and obscures women's lives. Elements of both models have existed in uneasy tension on most campuses, with one or the other dominating at specific moments. The contemporary feminist educator must confront the implications of these seemingly irreconcilable assumptions and attempt to bring together the sensitivity to women's experience of the first model while retaining the commitment to equity of the second. Education for diversity *and* equality is the challenge facing institutions committed to educating women (and men) in the last decades of the twentieth century. The Stephens experience of the last fifteen years reflects the conflicts engendered by changing definitions of education for women and suggests some directions for all institutions committed to diversity and equality.

Education for Women and Changing Times

Stephens College chose to build a curriculum for women during two significant periods of educational and societal change. The first occurred in the 1920s and 1930s and embodied the best of the first, or woman-focused, model. In 1921, W.W. Charters, Dean of Research at Stephens College, began the research task of identifying the "nature and range of the aptitudes, responsibilities, and problems of women." Charters and President James Madison Wood, following the theories of John Dewey, believed that education should be related to the real-life problems and situations of students. By collecting data from women's diaries and letters, Charters was able to develop a curriculum that he and President Wood believed would prepare women to enter traditional professions for women or to become homemakers. This two-year curriculum reinforced community responsibility, holistic thinking, valuing of self and others, and "proper" female behavior. Progressive educational philosophy enabled Charters and Wood to design a curriculum that recognized the needs of the women students they hoped to serve, while reinforcing the dominant social structure of the time.

By the early 1970s, society, the structure and substance of women's lives, and Stephens had changed significantly. No longer a junior college, Stephens had a student body that was more diverse in terms of age, race, and class. The faculty was changing from a junior college faculty to a four-year liberal, fine, and performing arts faculty. The tradition of student-centered learning at Stephens was being challenged in two ways. First, the student body was composed of more diverse individuals than the traditional-aged, middle-class, white women whose needs and expectations shaped the earlier educational experience. Second, as the college struggled to become a four-year liberal arts college, it moved away from woman-centered learning and adopted the values of the dominant educational community. Largely unconsciously, Stephens moved toward the second model for women's education, valuing the traditional, male-defined, liberal arts curriculum, negating traditional women's activities, and cultural production, and aspiring to intellectual elitism.

Student-centered learning became identified for Stephens faculty with a traditionalist view of women's education that trained women for sex-segregated social roles. Academic responsibility was identified with a curriculum where, in order to be equal to men, women were denied access to their own experience. Three key moments in the struggle of the last fifteen years to negotiate those differences and to define a new curriculum that would be both student-centered and academically respectable have led, at Stephens, to the emergence of a third model for women's education that could serve to renew education for all students in the next decades. The first moment involved the conflict between a traditionalist definition of education for women and the new insights of women's studies in the early 1970s. Sources of resistance to implicitly feminist education surfaced in the second moment (the mid- to late '70s) as the college faced material difficulties such as budget freezes and faculty cutbacks. Finally, in the early '80s a new "transformed" curriculum was hammered out through a participatory process enhanced (and threatened) by different strategies for faculty development.

Change Agents and Traditionalists

During the period from 1973 to 1975, the establishment of a women's studies program and the appointment of a new president crystallized the debate between change agents and traditionalists. In the early '70s, the English Department began teaching a first-year course using women writers. Although three courses on women in the curriculum had already been in place for nearly ten years, they were, from the perspective of the rapidly growing group of feminists on campus, conventional, in the traditionalist women's college mode. A new approach to the study of women was needed. Following the English Department's experiment in curriculum integration, a group of women administrators and faculty members from several departments proposed a new interdisciplinary course that would serve as an introduction to women's studies in 1973. This group generally met openly during their period of planning; however, nostalgic stories are told of the first meetings among students and faculty at night on the roof of the library.

Following the model of women's studies courses on other campuses, the course used faculty from all departments of the college.

Each was asked to address the implications of the study of women in her field. In the first year nearly 500 students took the course, which met in the evening, outside regular class hours. Fifty-two different faculty members and community women taught some portion of the course. Although the course has undergone some changes since, it still serves, as it did in the beginning, as a valuable orientation for new faculty members interested in women's studies, because it is a cooperative teaching venture. It also exposes a diverse group of students and faculty to basic assumptions and methodologies of feminist scholarship in a variety of academic fields, thus introducing women's studies to both students and faculty who might later develop more advanced courses in their own fields of specialization.

The same year that the course was established, the college began a search for a new president. Other than one woman who had served as acting president for a short time, all the presidents since Stephens's founding in 1833 had been men. While both faculty and students favored the same woman among the final three candidates (two female, one male), she was passed over in favor of the man, who had historic connections with the college. Many faculty and students believed that gender as much as qualifications had played a role in the decision. As a result, the president, who remained in office for ten years, was never accepted by the faculty. He represented a traditionalist view of women's education that the faculty rejected in separately defining the college's educational goals.

His appointment sharpened the growing debate about women's education. Faculty who might have preferred to ignore the women's movement entirely readily identified themselves as emotionally opposed to the traditionalist women's education the president favored. It is ironic that the new president, because his appointment had been fraught with so much controversy, may have felt more pressure to appoint women to administrative positions and authority roles, such as the Board of Curators, than his conservative perspective would have predicted. The backlash from the faculty to the appointment of a traditionalist male president and his attempt to minimize faculty opposition were to have long-range implications for the development of a moderately feminist educational environment.

This climate enabled the Board of Curators to appoint a Committee on Women's Education composed of faculty, students, curators, and alumnae to redefine the college's mission. The mandate asked the committee to "develop a working definition of women's education as the mission of Stephens College. Restatement of the College mission must take into account the major social, economic, and cultural forces generated by the women's movement and their impact on women's lives." The membership of the committee was diverse and included many people who had worked on women's issues in and out of feminist organizations. The statement they presented to the faculty was approved by the Board of Curators in 1977:

> Stephens College, an undergraduate women's college, is dedicated to the dignity and equality of women and to an educational program that embodies this dedication. To address the changing needs, roles and aspirations of women, the College is committed to rigorous examination of its existing programs and experimentation with new ones. Stephens endeavors to:
>
> 1. Promote standards of intellectual and creative excellence and the development of critical thinking.
> 2. Include students as partners in scholarship and support them in serious examination of their own experience and its intellectual and spiritual significance.
> 3. Offer liberal and specialized education designed to enable women to be independent, self-fulfilled, contributing members of a world community.
> 4. Encourage women to perceive learning as a lifelong process that requires continual re-evaluation of goals and directions.
> 5. Provide an academic and residential environment in which women of all ages and backgrounds assess values and beliefs and develop a sense of self and of responsibility to others.

By the mid-70s, then, the faculty and Board of Curators had committed themselves to an educational environment supportive of women, sensitive to diversity, and attentive to change.

With the Best Intentions: Doing Good and Feeling Bad

Although the new mission statement was in place and full of promise, it had yet to be fully translated into the curriculum.

Nonetheless, students and faculty members together worked on both curricular and noncurricular issues to produce a supportive environment for women. The mid-70s, unfortunately, also brought pressures from the outside that led to a freeze on faculty raises, cuts in the faculty, and a drop in student applications.

The low morale that resulted from these conditions contributed to scapegoating. The implicit feminism of the new mission statement, unsupported by curricular reality and widespread faculty education, was suspect. The Women's Studies Program, begun in such enthusiasm, struggled to survive even as the authority of the male Dean of Faculty, who had supported it, was diminishing. Individuals in the administration who feared the presence of lesbians on campus appeared to be starting a witch hunt. Women who were identified as feminists became targets of criticism; women's studies positions or budgets that were not a secure part of the regular college structure were threatened and sometimes cut without notice. Two positive steps helped to dissipate the climate of fear and reaction that threatened the campus and to restore the support for feminist education articulated by the mission statement that continued despite structural chaos.

First, a long-range planning committee made up of administrators, elected faculty members, and students produced a document in 1979 that would help shape the curriculum two years later, and second, a project begun with support from the National Endowment for the Humanities laid the groundwork for the planning and implementation of a new curriculum. The 1979 long-range planning document (see appendix), even more strongly than the mission statement, affirmed dedication to the dignity and equality of women. It explicitly called on the faculty to incorporate the "new scholarship on women" in the curriculum.

One reason the implicit feminism of the earlier mission statement was scapegoated as soon as the college faced crises in the mid-70s may have been that only a small number of faculty members (those who participated in the interdisciplinary women's studies course) and some administrators (women for the most part) had first-hand experience with the "new scholarship on women." Others felt excluded or failed to see its relevance to their own work and goals. Fortunately, during the same year that the long-range planning committee was working on its report, the

National Endowment for the Humanities funded a project at Stephens on "Implementing the Goals of Women's Education in the Humanities." Nine faculty members, both women and men, from the social sciences and humanities met for one day each month to give papers on the issues of women's education in their own fields. This was the first ongoing program to provide the men of the faculty a forum for examining their own disciplines, and an intellectual context in which to analyze how methodological assumptions shape our understanding of women's (and men's) lives. Thanks to an alumnae gift supporting faculty development in women's studies, the faculty development begun by the NEH project was extended for three years and was expanded to include non-liberal arts faculty and administrators. Sixteen men and sixteen women participated in this program, whose goals included:

- to gather information about the history and culture of women,
- to gain awareness of the experience of women as a subculture within a dominant, male-oriented society,
- to enhance the ability to empathize with the student in her life-situation and to develop teaching methods relevant to her experience and her developmental needs, and
- to bring critical judgment to bear upon one's own academic discipline or administrative responsibility, using the new tools of women's scholarship.

As a model for faculty development, this four-year effort provides both constructive guidelines and a warning. Several key elements contributed to the overall success and usefulness of the effort: (a) participants were invited but not coerced to take part in the workshops, and both men and women participated in equal numbers; (b) the workshops extended over a long enough period of time to allow for in-depth study; and (c) participants came not only from a variety of departments, allowing for interdisciplinary exchange, but from the administration so that different sectors of the college community were involved and communicating with each other about issues central to the college's mission.

Other aspects of the program were more problematic. What looked like an initial blessing became a liability. A sense of "shared ownership" existed because no specific office, person, or program was responsible for coordination and planning. The workshops were parallel to the Women's Studies Program and compatible with it, but structurally separate. Although the non-hierarchical, collaborative nature of the workshops was attractive for outreach and worked for four years, the lack of structural responsibility meant that the workshops ended when the one administrator who informally looked after them moved out of her position. For continuing faculty development, then, responsibility and authority need to be visibly linked to a stable program or office that enjoys the respect of a wide spectrum of faculty and administrators.

In sum, this "second moment" in Stephens's recent history—when material adversity led to the scapegoating of feminist issues—led to the writing of a long-range planning report that could help implement the earlier mission statement, and produced a four-year sequence of workshops that laid the groundwork for broader support for curricular reform based on the principles of the long-range report.

A New Curriculum

In 1980, the various elements of Stephens's identity as an institution merged in efforts to develop a new curriculum. The long transition from a two-year to a fully recognized four-year liberal arts college, the need to incorporate Stephens's mission as a college for women through changes in the male-defined liberal arts curriculum, and the diverse efforts to engage the faculty in a participatory, "shared ownership," policy-making process all converged when the faculty decided not to accept a curriculum proposal drafted at the faculty's request, but without faculty participation in the Dean's Office, and returned the process to the faculty Curriculum and Instruction Board (CIB).

As the newly elected chair of that board, and as a person committed to shared ownership and shared leadership, I saw this mandate as an opportunity to engage the entire faculty in the kind of participatory decision-making we had practiced in women's studies. The CIB established a process for the curriculum revision that involved task forces, workshops, and straw votes of the faculty as a whole so that no motion for approval of any segment of the new curriculum was made until all faculty members had had an opportunity to express their thinking. Although slow, the process permitted the faculty to reach near consensus on most of the decisions. The Long-Range Planning Report provided language for educational assumptions underlying the rationale of the new curriculum. The new curriculum specifically recognizes the changing role of women, obstacles to equality, and the obligation of a women's college to enable students to understand their situation as women and to prepare them to use their intelligence and talents as fully as possible.

Two new aspects of the curriculum brought together most dramatically the efforts to incorporate the insights, perspectives, and data from the new scholarship on women as an integral part of a liberal arts curriculum. First was the establishment of the liberal education requirement. Women's studies was identified as one of seven "lower-level liberal education areas." Second, all courses approved as liberal education courses are required to "include information and values relevant to women and ethnic minorities." Because the commitment to women's education was by now a strongly shared sentiment in the college community, relatively little opposition (or even discussion) surfaced when these requirements were proposed. Nonetheless, it is possible that faculty members who had not yet participated in workshops on the new scholarship did not realize what it would take to implement this proposal responsibly.

At the upper level of the curriculum, the faculty proposed an upper-division education requirement for all Bachelor of Arts candidates. The innovative new requirement for B.A. students would implement one of the assumptions of the new curriculum: "an educated woman should be able to integrate what she learns in college with her life plan. She should have a sense of direction for herself in terms of work." The course, called simply the *Senior Colloquium*, was placed under the administration of Women's Studies.

Using case studies and simulations developed from the actual experience of young women similar to themselves, students apply knowledge and skills gained in their liberal education courses and in their major to solve problems common to college-educated women. Like W.W. Charters's experiments in the 1920s, this course uses women's accounts of their experience as a basis for education. But whereas Charters's student-centered learning was

designed to fit women to the status quo, this student-centered
learning engages students in the process and seeks to make them
active participants and change agents in their society.
The real test of the easy assent to the inclusion of women and
ethnic minorities in the rest of the curriculum came as specific
liberal education courses were submitted for approval. All proposals had to demonstrate how information and values relevant to
women and ethnic minorities were to be included in the course.
Failure to meet this criterion had to be justified by the department submitting the proposal. While opposition to the principle
of including this information and this perspective had been virtually nonexistent, when the time came for actual implementation
many reasons for the non-inclusion of women and minorities
were articulated.

Resistance took two forms that seem typical of this process on
other campuses as well. First, faculty members objected to what
they perceived as a breach of academic freedom. The autonomy
of the teacher in the classroom is well protected at Stephens, and
the directive by the CIB to include certain types of information
was seen as an intrusion. Second, faculty members perceived this
requirement as a demand to include additional material in their
courses. In the interest of coverage they argued that introductory
courses, in particular, already had syllabi that filled all available
time. Through a long process of negotiation, these objections were
overcome, and all the approved courses (including geology and
calculus) have some content or method relevant to women and
ethnic minorities.

Although the approved courses have been largely successful, no
systematic attempt to help faculty revise their courses exists. A
one-day workshop developed by the Women's Studies Program to
assist these faculty members ended up raising the resistance level
of the participants and might serve as a cautionary tale for other
programs.

At least two-thirds of the participants in the workshop for
faculty members teaching the liberal education courses had not
been involved in any previous development efforts related to
women's studies. Also, unlike the earlier, successful, year-long
programs, this one involved a large group with no chance for the
small-group exploration that had previously worked so well. Ear-

lier programs had provided a sense that faculty members were serving as a resource to each other, whatever their level of sophistication about feminism; this time because outside "experts" from the community were brought in, the participants felt they were being told how to teach, even though they believed they were already competent teachers. Consequently, they resisted the observations of the visitors—a psychologist, teachers from black studies and women's studies, and a panel of students. Because their resistance was high, the participants criticized the methodology of the psychologist, dismissed the black studies approach as simplistic, and characterized the students' descriptions of classroom experience (especially the black students') as idiosyncratic. The negative experience of this workshop reinforces the lessons learned from the earlier, successful programs: (a) participants need to feel invested in the work being done, to have their own areas of expertise validated; (b) opportunities for small-group interaction should be built in; and (c) follow-up or long-term work is needed to assure in-depth participation.

A New Model for Women's Education

In assessing the varied experiences of Stephens's transition from a two-year college to a four-year liberal arts college, from a traditionalist college for women to a college for women informed by feminist insights, we can begin to see the basis for a new model for women's education that would make coeducation more responsible as well. The first obstacle we needed to overcome was the largely unarticulated belief that the models for women's education were limited to the two that had dominated until the mid-twentieth century: a curriculum different from that offered to men, which assumed a lesser status for women, or a curriculum equal to men's education which obscured women's experience altogether. We've learned that student-centered education in a women's college need not perpetuate the status quo. By recognizing and planning for the diversity in our student body, the changes taking place for women in our society, and the insights of feminist scholarship and pedagogy, we can design dynamic, student-centered learning.

The second obstacle we had to overcome was the unstated assumption that "exellence" and "rigor" in the liberal arts were defined by the conventional liberal arts curriculum. In-depth, extended faculty development in the new scholarship on women provides new perspectives as well as new information that enable teachers to present the methods and criteria of the traditional disciplines with a much sharper focus.

The last fifteen years also taught us the strengths and limitations of changing forms of authority and decision-making. In the early years of developing consciousness and women's studies on the Stephens campus, informal meetings of groups outside the regular structure of the college, without any policy-making authority, allowed us to experiment with collective decision-making and nonhierarchical structures. As the ideas these groups lobbied for became part of the institutional agenda, our subordinate, outsider status shifted and issues of leadership surfaced. We were able to bring some of the principles of shared ownership with us as we became more a part of the institution itself, but at the expense of a cohesiveness that in fact obscured the differences among us. The traditional distrust that separates the faculty from the administration did not diminish as we tried to change the forms of authority. The challenge facing the Stephens community now is the development of a kind of faculty feminist leadership with legitimate authority that can function as both critic and guide to the institution's feminist consciousness.

Appendix

Stephens College
Long-Range Planning Report 1979

Stephens College will continue to be a college dedicated to promoting "the dignity and equality of women." Although the position of women in our society will improve, the attitudes of the past and their impact will not be corrected quickly. Therefore, Stephens will seek to:

1. Provide an environment free of prejudice, an environment that nurtures, supports and encourages women to create their own identities.

2. Teach its students to recognize the mechanism of sex-role stereotyping and to cope with its consequences.

3. Acknowledge, support and promote the right of women to equal opportunities in work and to equality with men in the social, legal, economic and political spheres.

4. Embody its commitment to women in its organizations, staffing, curriculum, and attitudes toward students and women faculty and staff members.

5. Promote, encourage and reward research that incorporates the "new scholarship" on women into the subject matter and the methodology of the disciplines and therefore of our teaching. This means the introduction of material by and about women not included in the traditional disciplines, the critical examination of this new material according to the standards and criteria used in the traditional disciplines, and the reevaluation of the traditional disciplines in the light of both.

6. Promote, encourage, and reward research on the education and status of women.

7. Provide a basis for a critique of traditional social structure through the redefinition of current values (for example, the concepts of individuality, leadership, success) and the examination of alternative values.

5

Women's Studies/Black Studies: Learning from Our Common Pasts/Forging a Common Future

Margaret L. Andersen

Black Studies, White Studies: Revised. What is the curriculum, what are the standards that only human life threatens to defile and 'lower'? Is the curriculum kin to that monstrous metaphor of justice, seated, under blindfold, in an attitude and substance of absolute stone? Life appealing to live and to be, and to know a community that will protect the living simply because we are alive: This is the menace to university curriculum and standards. This is the possibility of survival we must all embrace: the possibility of life, as has been said, by whatever means necessary.

June Jordan, *Civil Wars*

Jordan's prose begs us to ask, "What is the impact of a curriculum that denies the culture—indeed, the very existence—of most of the world's population?" How, as educators, do we begin to alter a curriculum whose standards emerge only from the experience of a few? And how, in this process of change, do we create dynamic accounts of race, culture, class, and gender in the development of a sound curriculum—one that is rooted in the multiracial, multicultural, and gendered character of the total range of social experience?

The current movement among women's studies scholars to transform the curriculum by integrating research on women is an important step in the reconstruction of education. This effort is occurring alongside the historical development of black and ethnic studies programs, which also seek to balance the curriculum by being more inclusive of Afro-American, Asian-American, Hispanic, and Native-American experiences. The work to balance the curriculum requires that women's studies and black studies become allies in the process of change. Typically, women's studies and black studies have worked as separate programs, resulting in the too-common problem of treating race as if it were one feature of experience, and gender, another. In the next decade the greatest challenge to feminist and black scholars and educators is to transform the curriculum in ways that make the dynamics of race, class, and gender central to students' learning experience.

The Challenge of Collaboration

The collaboration of women's studies and black studies suggests several strategies to ensure that the transformation of the curriculum will accomplish educational change that is inclusive of all persons. Genuine collaboration, rather than merely trying to enlist support for separate agenda, requires ongoing dialogue between the two and constant reevalution of what we already know. As reformers of educational institutions we share a belief in the liberating opportunities of education for making social change possible. Yet the urgency of our commitment to reforming the curriculum comes from our conviction that these institutions have short-changed us. There is, as Marcia Westkott has suggested, a breach between our consciousness and our activity within these institutions, since women and blacks have not had the power to implement their consciousness through activity in existing institutions.[1] Our specific strategies and philosophies for change emerge from the particular context of being alienated members of these institutions.

Both black studies and women's studies center their intellectual foundation on a critique of the singularity and exclusiveness of the standard canon. Each rests essentially on the premise that the experience of traditionally excluded groups has been denied, ignored, and undercut by traditional knowledge; thus, reconstruction of the curriculum begins through developing a more pluralistic body of knowledge. As a result, the demand for integration of the women's studies and black studies perspectives becomes a multidimensional process that need not imply acceptance of the status quo. We seek both admission to *and* transformation of dominant institutions, and these dual strategies are reflected in our programs for integration and change.

OUR CONNECTED PAST

As we recover the histories of individuals and groups for the good of the core curriculum, we need to remember clearly, for our own good, the many links in the histories of black studies and women's studies that have shaped our political analysis and that could strengthen our combined force now. In the nineteenth and twentieth centuries, the feminist movement emerged from black liberation movements. In the nineteenth century, although feminists failed to develop an analysis that incorporated the unique experience of black women, the institutional perspective of the antislavery and black freedom movements influenced feminist political theory. And in the contemporary period, the civil rights and black power movements heightened women's awareness of gender oppression and influenced the direction of the second wave of feminism.[2] From the black power movement the feminists took their analysis calling for collective action, self-determination, power, and the restructuring of social institutions.[3] Additionally, the women's movement has built on the black movement by recognizing the "missing curriculum" that includes women, black, Third World, gay, and lesbian people. It is the missing curriculum that feminist and black scholars have sought to reclaim.

The Example of Black Studies: Becoming Visible

The development of black studies in the late 1960s and early 1970s found black students demanding that "all of the study of America and the world be saturated with the significance of the black presence, so that every relevant event, man, and movement is re-evaluated."[4] Clearly, the importance of this project was to create what feminists now call a "balanced curriculum." As one of the early educators in the black studies movement put it, "The significance of the establishment of Afro-American Studies at institutions of higher learning would be a balanced education for everyone involved—both blacks and whites."[5] Like the proponents of the women's studies movement, those articulating the philosophy of black studies saw new scholarship as correcting the race-bound assumptions of previous studies and adding new material and ideas where omissions had existed. Also like women's studies, the black studies curriculum was clearly and consciously linked to the history and development of black protest. Advocates of the new scholarship in black studies perceived this movement as having dual objectives: counteracting the effect of white racism and generating a strong sense of black identity and community, both with the intent of building group power in the struggle for liberation.[6]

Thus, the evolution of new scholarship in black studies was wedded to the political goals for black liberation. While the establishment of black studies programs and departments represented a new development in black freedom movements, the underlying philosophy of advocating education as a means for social change was not new. Since slavery, education in the black community has been seen as essential to the struggle for freedom. Frederick Douglass learned this early. When his owner found his wife teaching the young slave Douglass to read, he said, "If he learns to read the Bible, it will forever unfit him to be a slave. He should know nothing but the will of his master, and learn to obey it. As to himself, learning will do him no good, but a great deal of harm, making him disconsolate and unhappy. If you teach him how to read, he'll want to know how to write, and this accomplished, he'll be running away with himself."[7] Throughout the development of black history, "education has persisted as one of the most consistent themes in the life, thought, struggle, and protest of black Americans. It has been viewed as a major avenue for acquiring first-class citizenship."[8]

The philosophy of black studies has, then, a two-pronged approach: to help provide the basis for radical social change, and to help black students acquire the personal and academic skills to integrate into American society. In the literature on black education, black studies at the collegiate level is clearly part of a larger theme of developing sound education within and on behalf of the black community. These writings reveal the persistent theme that education is a privilege in and of itself; therefore, it is no surprise that much of the literature on black education focuses on issues prerequisite to the college curriculum: the provision of good education for black students in the elementary and secondary schools.

The Example of Women's Studies: Becoming Central

For feminists, placing black studies in the context of long-range goals for black education can inform discussions about the integration of research on women into the core curriculum. Clearly, women's studies seeks to provide the knowledge that will help to create new patterns of gender relations in society. Also, the intellectual frameworks of women's studies stand in clear opposition to those of the male-centered, white, Western tradition upon which most educational institutions rest. Like black studies, women's studies has the multiple goals of preparing women to comprehend the world they face, of transforming the traditional curriculum to include everyone, and of providing the basis for liberating changes in society.

The educational history of women's studies dates to 1970 when women's studies courses and programs began to grow nationwide. Since that time, more than 450 women's studies programs have been established on campuses across the country. The early purposes of women's studies included raising the consciousness of students to become aware of sexism both in the curriculum and in the society at large. The first thrust of the women's studies curriculum was to develop courses to supplement the traditional curriculum by adding material on women and establishing women as a legitimate topic for study and research.[9] In the brief period of time since, women's studies has flourished as an area for scholarship and critical inquiry such that, like black studies, it is now a field in its own right, although one that overlaps with scholarship and teaching in traditional disciplines. More recently, as scholars demonstrated that the new scholarship on women challenged the existing concepts and theories in the disciplines, they began to envision women's studies as altering the core content of previously androcentric fields. Women's studies scholars have adopted the language of "integration" to describe this process of transforming the traditional curriculum.

Risks of Integration: Cooptation and Assimilation

Some women's studies scholars caution that projects that seek to integrate research on women into the curriculum cannot, at the same time, maintain the more radical goals of the women's studies movement.[10] This fear stems in part from the concern that, to make women's studies more palatable to those who control higher education, the political goals of women's studies will become diluted and the difficult issues of racism and compulsory heterosexuality will be left out. These concerns are important ones and should be kept constantly in mind as we take on transformation of the curriculum. They also underscore the importance of having women's studies and black studies work hand-in-hand in the development of a new, more liberating curriculum for our students. Furthermore, as women's studies educators review the development of black studies, they will see new meaning in the language of integration that they use to describe their educational programs for change.

Understanding Integration:
The History of Black Protest and Black Studies

Throughout the history of black protest, integration has been a widely held value—one that refers to the process of acquiring equity for black Americans in all areas of American society. Political differences in the black community exist, to be sure, but the struggle against racism is so enormous that, if we look closely, we find multiple approaches and a wide degree of tolerance for diverse efforts to create liberating social changes. Moreover, throughout the history of black protest, the majority of black Americans have continued to support the goal of integration, while also adopting more radical analyses.

Studies of black student attitudes illustrate that integration has a more complex meaning than assimilation into a dominant culture. One survey of black college students, taken in 1974, found that most students perceived the black movement as having changed for the better. These students found "system-oriented" change as preferable to total separation, even while they expressed alienation from the dominant culture.[11] Another study of black students has found that to them integration does not mean giving up their racial or cultural heritage, as is sometimes assumed. Rather, for the students studied, integration implies the free association of people on all levels of life, along with open acceptance of other people and other racial and cultural heritage.[12]

In the development of black studies, integration and separatism are not either/or strategies, although they do at times reflect different emphases in black political philosophy.[13] A separatist approach has the benefit of ensuring black control over the content of black studies and emphasizing the development of black values and community identity. Nonetheless, most statements of the educational philosophy of black studies also emphasize that students need preparation in traditional majors and in the acquisition of academic skills to complement their education in black studies. Realistically, black studies programs, like women's studies programs, are typically not autonomous units within universities. Since none of us lives totally outside these institutions, our unique position as critics and transformers is to work with a dual vision—one that enables us to work together within existing imperfect institutions at the same time that we work to change them.

The idea of integration, if we look at its evolution through black political activity, will involve a complex educational strategy to put women's studies and black studies into the curriculum of every student, while at the same time to continue a critical examination of existing bodies of scholarship. When examined in the fullest context, integration becomes a more radical concept—one not necessarily implying acceptance of existing social, economic, and political institutions. Surely, an integrationist approach would be inadequate if it only meant being included in the dominant system. Developing women's studies and black studies within the curriculum will certainly generate more radical changes because, when race and gender are taken seriously in research and theory, radical transformations of the content, epistemological foundations, and theoretical questions of disciplinary paradigms have already begun and are likely to proliferate.

A Collaborative Model for Transformation

For white feminists this effort requires building a multiracial analysis into feminist studies. Feminist efforts to transform the curriculum that include only the experience of white women must be seen as inadequate since they ignore the fact that women of color constitute the majority of the world's population. Moreover, knowledge that is centered exclusively on the lives of white women perpetuates the problem of generalizing from the lives of a few. For example, the common feminist argument that women's secondary status derives from their exclusion from the public labor force clearly ignores the experience of the overwhelming majority of black women who have always worked outside their homes. Similarly, a more global perspective in feminist studies would tell us that education for women must include programs for the development of literacy and basic skills and would recognize that the focus on collegiate curriculum is particular to the lives of privileged women in the Western world. As Margo Culley, codirector of the "Black Studies/Women's Studies: An Overdue Partnership" project at the University of Massachusetts, Amherst, has concluded, mainstreaming women's studies should mean making women's studies multiracial and multicultural.[14] Her statement underscores the urgency of developing an integrated analysis of race, class, and gender in women's studies; it is just as imperative to build a multiracial analysis into feminist studies as it is to create gender balance in the core curriculum.

Similarly for black studies scholars, it is equally imperative that women are not ignored in the agenda for a curriculum focused on the experience of Afro-Americans. With women's studies focusing on white women and black studies focusing on black men, women of color disappear from the scene. A male-dominated curriculum in black studies results in the exclusion of black women from courses such as "Black Literature" or "Black History." And, like the related trend in the male-centered curriculum, the only black women who are mentioned stand out as historical exceptions. Black women's studies promises to put black women and other women of color back into our vision and to do so in a way that explores the experience of ordinary women acting within the fabric of their everyday lives. The recent development of black women's studies at Spelman College, for example, speaks to this need. A full program in black studies would acknowledge the ordinary activities of women and men of color, as well as the exceptional contributions of those who led remarkable lives.[15]

Planning for the Future: Multiple Strategies for a Radical Mission

Working together, black studies and women's studies can coordinate projects to ensure that both race and gender will be the basis for transforming the curriculum. We must expect and even encourage in this process the adoption of multiple strategies and intellectual perspectives, since it appears that movements for social change are stronger when they entail multiple purposes and philosophies. This was the case for the nineteenth-century women's movement, and it also appears true if we examine the diverse perspectives and programs that constitute contemporary black and feminist movements. Intellectually, this encourages a pluralistic approach to our studies, since it recognizes multiple realities in people's lives; a diversity of intellectual perspectives provides a rich account of these experiences.

Through cosponsorship of faculty development programs, black studies and women's studies will each best accomplish the goals they have historically defined for themselves. Their cooperation will not only require the political and administrative acumen to maneuver through educational institutions, but it will also require personal and intellectual changes to override the racism and sexism inherent in much of our own work. If we keep in mind that we are educating students for a world which is neither all-white nor all-male, then we will have to realize that we can no longer certify students as educated if they know nothing of the history and contemporary facts of racism and sexism. The commitment of women's studies and black studies to humanistic and liberating values will continue to be the heartbeat of this work.

The ultimate radicalism of efforts to transform the curriculum is revealed when we see how the goals of women's studies and black studies are contrary to those of dominant institutions. Transforming these institutions means we embark on projects that radicalize us because they show how our experience has been denied in the past. Black studies and women's studies do not cancel out our differences, but show us how contradictions and differences enrich the whole fabric of our experience.[16] Together, black studies and women's studies show the specificity of the traditional curriculum, even when it claims to be absolute and universal. We know this to be a myth and are committed to revealing it. The ultimate contribution of black studies and women's studies is in showing how race, class, and gender are fundamental and interlocking systems that define us all.

Notes

1. Marcia Westkott, "Feminist Criticism of the Social Science," *Harvard Educational Review* 49 (1979): 422–30.
2. See Ellen Carol DuBois, *Feminism and Suffrage* (Ithaca: Cornell University Press, 1978); and Sara Evans, *Personal Politics: The Roots of Women's Liberation in the Civil Rights Movement and the New Left* (New York: Knopf, 1979).
3. Shirley Weber, "Black Power in the 1960's: A Study of Its Impact on Women's Liberation," *Journal of Black Studies* 11 (June 1981): 483–97.
4. Vincent Harding, "Black Studies and the Impossible Revolution," *Journal of Black Studies* 1 (September 1970): 82.
5. Boniface Obichere, "The Significance and Challenge of Afro-American Studies," *Journal of Black Studies* 1 (December 1970): 171.
6. Russel Adams, "Black Studies Perspectives," *Journal of Negro Education* 46 (Spring 1977): 99–117.
7. Frederick Douglass, *Life and Times of Frederick Douglass* (New York: Collier Books, 1962), p.79.
8. Bettye Collier-Thomas, "The Impact of Black Women in Education: An Historical Overview," *Journal of Negro Education* 51 (Summer 1982): 173.
9. Florence Howe, *Seven Years Later: Women's Studies Programs in 1976* (Washington, D.C.: National Advisory Council on Women's Educational Programs, June 1977).
10. Gloria Bowles and Renate Duelli-Klein, "Theories of Women's Studies and the Autonomy/Integration Debate," in Bowles and Duelli-Klein, eds., *Theories of Women's Studies* (Boston: Routledge and Kegan Paul, 1983), pp.1–26.
11. Ronald Walters and Robert Smith, "The Black Education Strategy in the 1970's," *Journal of Negro Education* 48 (Spring 1979): 156–70.
12. Leonard A. Marascuilo and F. Dagenis, "The Meaning of the Word 'Integration' to Seniors in a Multi-Racial High School," *Journal of Negro Education* 43 (Spring 1974): 179–89.
13. James Newton, "A Review of Black Studies as Related to Basic Elements of Curriculum," *Journal of Negro Education* 43 (Fall 1974): 477–88; Clemmont Vontress, "Black Studies—Boon or Bane?" *Journal of Negro Education* 39 (Summer 1970): 192–201; Joyce E. Williams and Ron Ladd, "On the Relevance of Educa-

tion for Black Liberation," *Journal of Negro Education* 47 (Summer 1978): 266–82; and Louis Williams and Mohamed El-Khawas, "A Philosophy of Black Education," *Journal of Negro Education* 47 (Spring 1978): 177–91.

14. Margo Culley, "Black Studies/Women's Studies: An Overdue Partnership." Paper presented at "Moving Toward a Balanced Curriculum" Conference, Wheaton College, Norton, Mass. June 1983.

15. Gloria T. Hull, Patricia B. Scott, and Barbara Smith, eds., *All the Women Are White, All the Men Are Black, But Some of Us Are Brave: Black Women's Studies* (Old Westbury, N.Y.: The Feminist Press, 1982).

16. Johnnella Butler, "The Difference It Makes in the Humanities." Paper presented at "Moving Toward a Balanced Curriculum" Conference, Wheaton College, Norton, Mass. June 1983.

6

Complicating the Question: Black Studies and Women's Studies

Johnnella E. Butler

Many of us who grew up in the sixties, inspired as we discovered Charlotte Perkins Gilman and Charlotte Forten Grimke, Emma Goldman and Shirley Chisholm, W.E.B. DuBois and Simone de Beauvoir, seek to know more about our pasts and present as women, as members of racial, cultural, and ethnic groups. We need also to find a means to reinterpret cultural history in order to effect social change and achieve a plural, equitable society. As teachers and scholars we seek conceptual frameworks to reshape the curriculum so that it will reflect the multicultural reality of the world and the experience of men and women. New frameworks are necessary, for much that has been immortalized in the liberal arts curriculum as "truth" is, in reality, vicious, self-serving fiction.

Scholars and teachers in black studies and women's studies have been working to develop frameworks that not only account for the additional data gathered about Black culture and women's experience, but that reinterpret all cultural history through a truly multicultural perspective. Black studies and women's studies professors have led the way in identifying the changes in content, method, and pedagogy that must take place for the liberal arts curriculum to reflect fully the truth about humanity. Yet no formal, full-scale, faculty development project bringing those two groups together was made until 1981. That was the first year the

Fund for the Improvement of Postsecondary Education (FIPSE) sponsored "Black Studies/Women's Studies: An Overdue Partnership," which I codirected with Margo Culley in the Five College consortium.[1] An analysis of why we undertook this project, our goals and expectations at its outset, what we learned with the twenty participants during our two years together, and how the teaching of a course growing from the project expanded my understanding of the curriculum transformation process clearly reveals the difficulty and necessity of pursuing this work.

Why Black Studies and Women's Studies?

In black studies, we have set many tasks for ourselves: to correct distortions, to revise the history and other studies of people of African ancestry, and to critique the educational process itself by identifying how the colonization of minds is characteristic of American education. Black studies gives us the underside of what has been touted as American reality, past and present. It reveals the lies of the so-called mainstream in society and in the curriculum. Part of the burden for other black studies professors like myself, as the first generation of blacks to teach in significant numbers on predominantly white campuses, has been to act as "cultural translators" even as we advocate a transformation of the curriculum.

Black studies professors are good translators because we understand the interaction of community and culture. Our recognition of the need to examine curricular content contextually emerges from a study of African traditional thought and its expression in the diaspora and from the experience of teaching black studies. Culture is seen as a dynamic process composed of interdependent systems: belief, economics, politics, the arts, language. Cultural pluralism, from this perspective, is a generative process, promoting change and valuing difference.[2]

In women's studies, the need to recover and reconstruct the past, to correct distortions that have come about through the omission of women's experience has also led to a reconsideration of the liberal arts curriculum. Many white women scholars document in their work and realize in their lives the extent to which women are considered "other" in the dominant culture. They understand how the experience of women is systematically devalued in white American culture. They have thus been able to hear and accept the assertions of Afro-American women's studies scholars who warn that women's studies must not be exclusively white and middle class, but must strive for diversity. Reading their own lives contextually, reconsidering claims of "universality," and identifying systematic gender discrimination have led to the desire for conceptual frameworks that are inclusive of difference, in order to understand as fully as possible human acts and creations.

Black studies and women's studies have clear affinities. Both enterprises have strong roots in movements for social change, both cement the connections between theory and practice, between the academy and the world. Black studies and women's studies offer definitions and critiques of culture, analyses of oppression and, as interdisciplinary undertakings, challenge the traditional compartmentalization of knowledge. For these reasons, as well as for reasons having to do with the persistence of racism and sexism within the academy, black studies and women's studies programs and faculty have too often remained on the periphery of educational institutions and have even been forced to compete for the limited resources available to "peripheral" programs.

Black studies and women's studies, despite many affinities and common agendas, also have their own biases and blind spots. Just as black studies as a discipline has too often focused largely on the contributions of black men, women's studies is marked by its early focus on white, middle-class women. Although educators working in these two fields need each other's expertise, they often work in isolation from each other, and have sometimes regarded each other's enterprise with a suspicion that blocks mutual learning.

We undertook the FIPSE project because we felt that neither black studies nor women's studies alone could produce a transformed curriculum and pedagogy. We asked, how can black studies and women's studies transform each other to bring about social, cultural and curricular change so we can know and tell the full truth of human experience? How can the experience of black studies and women's studies teachers working together lay the groundwork for more interdisciplinary work involving other ethnic studies?

An Overdue Partnership: Goals, Expectations, Lessons

Jointly sponsored by the Afro-American Studies Department at Smith College and the Women's Studies Program at the University of Massachusetts in Amherst, the project brought together twenty faculty members from five area colleges in a two-year effort to build the intellectual, methodological, curricular, and pedagogical connections between the interdisciplinary fields of black studies and women's studies.

GOALS AND GUIDELINES

After reviewing other projects that had brought women's studies and/or black studies to the attention of a wide audience of students and teachers, and after assessing the strengths and weaknesses of previous faculty development efforts in our area, we determined that the FIPSE project needed to:

1. Provide a *sustained context* beyond the successful but isolated and occasional events that had focused on the issues of race and gender in our area.
2. Be oriented toward *products*: annotated bibliographies, new courses designed and taught in the home institution during the second year of the project.
3. Demand active participation of all members of the seminar, creating a *learner-centered* experience in which faculty members become resources for each other.
4. Make available to a wider group of faculty members both the thinking and the products of the seminar through a *regional dissemination conference.*
5. Incorporate regular *evaluation* components throughout the two years: entry and exit statements by participants, review of new courses while in progress, on-site visits by outside evaluators.
6. Demonstrate the importance of interdepartmental, interinstitutional, as well as interpersonal cooperation through a *co-directorship.*

The Five College area was ready for this type of faculty development, we felt, because conferences, colloquia, and lectures had already focused on issues of race and gender. Also, the many faculty members in the Five Colleges who had done research and/or teaching on race and gender provided a solid base of local expertise that we could draw on and develop further.

PARTICIPANTS

We publicized the project to all area faculty working in black studies and/or women's studies whether or not they were formally connected to programs or departments. We asked applicants to submit a statement of interest that would include a proposal for a curriculum development project. Selection was based on the strength of the statement of interest and the proposed project as well as on the applicant's demonstrated achievements in black studies and/or women's studies. We also wanted to achieve a balance of black and white participants, a variety of disciplines within these two fields, a mixture of male and female participants, and representation from each of the five area institutions.

Forty area faculty members submitted applications. We chose twenty participants, including four black women, four black men, and twelve white women, all of varying ethnic backgrounds. Two white males were among the forty applicants; neither was accepted. In retrospect, we think we should have accepted at least one of them for the sake of balance.

COMPONENTS AND PRODUCTS OF THE PROJECT

Each semester of the two years, and the intervening summer, had specific goals and were oriented toward different products. The first year of the faculty seminar produced syllabi for new courses designed to be taught at the participants' home institutions the following year (see appendix). Discussions focused on theoretical readings and debates, such as the racism/sexism debate that has been pursued in both black and feminist scholarly publications.[3] We felt it was also desirable to go beyond the questions of racism within women's studies and sexism within black studies and to explore the theoretical and methodological affinities between the fields. The second semester was designed to focus more specifically on the topic of black women in an effort to assist participants in their efforts to create new courses.

The product at the end of the summer between the two years was an annotated bibliography by each participant focusing on race and gender in the area of a newly developed course. This facilitated in-depth preparation of the new courses and further encouraged participants to become resources for each other. Summer stipends helped to free participants from summer teaching responsibilities and provided a modest incentive for participation over the two-year period. We chose stipends rather than released time during the year because released time would have been too costly financially. Even more important, we could not afford to lose for two years the black studies and women's studies courses taught by the participants.

During the second year of the seminar, participants tried out their courses and prepared the regional conference that took place in April 1983. The focus of the second year was pedagogy, addressing issues such as:

1. *Ideology and Learning*: How does ideology (overtly or covertly) shape, motivate, hinder learning?
2. *Authority in the Classroom*: How are the claims of intellectual traditions and the claims of life experience balanced in the classroom?
3. *The Affective Dimensions of Learning*: How does one recognize and direct anger? How and why are feelings expressed and disguised in black studies and women's studies classrooms?
4. *The Insider/Outsider or Oppressor/Oppressed Dialogue*: What challenges does the white student in the black studies classroom pose, or the male student in the women's studies classroom? What are the challenges to a white instructor teaching black studies, to a male instructor in women's studies?

An explicit goal of the final semester of the grant (and the regional conference that followed) was to codesign strategies for survival within our institutional contexts, to address the long-term goal of moving the concerns of black studies/women's studies toward the center of higher education, and by realizing these goals, to transform the liberal arts.

SURPRISES AND LESSONS

The twenty participants who started in the project were tough-minded, eager to tackle difficult issues. Because we were committed to compatible goals, some expected trust at the start; but we discovered that trust is built only after shared experience. What was needed, rather, was real tolerance so that we could begin to listen to each other. We ultimately developed tolerance as participants became open and vulnerable to each other. One of the surprises of the project, however, was that even this highly select group of colleagues from neighboring institutions, all of whom had demonstrated a commitment, through scholarship and teaching, to issues of race and gender, had initial, sometimes volatile, problems listening to each other and learning from each other's experience.

At first we did not recognize the problem. After a number of confrontations and considerable reflection, we discovered that cultural differences, particularly in the area of styles of conflict and communication, were an initial obstacle even in a group that shared so much. Although committed to cultural diversity in principle, we failed at first to recognize the operation of difference in our own interactions. Styles of expressing conflict that were rooted in culture and manifested through body gestures, different tolerance of voice level, and interruption in debate became, in themselves, sources of conflict. Whereas black participants (male and female) were comfortable with interruptions and direct assertions, many of the white women preferred more controlled patterns of debate (such as hand-raising) and interpreted some gestures as negative when they were not intended that way. Only after we sorted out the origins and meanings of differing styles of conflict could we move on to fruitful examination of issues. Our recognition of the role of cultural diversity in the seminar was to prove useful later in discussions of pedagogy and the implementation of the new courses.

Similarly, as we moved to substantive discussion, we learned the importance of reading contextually, interpreting seemingly similar language according to cultural context. One example involved efforts of white women to equate their own experience of alienation, being relegated to the status of "other" in white American culture, to what black participants called "double cons-

ciousness." The black experience of "double consciousness," as
originally defined by DuBois, entails a constant awareness of
oppression, of outsider status in a racist culture. Black participants resisted equating the white feminist experience with their
own. They urged the white women to refine the meaning of their
own terms rather than falsely to conflate black and white experiences. "Otherness" is not constant in the same way for white
women as "double consciousness" is for black men or women,
because white women are nevertheless served by white American
culture; they benefit from racial privilege. Only by understanding
the differences in perception and experience that marked participants could we then move on to a useful discussion of commonalities.

In bringing together black studies and women's studies, we find
that we must reconstruct the past, redefine ourselves, extricate our
norms from the illusions and deceptions of history as it has been
taught, destroy cultural hegemony and cultural submission, classism, and gender discrimination, and recreate identities based on
truly pluralistic norms. What did we learn about transforming the
liberal arts curriculum? We must incorporate race, gender, class,
and culture as categories of analysis throughout the curriculum.

All this means simply that we are not alike. To include Afro-
American literature or sociology in established courses, for example, requires a thorough reading of scholarship on the Afro-
American literary tradition and the black family structure. It is
not enough to add on a unit to a course in literature or sociology;
to teach the material responsibly requires attention not only to
the black cultural context that shaped the literature or the family,
but to the interaction of that context with the dominant white culture. That requires, in turn, an explicit analysis of the cultural
norms that define white literature and social structures. Efforts to
transform the curriculum through incorporation of black studies
and women's studies reveal the need to reformulate and redefine
the disciplines.

Testing the Product:
Teaching Women and Philosophy

The course I developed in the seminar with Vicky Spelman of the
Smith College Philosophy Department, and that we've now

team-taught, is an interdisciplinary course called "Women and Philosophy." We wanted to pay explicit attention to ethnicity and how it operates, to challenge conventional definitions of philosophy and of feminism, to engage the students in a generative process moving from the familiar to the unfamiliar. The class was mixed by race, ethnicity, and class, and it struggled in microcosm to achieve the dialogue we seek between women's studies and black studies, much as the faculty seminar had.

Students were hampered, as we all have been, by an inadequate definition of culture and ethnicity due to the tendency to see people in an either/or (rather than a richer, both/and) fashion. We confuse ethnicity with geographical distinctions and further distort perception by our simplistic reduction of everything to the racial. African traditional thought has produced in the New World, West Indian culture, Haitian culture, Brazilian culture, and Afro-Brazilian culture, among others. Asian traditional thought (which we reduce to a monolith called Eastern thought) has produced in this country Japanese-Americans, Chinese-Americans, Korean-Americans, Filipino-Americans, Vietnamese-Americans. Native-American worldviews are, in a sense, the least accessible in what we call American culture because of the history of American Indian persecution.

This brief listing of cultures that are American illustrates that the insights of black studies (and other ethnic studies) complicate the question of what is American. Even in a classroom where there is ethnic diversity, habits of reduction keep students from understanding the complexities of American culture. We have Euro-Americans of various European-based ethnic backgrounds, an Anglo-American ethnic-value dominance, and people of color, of varying types and degrees of color, who share some combination of the Euro-American, Afro-American, Native-American, Asian-American, and Hispanic-American ethnicities. The complexities of culture are particularly acute for those whose ethnic sensibility is based on a European continuum as well as an African or Asian continuum. The negation of the both/and possibility is central to the oppression of black Americans; it means, for example, that I cannot be perceived as racially and culturally of African and Euro-American descent. In our class, we learned to allow for the tension that emerges when WASP students discover the lie they've been told—that they are just American, the norm, and not that theirs is an ethnicity that holds power.

In the "Women and Philosophy" course we also wanted to complicate the question of what is feminism. For example, we put Toni Cade Bambara (*The Salt Eaters*) on the syllabus, as the first work to be read, to insist that the students begin the course dealing with feminism in a way that demands recognition of women other than simply white women. Virginia Woolf (*A Room of One's Own*) immediately followed. We felt that Bambara's work challenged Woolf's definition in serious ways, particularly in regard to racism and classism, and would facilitate a more inclusive, complex definition of feminism. Real transformation, we learned, requires a willingness to revise even while teaching, a willingness to be surprised.

We had not anticipated the loyalty that many of the students (white and black) felt toward Woolf. Because we challenged that loyalty, they resisted the effort to articulate a new definition of feminism. We learned through the experience that we should first validate the students' feelings and understand their basis and origins, and *then* engage them in imagining an expanded definition of feminism. The incident brought into sharp focus a problem central to the transformation process: establishing credibility with a class. Briefly, a black professor teaching black literature and favoring a specific text risks being dismissed as chauvinistic. A white professor challenging conventional expectations may be dismissed as idiosyncratic. Identifying and engaging the students' feelings is not only a means of validating them, but also of establishing the teacher's credibility.

Ultimately, the students identified insights they had gained through our dialogue with one another on issues of feminism:

1. We cannot assume that friendship alone, or the desire for friendship, will bring about either knowledge or transformation.

2. Good intentions are important, but are not sufficient to help move beyond the guilt felt when one confronts the fact s/he may belong by birth and color to an oppressive group. Guilt encourages inertia rather than responsible action.

3. Recognizing and understanding cultural differences does not hinder growth. Cultural differences prevent growth only when

they are made into deficits or benefits that create structural inequalities.

4. Insisting that we are all "just" human and implying that we are color-blind and not culture-bound or class-bound does not lead to cooperation and understanding, because societal restrictions and our history do not allow us to act in human ways toward each other without a concerted effort.

5. Each of us must recognize (and resist) the ease of falling back into the system. Beliefs are not easily changed; to do so involves a conscious process that encourages people to think critically.

6. We cannot assume that people are well-meaning or that mutual trust is a given. Our society does not encourage mutual trust; it must be worked for.

Underlying these observations is the realization that most human beings desire to see information as finite and define progress in terms of material comfort. Frequently, when we speak of "gaining knowledge for progress in human affairs," we are not talking about progress at all, but about how to use knowledge for a more elegant order. For women's studies and black studies, the desire for such an artificial order is a trap we must not fall into. We are not engaged in the pursuit of order; we must, rather, be genuinely interested in progress, even if it produces the *appearance* of turmoil and chaos. We do not yet have the knowledge or conceptual frameworks necessary to define a truly inclusive, pluralistic order. What we are engaged in is a long journey toward understanding the diversity within and the complexities of women's studies and black studies, both as separate entities and together. We are working toward the end of understanding the diversity of the human universe in order to create a more humane world and a more truthful curriculum.

Notes

1. The Five College consortium is comprised of five institutions in the Connecticut Valley: the University of Massachusetts, Amherst, a large, public university; Amherst, a small, formerly men's college; Hampshire, a ten-year-old experimental college; Mount Holyoke, the oldest women's college in the country; and Smith, the largest private women's college in the United States.

Much of this essay grows out of my collaborative work with Margo Culley. We are currently editing a volume of materials produced by the FIPSE project that further analyzes the experience: *Black Studies/Women's Studies: An Overdue Partnership.*

2. See, for example, Johnnella E. Butler, *Black Studies Pedagogy and Revolution* (Lanham, Md.: University Press of America, 1981); Philip T.K. Daniel, "Theory Building in Black Studies," *The Black Scholar* 12, no. 3 (May–June 1981): 29–36; Charles A. Frye, *Towards a Philosophy of Black Studies* (Saratoga, Calif.: R. and E. Research Associates, 1978); Merrill Harvey Goldwyn, "Teaching Literature and Human Rights Curricular Possibilities," *Improving College and University Teaching* 31, no. 4 (Fall 1983): 149–54; and Thaddeus H. Spratten, "The Educational Relevance of Black Studies: An Interdisciplinary and Intercultural Interpretation," *Western Journal of Black Studies* 1, no. 1 (March 1977): 38–45.

3. See, for example, Robert Staples, "The Myth of Black Macho: A Response to Angry Feminists," *The Black Scholar* 10, no. 2 (March–April 1979); responses to the Staples article in *The Black Scholar* 10, no. 3 (May–June 1979); and Elly Bulkin, "Racism and Writing: Some Implications for White Lesbian Critics," *Sinister Wisdom* 13 (Spring 1980): 3–22.

Appendix
Black Studies/Women's Studies: An Overdue Partnership

COURSES ADDRESSING ISSUES OF RACE, GENDER, AND CULTURE

AFRO-AMERICAN CHURCH MUSIC. Horace Clarence Boyer, Music, University of Massachusetts.

THE AFRO-AMERICAN WOMAN AND THE FEMINIST MOVEMENT. John Walter, Afro-American Studies, Smith College.

BLACK FEMINISM. Arlene Avakian and Mary Ruth Warner, Women's Studies, University of Massachusetts.

BLACK SOCIOLOGICAL THOUGHT. John Bracey, Afro-American Studies, University of Massachusetts.

COMPARATIVE BRITISH AND AMERICAN WOMEN'S HISTORY. Joyce Avrech Berkman, History, University of Massachusetts.

ETHNIC LITERATURE OF AMERICAN WOMEN. Margo Culley, English and Women's Studies, University of Massachusetts.

FEMINISM, BLACK NATIONALISM, MARXISM. Sara Lennox, John Bracey, Dan Clawson, German, Afro-American Studies, Philosophy, University of Massachusetts.

FEMINIST THEORY. Arlyn Diamond, English, University of Massachusetts.

THE LITERATURE OF THE BLACK WOMAN. Johnnella Butler, Afro-American Studies, Smith College.

PHILOSOPHY AND WOMEN. Ann Ferguson, Philosophy, University of Massachusetts.

THE POLITICAL ECONOMY OF WOMEN: CROSS-CULTURAL PERSPECTIVES. Amrita Basu, Amherst College.

THE PSYCHOLOGY OF WOMEN. Carla Golden, Psychology, Smith College.

RACE AND ETHNICITY IN AMERICAN LIFE. Laura Wexler, American Studies, Amherst College.

RACE IN POLITICS AND CULTURE OF THE UNITED STATES: 1920–1980. E. Francis White and Allen Hunter, Social Science, Hampshire College.

RACE, SEX, AND COMMUNICATION. Fern Johnson and Charlena Seymour, Communication Studies and Communication Disorders, University of Massachusetts.

THE SOCIO-CULTURAL DEVELOPMENT OF THE AFRO-AMERICAN WOMAN. Carolyn Jacobs, School for Social Work, Smith College.

THEM: MINORITY IMAGES IN AMERICAN FILM AND LITERATURE. Joseph T. Skerrett, Jr., English, University of Massachusetts.

THIRD WORLD WOMEN WRITERS IN THE UNITED STATES. Roberta Fernandez, Afro-American Studies, Smith College.

TWENTIETH CENTURY AMERICAN AND BRITISH WOMEN'S EXPERIENCE. Joyce Avrech Berkman, History, University of Massachusetts.

UNIVERSITY WITHOUT WALLS: CROSS-CULTURAL SEMINAR. Arlyn Diamond, English, University of Massachusetts.

URBAN POLITICS. Martha Ackelsberg, Government, Smith College.

WOMEN AND PHILOSOPHY. Johnnella Butler and Elizabeth Spelman, Afro-American Studies, Philosophy, Smith College.

WOMEN AND REVOLUTION: CROSS-CULTURAL SEMINAR. Joyce Avrech Berkman, History, University of Massachusetts.

WOMEN OF THE PORTUGUESE-SPEAKING WORLD. Alicia Clemente, Spanish and Portuguese, Smith College.

WOMEN'S FOLK MUSIC: THE BLUES. Mary Ruth Warner, Women's Studies, University of Massachusetts.

II

Faculty Development:
Models for Institutional Change

7

Changing the Institution

Marilyn R. Schuster and Susan R. Van Dyne

Transforming institutional structures in order to translate the insights of feminist scholarship and pedagogy effectively is a particularly difficult task at this historical moment. External and internal forces have created a context of crisis in American higher education that imperils progressive change. Budget cuts, retrenchment, a steady-state faculty, a shrinking pool of applicants, the changing expectations of women and men students: the crises that beset American higher education in the eighties have put many faculty members on the defensive, making them more protective of their own special interests at the very moment that interdepartmental cooperation and a broader institutional vision are called for.

The intellectual and structural provincialism created by this defensive posture is aggravated as aging faculties find themselves caught between rapid disciplinary changes, on the one hand, and shrinking financial resources, on the other. In *The Academic Tribes* (1976) Hazard S. Adams recognized that "the diminishment of organizational allegiance" was an influential principle of academic politics. According to this principle, "the fundamental allegiance of the faculty member will be to the smallest unit to which he or she belongs."* The curriculum transformation plans described in Part II suggest antidotes to faculty isolationism.

---

*Adams developed this principle further in an article for the annual MLA publication *Profession '83:* "How Departments Commit Suicide," pp. 29–35.

Plans to integrate women's experience in the liberal arts curriculum address many of the problems colleges and universities are facing in the last two decades of the twentieth century. These plans acknowledge the growing numbers of women students (both traditional-aged and returning students), provide means for retraining faculty, maximize the use of internal resources, and create a context in which faculty members work across departmental boundaries toward shared intellectual and institutional goals. Because the new scholarship on women is by nature interdisciplinary, and because women's studies has stressed the interrelationship of the new scholarship and pedagogical change, plans to integrate that scholarship throughout the curriculum provide a means for faculty renewal in research and teaching. The essays in this section analyze the experience of projects in colleges and universities throughout the country: public and private, coeducational and women's. Although most of these projects began with external funding from NEH, FIPSE, Ford, Mellon, WEEA and Carnegie, for example, many have been successfully institutionalized, and their experience can provide models for internally funded projects on other campuses.

The Beginnings of Integration Projects: Common Elements

The centerpiece of all integration projects is faculty development. In an era of steady-state faculty, colleges cannot depend exclusively on new personnel or outside consultants to effect the kind of long-range change these models aim for. Some plans include only tenured faculty on the assumption that these are the teachers with the longest range commitment to the institution and with the level of responsibility and power over the curriculum necessary to make changes. This may, however, isolate and alienate junior faculty. It's worth remembering that in traditional departmental hierarchies, junior faculty members most frequently staff the basic courses of departments that need to be transformed to touch the greatest number of students. Betty Schmitz, Myra Dinnerstein and Nancy Mairs examine the experience of a wide range of projects in public institutions in the western states that targeted different types of faculty through a variety of recruitment strategies.

A primary vehicle for faculty development on many campuses, as these essays illustrate, has been a seminar or workshop. The most effective of these seminars have been interdisciplinary and ongoing (in the summer or through the term, supported by released time or a stipend to participants). This environment frees faculty members from a narrow, departmental perspective. In interdisciplinary study and work groups, faculty members become engaged in a common intellectual undertaking in which they can exercise their own expertise, develop new ideas, and attempt to establish a mutually intelligible vocabulary. Many seminars include visiting outside experts, putting faculty in commerce with leaders in women's scholarship. Visits from outsiders can simultaneously validate local feminist faculty members. Faculty members whose research and teaching are women-focused have expertise that makes them essential to any form of transformation project. While these internal resources must be central to any integration project, administrative support needs to be explicit so that the project is recognized as an institutional priority and not merely the personal priority of feminist faculty.

The seminars that have produced the most lasting consequences have required some tangible product of participants: a bibliography for their specific teaching field, a syllabus to be implemented within the next year, a paper, or participation in a new, shared teaching experience. These tangible outcomes assure that the faculty make the newly learned material their own through teaching it, and prompt a degree of reflection to help faculty members analyze the process of change, including their own resistance and incentive for development. Since the curriculum is at the heart of a college's mission and depends on institutional support systems, the most effective plans also involve administrators, librarians, and other non-faculty personnel so they are all informed and engaged in what is ultimately an institutionwide effort.

A final element shared by all projects is a concern to assure progeny. The long-range nature of curriculum transformation requires that some means be found to continue to involve more faculty and administrators in the enterprise. As Schmitz, Dinnerstein, and Mairs point out in their analysis, realizable short-term goals (changing a specific syllabus, mounting a seminar around a certain set of issues) should not be confused with the long-term objective of involving ever increasing numbers of faculty members in projects that will help them inform their courses and teaching through feminist scholarship.

Curriculum Transformation Comes of Age: Three Models

The curriculum transformation projects analyzed in these separate essays, and throughout the anthology, represent some of the best work that has been done in the last five years. A review of these projects and others suggests three primary models that have been tried in a variety of contexts. While these essays develop, in detail, complex and diverse strategies for undertaking transformation work within very different institutions, with marked differences in local resources and political climates, we think it is useful to propose an overview of the models that are emerging from these and other projects. Such an overview can serve to clarify options for those committed to this work and enable them to share successful strategies. Our effort here is descriptive, not prescriptive. Each model has its strengths and inherent risks, as the essays in this section demonstrate. From the more than fifty curriculum projects undertaken since the late seventies, three models stand out:

A top-down model that begins with an administrative directive to make sweeping changes in the curriculum by integrating introductory courses in all departments or otherwise affecting a significant number of basic courses.

A piggy-back model in which interdisciplinary courses or programs already sanctioned within the institutional agenda are targeted by women's studies groups or by administrators as the best way to begin curriculum transformation and to reach a broad range of faculty.

A bottom-up coordination or consortial model that originates with faculty expertise and student interest and seeks to highlight, connect, and maximize internal or regional resources. Retraining is accomplished through collaboration among peers.

In thinking about these models we asked how each would answer these questions: Who can change? Where is the locus for change? What are the incentives for change? And how do we evaluate change? In seeking answers to these questions we've tried to bring into view the assumptions and priorities, the invisible paradigms, that may govern the outcomes of these important experiments.

THE TOP-DOWN MODEL

The top-down model is best illustrated here by the first stage of the Wheaton experiment that culminated in the dissemination conference analyzed in Bonnie Spanier's essay and by some of the initial projects sponsored by Montana State and the Southwest Institute for Research on Women.

A distinguishing characteristic of the top-down model is a comprehensive administrative mandate. The initial charge at Wheaton, for example, was "to integrate scholarship about women into the whole curriculum." Established departments or divisions are most frequently the locus for change in this model, with a special focus on the introductory courses within departments. This is partly determined by a desire to reach as many students and faculty as possible, as quickly as possible. The implied assumption here is that the answer to "who can change" is "everyone should."

The targeting of introductory-level courses, working within the departmental structure, and the broad mandate that characterize the top-down model serve to bring into sharp relief tenacious paradigms that have been invisible or at least obscured. The conventional introductory course in traditional departments, those designed to introduce students to the material and methodology of a discipline, are probably the hardest to transform. To transform their assumptions and organization requires rethinking the entire discipline and usually must wait until a significant proportion of the faculty has first-hand experience teaching scholarship on women in intermediate and advanced courses.

A second discovery is that using the departmental structure as a locus for change is not enough. Because this model is often adopted by institutions without a core of women's studies faculty, they discover they've tried to skip a step that is essential to effective transformation: the creation of women-focused courses that don't fit departmental categories. As Spanier's analysis of the Wheaton experience points out, the presence of interdisciplinary courses in feminist theory or focused on women's experience are essential for providing not only data, but strategies and theory for rethinking conventional courses. Although projects designed according to the top-down model, particularly those that require tangible products of faculty participants, do succeed in transforming some basic courses, the most positive outcome is likely to be the creation of a network of faculty members who might begin to provide the missing step: women-focused and feminist theory courses.

The top-down model almost inevitably generates faculty resistance and even backlash if the administrative initiative is perceived as an effort to tell faculty members what and how to teach. The best strategy for countering that resistance, as Schmitz, Dinnerstein, Mairs, and Spanier point out, is to minimize the top-down nature of the project by making participation voluntary and soliciting a wide range of faculty-designed proposals to compete for available resources.

THE PIGGY-BACK MODEL

Projects structured along the lines of the piggy-back model hope ultimately to transform the whole curriculum, but take as the locus for change a course or department that already stands outside the conventional disciplines and yet enjoys a privileged place in the institution's established agenda. Whereas the first model begins with a departmental base, this second model is interdepartmental or interdisciplinary at the start. The Lewis and Clark project that led to the reevaluation of coeducation (described in Chapter 3) started as a piggy-back plan targeting the General Studies Program, because it is interdisciplinary, multicultural, and involves a large number of faculty who teach in teams. The objective was to train faculty participants who would bring their new knowledge back to the General Studies Program, and who, while team-teaching, would in turn teach the others what they'd gained in the seminar. The program organizers hoped that faculty participants would also spontaneously transform their upper division courses.

The results of another piggy-back project underway at Alverno College in Milwaukee are described in "Transforming the Social Sciences" (Chapter 17). Their locus for change is an important interdisciplinary program, the Social Sciences and Policy Studies Department. Here the locus for change was less the faculty than the students, whom they hoped to change by engaging them directly in a participatory learning/teaching process. Explicitly using gender as a category of analysis helped them make two important discoveries. First, students became more personally engaged in their learning, deriving definitions of political power and social systems from their own experience, and became more politically active by transgressing the conventional boundaries between the classroom and the world, intellectual reflection and political action. Second, issues even the organizers had initially perceived as gender-neutral (urban policies in housing and transportation, for example) were found to affect the lives of men and women in markedly different ways. The Alverno project, like the one at Stephens College described in Chapter 4, explicitly recognized that by transforming the curriculum they hoped to empower women students to participate more actively in the world and become change agents in their communities.

The clearest advantage of the piggy-back model is the legitimacy and visibility afforded by association with a strong requirement or program that is already central to the institution's curriculum. A risk of this model is that the program or core courses it targets will swallow up the entire integration effort. If faculty members change their view of their disciplines, however, they can carry what they've learned into their other courses. This translation requires conscious encouragement. The model also points to further ways to "piggy-back" institutionwide development efforts. For example, programs to improve writing across the curriculum or to develop computer literacy could profitably be linked to women's studies integration.

THE BOTTOM-UP MODEL

The bottom-up model presupposes a network, however loosely defined, of feminist scholars, women-focused courses, and other resources. All the questions—who can change, what is the locus for change, what stimulates change and how we measure it—are answered differently than for the other two models. The immediate objective of this model is to make visible and accessible all the resources within a region or institution that facilitate curriculum transformation in order to create a community for previously dispersed feminist scholars and teachers, and then to include others who are new to women's research and teaching in the community.

The Smith plan analyzed in Chapter 8 illustrates the adoption of this model on an individual campus, and the Great Lakes Colleges Association Summer Institute discussed in Chapter 10 exemplifies this model on a regional scale. The Western States project described by Schmitz, Dinnerstein, and Mairs in Chapter 9 is also a regional, consortial model that makes the best use of resources and experience throughout a large area of the country. These projects attempt to create a new locus in which to operate and effect change. Just as the top-down model is departmental and targets introductory courses, and the piggy-back model is interdepartmental, the bottom-up model is counter- or extradepartmental.

The Wheaton project, begun as a campus project along the lines of the top-down model, culminated in a national conference described in Chapter 11. In a sense the conference created a hybrid model. The organizers planned it according to the principles of the consortial model, making disparate resources available to a broad network of institutions. At the same time they required participating schools to send teams made up of administrators, women's studies faculty, and faculty new to feminist scholarship. In this way they sought to foster the kind of coalition necessary to initiate top-down or piggy-back projects on local campuses.

Models for the Future

Because true transformation is a long-range undertaking and must be ongoing to be effective, and because external sources of funding are drying up, we need to look to the experience of successful programs for models that can be undertaken economically within our current institutional resources. The commitment to research and teaching about women, which is easy to articulate when an outside funding agency is paying for it, must become an integral part of fund-raising objectives, of appeals to alumni donors, and of the operating budget when no more grants are forthcoming.

The essays in this section begin with campus-based projects and then move outward to regional efforts, ending with the national conference sponsored by Wheaton. Each essay seeks to identify ways to assess local conditions and to maximize internal and regional resources so that new projects may be undertaken and established ones continue, even as outside funding sources diminish.

It's important, as Schmitz, Dinnerstein, and Mairs argue, not to confuse transformation of the academic disciplines and institutional power structures with mere assimilation of what's most affordable or readily acceptable of women's studies. We need to be particularly insistent that what we have to offer is an inclusive vision of the complexity of gender as a category of analysis, not merely white women's studies. As Johnnella Butler and Margaret Andersen point out in Part I, we need to be clear that race and class are not merely adjuncts or liberal afterthoughts to a concern for gender, but the essential means for understanding the diversity of women's experience and the experience of other subordinate groups. We need to protect and speak up for our own often-silenced minorities, such as lesbians, and not allow their presence and identities to be submerged in the name of short-term political compromises.

Whether located within departmental structures, in concert with preexisting interdisciplinary programs, or in new structures outside the usual avenues of curriculum design, the experience of all these models has shown that when real transformation begins to happen, we become even more aware of the breadth and tenacity of the invisible paradigms of our institutions, our disciplines, and our own social and psychological construction. We need to recognize, in short, the pervasive and unconscious forms in which the dominant culture is reproduced in the curriculum and the classroom, even as we have as our conscious goal the transformation of our culture's understanding of women.

8

Beyond Departmental Boundaries

Marilyn R. Schuster and Susan R. Van Dyne

Building from Strength

The Smith curriculum transformation plan seeks to build on existing strengths and to facilitate interdisciplinary teaching and learning in an institutional context structured by academic departments. Throughout the seventies, individual faculty members in separate departments had developed women-focused courses that reflected both their research interests and growing student demand for attention to women's experience in the curriculum. We saw the need, partly through student prompting, to build a more formal community for interdisciplinary exchange among these teachers, to learn from our collective experience, and to share the insights we were gaining in women-focused courses with faculty members whose own research had not led them in that direction.

We started with a strong women's studies base (about two dozen women-focused courses offered each year) and the conviction that as a women's college, Smith has a special responsibility to offer our students an inclusive vision of human experience. We wanted to develop a model that would accomplish these goals:

- provide a forum for interdisciplinary exchange among women's studies teachers,
- enable faculty members whose research did not focus on women's experience to learn how feminist scholarship might inform their courses,

- bring faculty members from a variety of departments together to test the findings of scholarship on women and insights from feminist pedagogy through interdisciplinary teaching, and
- provide a common interdisciplinary educational experience that incorporated the study of women for a sizable number of students and faculty members.

To accomplish these goals we developed a model that combines mechanisms for faculty development that had already proven successful for Smith faculty with a curricular experiment that provides a new approach to course organization and joint teaching. The model has three tiers that represent sequential involvement: introductory workshops, faculty development seminars, and an annual course cluster.

The Model

FACULTY DEVELOPMENT: THEORY

We recognize that most faculty members are not engaged in research that focuses on women; further, they are often intimidated by the quantity of research that has become available in the last two decades, and because this work is frequently interdisciplinary by nature, they are often unsure how it might relate to their own research and teaching. Because a growing percentage of the total faculty at Smith, as at many other institutions, is tenured, in-service retraining becomes essential for any fundamental restructuring of the curriculum. To engage established teachers whose graduate training did not include work on women, without benefit of large outside funding, was central to the conception of our model and to the ultimate production of large numbers of transformed courses.

For the last three years we have offered intensive five-week faculty seminars in the fall semester, taught by Smith faculty whose own research and teaching focuses on issues of gender, race, and/or class, and open to anyone who is willing to make the commitment to five weeks of interdisciplinary readings and discussions. The presenters received a modest stipend. All participants were given a copy of our *Selected Bibliography for Integrat-*

ing Research on Women's Experience in the Liberal Arts Curriculum to guide their library search for course materials and background reading. The primary incentive for participation, we found, was the possibility of engaging in intellectual inquiry with peers.

Each seminar focuses on "the difference it makes" to include women in the curriculum. Presenters from different fields demonstrate how the new scholarship has changed the shape of knowledge in their field; for example, how the definition of "politics" changes when the experience of the family and women are taken into account, how definitions of "genre" and conventions of interpretation shift when women's writing is studied on its own terms.

The purpose of the seminar is to expose basic theoretical questions that have emerged in feminist scholarship and to work together to see how they apply to the fields of the seminar participants. In the first seminar, for example, we focused on feminist literary criticism. Initially the presenters, whose work is in literature, illustrated the ways in which women's texts and feminist literary criticism have changed the questions we ask of texts, placing, for example, a more important emphasis on the cultural context of both the writer and the reader, and showing the ways in which gender is inscribed or disguised in texts by women and men. Then the participants supplied readings from their own fields (such as history, philosophy, psychology, sociology, or music) and together we applied strategies of interpretation that had originated in literary criticism but which shed new light on the making of meaning in all texts.

The second and third years, presenters from eight different fields (literature, anthropology, psychology, black history, biology, art history, politics, and philosophy) discussed "the difference" feminist scholarship had made in their disciplines by leading discussions of key essays in each field. They demonstrated how this scholarship could provide frameworks for incorporating gender, race, and class as categories of analysis in traditional courses.

Discussion in each seminar offered so far, particularly around issues as explosive as gender and race, was often heated, illustrating the diversity of views encompassed by feminist scholars, the different weighting of priorities, and also the difficulty of speaking across disciplines. Hammering out what the criteria for "evidence" are in one field as opposed to another, discovering in practice what it means to be shaped by a discipline that forefronts method (like the sciences), or causality (like the social sciences), or meaning and interpretation (like literature), or esthetics (like the arts and music) helped all the participants see more clearly their own working assumptions as well as those of other fields. Although some of these issues would surface in any interdisciplinary seminar, they surface with more urgency in an interdisciplinary seminar focused on women and minorities because feminist scholarship is testing the underlying assumptions of the disciplines, and because our personal, psychological assumptions about gender, race, and class are so often unconscious.

The participants represented twenty departments and also included the head librarian and the director of Career Development. The most common response of the participants was enthusiasm at the opportunity of meeting in an interdisciplinary forum that focused on intellectual issues. "We so rarely get to talk about teaching, much less see each other teach," was a typical response. At the end of the spring semester participants wanted to meet again to compare notes on how insights gained from the seminar had affected the teaching of their regular spring semester courses.

The intensive faculty development seminar, then, provides a theoretical base for faculty members who are interested in scholarship on women, but whose own research is not focused on women, to reexamine the courses they regularly teach. We found that a sizable group of faculty members from the three main divisions of the college (science, social science, and the humanities) were interested in taking such a seminar. After three more years our seminars will have reached seventy-five faculty members (about a third of our full-time faculty), with a potential impact on more than 350 courses.

In 1985 we began a second type of faculty outreach in a format familiar to Smith faculty members: an introductory facultywide workshop. In January, for example, we offered a one-day workshop for forty or fifty participants during which outside con-

sultants presented the fundamental questions raised when we try
to incorporate material about women and minorities throughout
the curriculum. In this format, requiring a less sustained initial
commitment, we hope to attract, on a voluntary basis, an even
broader group of faculty members, perhaps more skeptical, than
the teachers who made a five-week commitment, and less conver-
sant with feminist scholarship. We anticipate that future seminar
participants will emerge from the workshop group. We feel that
the introductory workshops should be run by someone from outside the Smith community to avoid the possibility that internal
political issues automatically associated with anyone from within
the faculty will obscure the presentation of the issues.

Why didn't we implement this introductory stage of faculty
development first? Although introducing the fundamental questions would seem a logical first phase of faculty development, we
have saved it for last in our implementation schedule for political
reasons that may well pertain on other campuses. Our plan is
what we have termed a "bottom-up" model. Although we had
administrative approval for the integration plan, the impetus,
resources, and implementation came from the faculty. We felt we
first needed to consolidate our strengths by connecting the
women-focused courses we had developed individually and by
creating an extradepartmental structure. Then we wanted to build
a base of faculty members seriously committed to reconceptualizing their traditional courses through the incorporation of scholarship on women and non-white cultural groups. At Smith as elsewhere, incorporating a feminist perspective in the liberal arts
curriculum is a volatile political issue, primarily because of misconceptions about what feminist scholarship is and how it relates
to course design and pedagogy. Given only tacit administrative
support, if we had started by offering a facultywide workshop
without first creating a solid base of support, the resistance might
have been stronger because fewer faculty members would have
understood what transformation is really about. After three fall
seminars we believe enough teachers in different departments are
committed to the task and informed about it to persuade other,
more skeptical colleagues that it is worth the investment of one
day to learn about the basic questions.

THE COURSE CLUSTER: PRACTICE

The curricular core of the Smith model, the place where students and teachers, theory and practice come together, is the Course Cluster. Since 1982, four established courses (often two women-focused and two transformed) from different departments have been chosen to form a "cluster" of courses in the spring semester. A student may take one or more of the courses, which are linked by a public lecture and discussion series around an interdisciplinary theme relevant to each of the courses: "Women and Power" in 1982, "Women: Image and Identity" in 1983, "Culture Constructs the Female" in 1984. (The complete programs for these three years are listed in the appendix.)

To help students and faculty members become aware of the resources we have at hand in the area of feminist scholarship and political action, the instructors have chosen members of the Smith or Five College faculties or, in one case, a political activist from the local community to give the lectures. The lecturers are asked to look critically at their discipline and to ask, for instance, how raising questions about women has altered their sense of their discipline and of themselves as teachers and researchers, and how disciplinary questions are reshaped in order to account for women's experience. For example, for the "Culture Constructs the Female" lecture series, each lecturer was asked to address questions such as, how do you understand "culture" with reference to your field? Has the study of women altered your understanding or perception of "culture" as it affects definitions of the individual? What terms do various cultural contexts provide for defining women? How have women in those contexts understood, confronted, adapted, or transformed those terms of definition?

Immediately following each lecture, the students divide into small groups to discuss what they have heard, and to relate it to their courses and to the other lectures in the series. Each discussion group is led by an interdisciplinary team of two faculty members. For faculty, the lecture and discussion series is a formal extension of the interdisciplinary exchange begun in the fall seminar. It also gives us a chance to teach together, to see each other teach, and to put into practice principles we had discussed in theory. At the same time, the series provides a common educational experience for students unlike any other they are likely to have, in which a large group of faculty and students address interdisciplinary issues together and think through the study of women's lives.

The discussion sections by their very structure provide an opportunity not only for reflecting on the lecture series, but for analyzing the conventional classroom. With two professors in the room who are not responsible for grading the students, who come from different disciplines and perhaps not from the discipline represented by the lecturer, the usual sources of authority (grading, special expertise) are removed. Often some of the students in the room are more informed about the topic just presented than are the professors.

To make the most of this unconventional teaching situation, the discussion leaders, course instructors and, often, the lecturers have luncheon meetings before the lectures to prepare discussion questions, and afterward to reflect on how the lectures connect and how the students are relating to the issues and to each other in the groups. These sessions are particularly useful for discussing pedagogy and research, bringing the classroom experience and the presentation of research findings together.

To make explicit connections among the cluster courses and between the lecture/discussion series and the courses, the instructors of the four courses form a panel and raise issues for the entire group in a final public meeting. They may each begin, for example, by answering a question such as, what did each of us learn from a lecture outside our discipline that helped us to see our own work in a new light? This type of question again forefronts methodology in an interdisciplinary context. They then address questions suggested by students and open up discussion to the whole group. The instructors, in a sense, model an ideal student outcome: they forefront methodology and contrast the assumptions of various disciplines, they relate the issues of the series to their own intellectual work and lives, and they tie together the different elements of the cluster experience. As in the faculty seminar, faculty members made discoveries about their own disciplines by working together on a common task with colleagues from other departments. These discoveries were sometimes made when communication seemed the most difficult or blocked.

For instance, we began to define more vividly the differences in priorities set by each. Gender was the central issue for some of us, while class or race was the overriding issue for others. We recognized in debating these priorities how much our institutional environment, our disciplines, our social structure, and our personal histories have been built upon hierarchies of issues. In teaching together, by contrast, we wanted to work toward the use of gender, race, class, and culture as interrelated tools of analysis we all needed. In other words, we had to find a way to understand and support a real plurality of concerns rather than fall into a debilitating competition of concerns.

Obstacles, Resistance, and Conflict in the Classroom

As we have worked together on theory and course redesign in the faculty workshops, and on pedagogy and interdisciplinary teaching in the course cluster, we have become acutely aware of pitfalls, obstacles, and sources of conflict that threaten effective curricular change. One of the most useful, unforeseen side-effects of bringing together women's studies faculty with other faculty members, and of discussing candidly classroom problems and experiences, is that we have begun to perceive patterns in what had seemed to be idiosyncratic experiences. As faculty colleagues, we have recognized in practice the difficulties of interdisciplinary exchange and of restructuring our conventional course offerings. As teachers, we have identified sources of conflict that emerge in the classroom as we give women more than token representation on our syllabi.

THE BONDAGE OF DISCIPLINE

Two seemingly opposite dangers threaten effective interdisciplinary work at the outset: disciplinary solipsism and interdisciplinary arrogance. In fact, they both stem from the limitations of specialization. Disciplinary solipsism, usually unexpressed, is the assumption that the types of questions that concern you are the *really* important intellectual questions. Often this reflects other, pervasive paradigms of prestige (science is the "hard" stuff, politics is the "real" world), but frequently it is the understandable personal justification of a lifetime of commitment to a specific field. Interdisciplinary arrogance is actually just an extension of disciplinary solipsism. We are certain of the centrality of our own concerns, but we can see that a colleague in another field has some "language," a formulation, or a metaphor that appears to illuminate something we deal with, so we borrow that tool for our material. The danger here, of course, is that a concept or formulation painstakingly elaborated in one field carries with it theoretical associations that may not be immediately apparent to someone who is unacquainted with the literature of that field. A first trap to avoid in interdisciplinary exchange, then, is to allow concepts to be reduced to "buzzwords"; superficial adoption of each other's organizing metaphors is no substitute for real listening.

On the other hand, experience, and specifically women's experience, is not fully comprehended in any one discipline. Frequently research in one area is more advanced, more fully developed, than research in another when it comes to accounting for women's experience and gender. A sense of responsibility to one's own discipline and timidity in the face of new material often conspire to block faculty members whose intentions, motivated perhaps by a belief in affirmative action, are to include women in their courses. A sustained, interdisciplinary environment, such as a series of faculty seminars where peers who are experts in other fields serve as resources and guides, is needed to enable faculty members to take the initiative to learn and then apply insights from one field to their own, particularly if feminist research is less extensive in their field.

Disciplinary responsibility becomes an obstacle in another way as well. Having learned from other colleagues, having read in other fields, a faculty member returns to a syllabus for a regular departmental offering and is stymied by the "coverage" questions: "I'd like to incorporate women in this course, but if I'm going to be responsible to my students I have to cover certain basic material." This is a very real problem, particularly in introductory level courses. Two tentative solutions might be tried. First is to broaden the sense of responsibility from the way one's discipline has conventionally been defined to the way it is tested and redefined as gender becomes an explicit concern. Second is to suggest that the very same material can be presented in a new light, using gender as a category of analysis. For example, understanding that *Moby Dick* is a gendered text, or that scientific research is shaped by social context and has social consequences, changes the way we look at the core of our disciplines while allowing us to "cover the material."

CONFRONTING CONFLICT, UNDERSTANDING DIFFERENCE

Preparing faculty members theoretically is not enough. The experience of teaching a course in which women are more than a token presence is often tumultuous; making a central place for women and other subordinate groups on a syllabus or in the classroom, even when that place is shared with men from dominant groups, entails more conflict that is initially apparent. The experience of team-leading cluster discussion groups is a helpful preparation for this experience because it provides an ongoing opportunity for women's studies teachers and others to talk candidly while working together. They experience first-hand in a collaborative teaching arrangement problems that rarely surface in a regular course.

Conflicts that seem idiosyncratic emerge as patterns when taken out of isolation. For example, a teacher may not live up to a student's expectations of a particular discipline. A colleague in science reports that when, in an advanced seminar on immunology and mammalian reproduction, she tried to encourage students to think about the social implications of issues such as immunocontraception, implications that might very well involve them directly, one student became angry and said, "I want the facts; this other stuff is irrelevant to me as a science major." Similar resistance was encountered among students enrolled in the cluster courses themselves. Some asked, why we were paying "all this attention to women"; didn't that distort reality? Both these comments reveal the degree to which students assume that the norm is gender-neutral, that any attention paid to women and minority groups is a "special interest," peripheral to the real business of the course. Attention to women looms larger than its actual place in a specific course or in the student's overall educational experience exactly because it is absent or treated as peripheral elsewhere.

By far the most difficult issue is talking effectively about difference. The reflex reaction of most students who are, after all, trying to "fit in" is to look for commonalities as soon as difficult issues of difference arise. To push students beyond a surface tolerance to an understanding of real diversity (racial, cultural, sexual) is difficult because they feel they are being judged personally for social structures that oppress or repress difference. And yet if this discomfort is not addressed, if it is not made at least momentarily more intense within the classroom, it will seethe beneath the surface and subvert the entire learning process. The luncheon meetings where discussion groups are evaluated provide a place for working on strategies to use conflict in the teaching process rather than having it take over the classroom.

Participation in the cluster, often a common cauldron as much as a common educational experience, allowed a whole group of faculty members and students to work through these difficulties together instead of individual teachers feeling isolated with that tension in their separate classrooms. We tried to confront some of the difficult issues directly, right from the start. For example, the first lecture in the "Culture Constructs the Female" series was given by a black faculty member from the Smith School for Social Work about her research on black children developing a sense of ethnic self in a racist society.

The first exercise in the discussion groups was for teachers and students to identify their own ethnicity and to try to understand how their feelings about education, values, and family structure were related to ethnicity. Three important lessons came out of what was for many a very difficult process of disclosure and discovery. First, students and teachers who claimed no ethnicity because they were white, middle class, and mainstream had to realize that ethnicity shaped their sense of self and others.

Second, all participants had to become aware of the differences of background, family, class, and neighborhood that existed in what at first might have appeared to be a fairly homogeneous group. Finally, teachers and students all started the discussion (and series) speaking from the authority of their own experience, informed by the analysis that had preceded in the lecture, an analysis that grew out of black experience.

We have had student enrollments of more than 200 a year and the involvement of more than thirty faculty members in seminars and/or discussion groups (the equivalent of a large department). The model, especially as it is now institutionalized, realizes all the functions that a more traditional women's studies program would (encourages the development of women-focused courses, coordinates the courses that do exist, administers a minor in women's studies, sponsors public events) and also implements the transformation project. We feel that the flexibility and economy of the model transcend the divisive, fragmenting departmental structure of the college.

Making Changes: Institutionalization

To ensure that change continues and is not thwarted by the discouragement these difficulties often bring, there needs to be a continuing, institutionalized structure. The solution at Smith, after two experimental years, was to establish a standing faculty committee to design and implement faculty seminars, workshops, and the course cluster. Appointed initially by the president, the faculty committee operates on a modest budget, using internal resources and expertise.

The Smith model depends on the presence of a number of faculty members whose research already focuses on women and on the existence of a base of women's studies courses. It is a very economical model, even if seminar participants, lecturers, discussion leaders, and workshop leaders receive modest honoraria.*

---

*The cost of implementing the cluster—paying lecturers, giving discussion leaders a small honorarium, hosting a reception after the last panel, publicizing the events—is about the same as giving one professor released time from one course.

We feel that it is important to pay the lecturers even if they are on our faculty (which was contrary to custom) and to offer the discussion leaders a small honorarium to recognize that women's work should not be counted on as "volunteer work." The combination of faculty seminars, workshops, and the course cluster provides a way for faculty members to learn together about new scholarship, and to experience and reflect on transformed pedagogy, and for students and faculty members to understand more clearly the interrelatedness of issues in different fields and the pervasive importance of gender as a category of analysis.

Appendix

Course Cluster, Spring 1982, Smith College

WOMEN AND POWER

* * * *

LECTURE/DISCUSSION SERIES

February 9   *Self-Blame by Rape Victims: Power or Helpless-ness?* Ronnie Janoff-Bulman, University of Massachusetts, Department of Psychology

February 23   *Power and Politics: Feminist Contributions to New Perspectives* Susan C. Bourque, Government Department

March 16   *The Feminization of Poverty: Causes and Cures* Mary Wentworth, Everywoman's Center, University of Massachusetts

March 30   *Narrative Power and Sexual Politics* Deirdre David, English Department

April 6   *Women and Power,* panel discussion with Martha Ackelsberg, Susan Carter, Carla Golden, and Susan Van Dyne

Thursday evenings, *7:30 pm.*, McConnell Auditorium, followed by small discussion groups

* * * *

COURSES

ECO 221   HUMAN RESOURCES AND EMPLOYMENT POLICY, Susan Carter

ENG 239   AMERICAN WOMEN POETS, Susan Van Dyne

GOV 294   POLITICAL PARTICIPATION, Martha Ackelsberg

PSY 276   PSYCHOLOGY OF WOMEN, Carla Golden

To participate in this interdisciplinary study of women, enroll in one (or more) of the courses above. The lectures will be followed by small discussion groups led by teams of faculty members from a variety of departments. The lecture series and discussion groups give us a chance to see what questions are being asked about women in several different fields and how the methods and assumptions of each field shape our understanding of women's experience.

Course Cluster, Spring 1983, Smith College

WOMEN: IMAGE AND IDENTITY

In the spring semester, four courses that study women's experience will be linked by a special interdisciplinary lecture series for all students enrolled. Our theme is an exploration of women's identity and behavior in groups and in cultures within and beyond the American context.

* * * *

LECTURE/DISCUSSION SERIES

February 8   *Painting a Self*
Susan Heideman, Art Department

February 22   *Images of Afro-Caribbeans and Their Struggle for Identity in German Literature* Almut Wedekind, Department of German, Hood College; Gertraud Gutzmann, German Department; John Walter, Department of Afro-American Studies

March 1   *Walking Quietly Away from the Jargon: Toward a Phenomenology of Women's Experience of Self and Work* Gail A. Hornstein, Department of Psychology, Mount Holyoke College

March 8   *Personal Identities and Collective Visions: Reflections on Being a Jew and a Feminist* Martha Ackelsberg, Government Department

April 5   *The Contexts of Identity,* a panel discussion with
                 Johnnella Butler, Gertraud Gutzmann, Barbara
                 Kellum, Diedrick Snoek, Vicky Spelman

Thursday evenings, *7:30 pm,* McConnell Auditorium,
followed by small discussion groups

* * * *

COURSES

PHI/AAS 240   PHILOSOPHY AND WOMEN, Johnnella Butler and
              Vicky Spelman

PSY 278   BEHAVIOR IN ORGANIZATIONS, Diedrick Snoek

GER 227   TOPICS IN GERMAN LITERATURE: WOMEN
              UNDER NAZISM, Gertraud Gutzmann

ART 216   IMAGES IN ANCIENT ART, Barbara Kellum

To participate in this interdisciplinary study of women,
enroll in one (or more) of the courses above. The lecture
and discussion series gives us a chance to see what questions
are being asked about women in four fields and how the
methods of each field shape research being done on women.

Course Cluster, Spring 1984, Smith College

CULTURE CONSTRUCTS THE FEMALE

This semester, four courses that study women's experience
will be linked by a special interdisciplinary lecture and discussion series. Our theme is the ways culture constructs the
female and how women in a variety of cultural contexts
have understood, confronted, adapted or transformed the
terms that define them.

* * * *

LECTURE/DISCUSSION SERIES

February 2   *In Search of an Ethnic Self* Dorcas Bowles,
                Smith College School for Social Work

February 9   *Unequal Colleagues: Female Professional Culture*
                Penina Glazer and Miriam Slater, Hampshire
                College

February 23   *Women: Just Who Do We Think 'We' Is?* Vicky
                Spelman, Department of Philosophy

March 8   *The Gendered I* Marilyn R. Schuster, Department
                of French & Comparative Literature Program

March 29   *Culture Constructs the Female,* panel discussion
                with Bella Brodzki, Susan Carter, Rick Fantasia,
                Carolyn Jacobs and Frederique Marglin. Susan
                Van Dyne, Moderator.

Thursday evenings, *7:30 pm.*, McConnell Auditorium,
followed by small discussion groups

* * * *

COURSES

AAS 326   THE SOCIO-CULTURAL DEVELOPMENT OF THE
            AFRO-AMERICAN WOMAN, Carolyn Jacobs

ANT 243   WOMEN AND SEXUALITY: THE WESTERN AND
            HINDU TRADITIONS CONTRASTED, Frederique
            Marglin

CLT 223   WOMEN'S AUTOBIOGRAPHY, Bella Brodzki

PPL 255   EDUCATION AND PUBLIC POLICY, Susan Carter
            and Rich Fantasia

To participate in this interdisciplinary study of women, enroll in
one (or more) of the courses above. The lectures will be followed
by small discussion groups led by teams of faculty members from a

variety of departments. The lecture series and discussion groups give us a chance to see what questions are being asked about women in several different fields and how the methods and assumptions of each field shape our understanding of women's experience.

9

Initiating a Curriculum Integration Project: Lessons from the Campus and the Region

Betty Schmitz,
Myra Dinnerstein, and
Nancy Mairs

Montana State University and the University of Arizona were among the first campuses to initiate curricular change projects to expose non-women's studies faculty to feminist scholarship. Convinced that the new scholarship on women presents a fundamental shift in the ways students are taught to view the world, we began projects that assisted faculty to incorporate this scholarship into the courses they regularly taught. Then, encouraged by prospects for change, we developed new projects through which we could reach out to other colleges and universities in the western region to assist them in initiating curricular change. Like explorers, we've been disheartened at times by the unexpected bog or the face of a precipice that seems to offer no handhold; at other times, we've rejoiced in a sudden new vista. And like all explorers, we are anxious to make maps, or at least sketches in the sand for those who follow. What follows, then, are a few signposts.

Early Exploration: The Campus Projects

The project at Montana State University, "Seeking Women's Equity Through Curricular Reform," was funded by the Women's

Educational Equity Act (WEEA) Program, and began in 1979.[1] It
engaged forty faculty members for two years in a series of activities designed to culminate in curricular reform: seminars with
nationally known consultants in women's studies and curriculum
development, analyses of course content for sex bias, literature
reviews, research on women and gender, and revision of existing
courses or the development of new ones.

At the University of Arizona, "Women's Studies and the
Humanities Curriculum," funded by the National Endowment for
the Humanities (NEH) from 1980–85,[2] also has involved over
forty faculty members, about ten per year. Activities included an
orientation workshop, a summer program of intensive study, formal consultations with women's studies faculty, and workshops
with visiting scholars. Participants created annotated bibliographies of feminist scholarship in their disciplines and produced
and taught revised courses. An ongoing feminist theory group
provided them materials and support for further research and
course revision.

CHOOSING PARTICIPANTS

Project leaders at the two universities made different decisions
about who to involve in the projects. At Montana State, on the
hypothesis that allowing faculty to define the contours of their
change efforts would result in better quality, an open call for proposals was used to recruit participants. Encouraged by publicity
from an advisory board and a letter from the Vice President for
Academic Affairs, fifty-one applied, exactly 10 percent of the
full-time faculty. Forty faculty, twenty-two men and eighteen
women, were accepted. Although the hope had been to attract
senior faculty who hold the power in the institution and who
make decisions that affect women's lives, the call for proposals
resulted in the self-selection of faculty with a prior commitment
to women's equity and some knowledge of research on women in
their disciplines. The final group of participants overrepresented
women (40 percent, compared to 23 percent of the general
faculty) and the junior professorial ranks. In general, the greatest
faculty response came from those areas in which women faculty
and students are concentrated (the humanities and nursing) or in
which female student enrollment has sharply increased (business

and engineering). The participants at Montana State were motivated in large measure by the opportunity to increase their knowledge by broadening their base of information and discovering strategies to reduce sex bias in higher education. The stipend of $1500 a year for two years was also a critical factor because, by providing summer income, it allowed participants to devote time to new research.

For the first three years, the Arizona project also provided for each participant a stipend equivalent to the salary for one summer-school course. Project leaders chose participants solely from tenured faculty through discussions with department heads and women's studies faculty. Criteria included excellence in teaching and willingness to modify the curriculum. Approximately ten new participants from different disciplines were invited each year, and all but three remain engaged in project activities. All but two participants were male, and six were heads of departments. During a fourth-year extension of the project, instead of receiving a stipend, participants received released time for one course during a semester to attend a term-long weekly curriculum integration seminar.

MEASURING OUTCOMES

At both institutions, similar results emerged. Most participants made some initial pedagogical changes. A few made such astonishing professional leaps that not merely their courses, but their whole range of scholarly activities, including their research, reflected new vision and commitment. And a handful of faculty resisted fundamental change and were unwilling to deal with feminist concepts; beyond the addition of an occasional female figure, their courses remained untransformed.

Evaluations undertaken at Montana State indicate the extent to which the faculty changed as a result of project participation. On the Attitude Toward Women Scale[3] administered before and after their involvement, the faculty showed significant attitudinal change, even though they were more liberal to begin with than control groups. In interviews with the program evaluator, they also reported changes in their teaching behaviors, especially (a) modification of language style to avoid linguistic bias; (b) greater attention to nontraditional students in classroom discussions; (c) conscious efforts to place equal demands and expectations upon women and men students; and (d) attempts to modify traditional hierarchical structures in the classroom.[4] They also commented on changes in their personal and professional lives. Despite some negative impact in the form of discouragement and anger, lack of collegial support, and even hostility from peers, most reported greater insight into issues of sexism, professional development through research and writing, and improved courses. Although a number of those who revised courses showed at the outset the common tendency to add a separate unit on women, they soon recognized the insufficiency of such an approach and moved in subsequent revisions toward more integrated structures. Most were confident that they would continue to integrate their courses, and many have expanded their efforts toward curricular revision through consultancies, publications, and presentations at professional meetings.

Student reaction to revised courses was gauged at Arizona by students' evaluations in integrated and control classes. A consistent pattern emerged in student questionnaires. Students in the revised courses believed that these courses contained more material on women than did students in the control group. They also believed that their classmates were more interested in and their instructors more positive about these materials. Above all, students believed that this material decreased their misconceptions about women and increased their awareness of women's roles and status in the disciplines.

RESISTANCES

Another outcome of the campus projects was the uncovering of various levels of resistance to feminist scholarship among faculty. Initially we had anticipated a certain degree of ignorance among project participants about the new scholarship on women. But, we also expected colleagueship and lively and rigorous cross-disciplinary exchange as they read and reacted to the new material. These discussions were to result, we thought, in renewed intellectual excitement and commitment to change as faculty adopted the fresh insights of feminism and applied them to their teaching and research.

Very early in the projects, we began to realize that resistance to the material on the part of some faculty ran very deep. Despite their expression of interest in the project, some faculty could not get beyond their unwavering belief in the traditional standards of excellence that have shaped the curriculum nor in the current body of knowledge as representative of the best "man" has thought, created, and accomplished. This body of knowledge, they believed, was generated through objective modes of research and scholarship. In discussion about transforming courses, these faculty raised objections about "ideology" in the curriculum, about replacing superior works with inferior ones, and about "quotas" in the syllabus. For some, and this was a recurrent theme, the insurmountable intellectual barrier was a profound unwillingness to let go of the idea that culture is defined by inherent biological differences between the sexes.

Other faculty, while willing to accept the feminist analysis of traditional knowledge, hedged at applying this critique beyond a purely abstract realm. They showed a lack of connection with the material and its implications for both their professional and personal lives. Or, at the other extreme, for some faculty, discovering the systematic biases in the method and content of their work represented such a challenge to their interactions and relationships, that they lost heart and abandoned their efforts at change.

Recognizing these sources of resistance, we were able to minimize their effect on the group as a whole. We presented counterarguments in a scholarly manner. We became directive on occasion, abandoning a collegial tone and setting clear expectations for the kind of work we expected from participants. And, we elected not to spend too much time on faculty who, we judged, would not change. We focused on those who were interested and open to new ideas. This group, luckily the majority, became our allies and helped build a new community of scholars working toward curricular change.

Ensuring the Future of Curriculum Change:
Initiating Change in the Context of Dwindling Resources

The results of the Montana State University and University of Arizona projects demonstrate that, with ample resources, such as those provided by large, externally funded grants, the teaching behaviors and research priorities of individual faculty can be altered. But in an era of shrinking resources and retrenchment, is curriculum integration a realistic strategy for curricular change? How much faculty reeducation is possible without benefit of money for stipends? Our recent experience with regional consortia for curriculum integration suggests that even small amounts of seed money for initiating projects can result in concrete change.

THE NORTHERN ROCKIES PROGRAM ON
WOMEN IN THE CURRICULUM

In the fall of 1981, Montana State University received a two-year grant from the Fund for the Improvement of Postsecondary Education (FIPSE) to establish the Northern Rockies Program on Women in the Curriculum.[5] The Northern Rockies Program on Women in the Curriculum was designed to discover the conditions necessary for a successful campus-based effort to integrate women's studies into the curriculum. The program provided seed money, resources, training, and technical assistance to ten campuses in Idaho, Montana, Utah, and Wyoming to assist in developing projects to integrate women's studies into the curriculum. The program was cosponsored by the Northern Rockies Consortium for Higher Education (NORCHE), a regional consortium for interinstitutional exchange of faculty-development resources. The program hence sought to involve academic administrators as well as faculty at all stages of activity to create the internal institutional networks necessary to sustain change. Institutions were required to designate a project team including an academic administrator with resources to commit to the project and faculty with expertise in women's studies and curriculum development. This team attended, at institutional expense, a four day institute on women's studies held at Montana State University.

The financial assistance offered for institutional participation was relatively slim: a $2000 stipend for project activities and travel expenses to attend the two follow-up meetings. The Northern Rockies Program also made the experiences and resources of the Montana State University Project available to participants and attempted to substitute external validity and expertise for significant external funding. Association with NORCHE was critical in this process: several chief academic officers active in the organization served on the program advisory board and urged colleagues to support the projects that emerged on local campuses.

The participating campuses experimented with diverse approaches to transforming the traditional curriculum. Project goals fell into four categories: to integrate the study of women into core or departmental curricula (Lewis-Clark State and Western Wyoming Colleges, the University of Wyoming); to conduct faculty development programs aimed at general course revision (Central Wyoming College, Southern Utah State College, and the University of Utah); to build networks of faculty interested in research on women and course revision (Universities of Idaho and Montana); and to expand educational options for women students in nontraditional curricula (Montana College of Mineral Sciences and Technology and Weber State College).

Most campuses adopted program management ideas and resources proven effective at Montana State University and Arizona. Most of these second-generation projects began with a major faculty development workshop or seminar with a well-known consultant in women's studies, either for the entire faculty (from which a core group of project participants was later selected) or for a previously designated group of faculty in targeted departments. Strategies for eliciting faculty participation included small stipends or merit points for participation, letters from deans or department heads urging participation, calls for proposals of application to the project, research assistance in locating discipline-specific materials for course revision, and opportunities for interdisciplinary work or team-teaching.

In their final reports submitted in May 1983, local project directors reported as the most significant short-term outcomes the emergence of networks to facilitate change, including:

• increased communication among faculty and administrators interested in women's studies and/or curricular innovation;
• new networks for sharing information on campus, between nearby campuses, and at the regional level; and

• the acquisition, consolidation and improved access to campus resources in women's studies;

and heightened consciousness of several kinds, including:

• increased faculty (and in some cases student) awareness of both the nature and extent of bias in higher education and of resources in women's studies;
• increased recognition of the importance of women's studies to undergraduate education; and
• the establishment of a process to review courses and, sometimes, the revision of several courses.

THE WESTERN STATES PROJECT ON WOMEN IN THE CURRICULUM

The Western States Project on Women in the Curriculum, funded from 1983 to 1985 by the Ford Foundation and sponsored by the Southwest Institute for Research on Women (SIROW),[6] was a further extension of the Montana State and Arizona projects. With offices at both institutions, the Western States Project encompasses sixteen states: Arizona, Colorado, Kansas, Nebraska, Nevada, New Mexico, Oklahoma, Texas, and Utah in the Southwest; and Idaho, Montana, North Dakota, Oregon, South Dakota, Washington, and Wyoming in the Northwest. The Western States Project began with a small matching-fund grant program designed to fund two kinds of projects at four-year colleges and universities: new projects for initiating faculty development activities, and model projects for expanding and disseminating previous work. In addition to supporting campus-based activities, the Western States Project sponsored conferences in the Northwest and the Southwest in 1984, and a regionwide conference in 1985. Project publications included a directory of consultants in the region with expertise in incorporating the new scholarship on women into their traditional disciplines, as well as a collection of syllabi for integrated courses.

By attracting institutional attention through the offer of even a small amount of money, by providing encouragement and technical expertise, and by offering increased opportunity for communication within and among institutions, the Western States Project, like the Northern Rockies Program, provided the initial impetus for transformative work in the hope that each institution itself, once the work's weight and importance for the educational environment became apparent, would choose to sustain it.

Designing a Successful Project

We have learned a great deal from the successes and partial successes of these campus-based and regional programs, more than we could hope to summarize in this essay. We will therefore concentrate on those features we think essential to a successful curriculum integration project, regardless of its size or scope. Although there is no one "best" strategy for implementing a curriculum integration project, several characteristics of project design and management emerge from analysis of successful initiatives.

SETTING GOALS: CHALLENGE AND CONTROVERSY

Successful projects differentiated long-term goals, such as transforming the core curriculum through the incorporation of feminist scholarship, from short-term objectives, such as introducing faculty in specific departments to the new scholarship on women in their disciplines or establishing a computerized data base for accessing women's studies resources in campus libraries. Project leaders were careful not to set short-term goals that were too abstract or too ambitious, given the resources of the project; often they deliberately selected some short-term objectives that were immediately achievable to lay the groundwork for longer-term, more fundamental change and to provide some initial concrete rewards to the project leaders and participants.

It is important, we found, not to set short-term, "manageable" goals with no long-term vision. Once such immediate goals have been met, faculty and administrators might assume the project is over, even though no fundamental change has occurred. It is a particular handicap to equate long-term goals with a formal project, funded externally for a shorter period of time. Project leaders should plan from the outset of institutionalize their efforts in tangible ways that are clear and visible to both current and future participants. Revising policy or mission statements, designating funds for faculty development, and rewriting job descriptions with assigned responsibilities for curriculum integration efforts are some of the ways this can be done. Another hazard in goal-setting is the tendency to avoid controversial topics or issues in an attempt to win broad-based faculty support for the project. In general, projects that presented high quality feminist analysis of middle-class, white male bias in the structure and content of academic disciplines and in power structures within the institution, and raised critical and challenging issues were the most successful in engaging faculty in discussions that led to fruitful reform.

Initial discussion of project goals should include discussion of what success would look like. How do we know when "gender balance" in the curriculum has been achieved? How is this balance related to treatment of people of differing race, culture, class, or sexual preference? How will revised courses be judged? How will we know that faculty have improved their advising of women students? Questions like these will assist project planners in defining long- and short-term goals, and in focusing on collecting data that can be used for planning the implementation of long-term goals and new projects.

INTEGRATING THE LOCUS OF CHANGE WITH THE LOCUS OF POWER

Thorough knowledge of the power structure of the institution will allow careful assessment of the benefits and costs of alternative administrative locations for a curriculum integration project. The most successful projects were those placed within legitimate, high priority programs and were directed by persons reporting directly to a dean or department head with authority over the central areas of the curriculum to be affected. The directors had carefully assessed the administrators' commitment to the project before implementing it. Evidence of this commitment translated into matching funds, "mandates" to faculty to participate in seminars, and merit points that resulted in salary increments.

Early in the planning stages, project leaders should assess the interest and commitment of all those with a "stake" in the project and those who can provide human or financial resources. Consulting key actors in the system and allowing them to contribute ideas to the design of the project helps them to "buy into" the project at some level and ensures that they are informed about project goals, even if they adopt a "wait-and-see" attitude or offer only tacit approval. Broadly-based advisory boards are an excellent means to build interest and commitment for a project and to assess areas of support and resistance.

In seeking institutional support for a project it is more effective to show an administrator how the goals of the project, if accomplished, can help solve a problem or issue already acknowledged as an institutional priority rather than to seek to add another priority to an already long list. An institutional process may be underway that can be furthered or improved by a joint effort. At one institution, for example, project planners worked with members of the general education committee to improve the new core curriculum in arts and sciences by incorporating materials on women and minorities into new courses. Our project leaders were creative in using current campus concerns to the benefit of their own goals. These included accreditation reviews, institutional goals for affirmative action, goals for increased enrollments in specific areas, general education reviews, redefinition of institutional mission in relation to the liberal arts and professions, and concern for the quality of teaching and scholarship.

RECRUITING FACULTY PARTICIPANTS

Some projects, particularly those on small campuses, elected to begin with a general faculty seminar from which a core group of project participants was later selected. Others preferred to work from the outset with a small group of interested faculty. No matter where faculty recruitment begins, if the larger goal of a transformed curriculum is to be attained, a large number of faculty, including senior faculty, from all disciplines will have to be brought into the effort. Those projects with the most potential for ongoing change have invested at least some of their resources in people with the power to influence their peers or who are well placed to influence decisions about curriculum.

To select incentives that will appeal to faculty one must know where they are concerned intellectually and politically, and what sustains them in their work. Faculty do not respond to the same sorts of arguments for change as administrators. They are wary of political agendas and resist reshaping curricula in response to what they view as fads. Teaching-oriented faculty will respond to different incentives than research-oriented faculty. Projects provided a number of incentives to faculty: help in addressing an existing task or agenda, special seminars with outside consultants, resources or library search assistance, stipends, awards, and released time. Most successful projects used advisory boards to help publicize the project and recruit faculty participants.

From our experience, no rule has emerged about whether stipends are necessary to encourage faculty to participate in curriculum integration projects. Faculty do need time to read and reflect, and it helps to be able to offer them released time to do so. In one sense, no amount is sufficient to compensate faculty for becoming knowledgable about feminist theory, short of lengthy sabbaticals. On the other hand, once faculty become intellectually excited by a question, they refocus their work, set new research priorities, and use means available to them through departmental or general funds to support their nascent interest. Creating a sense of community and support on campus will go a long way toward replacing dollars. Resources are needed, however, to offer seminars and activities to capture their interest and to provide initial opportunities for professional development.

Intellectual content and quality of the program were critical in eliciting faculty participation. In publicizing faculty workshops, project leaders used language that invoked substantive issues in curricular reform, designed seminars around topics of intellectual interest to the faculty, and chose noted and respected speakers who could challenge the faculty with questions of substance.

Mapping the Terrain: Critical Conditions for Success

Here is the lay of the land as we've been able to sketch it so far. Although the individual characteristics and strategies of curriculum integration projects differ necessarily from campus to campus, our experience demonstrates that certain necessary conditions must exist for a project to be successful over time. These are the basic conditions we have found to be essential for initiating a successful project to integrate women's studies into the curriculum:

- a key group of committed individuals who will act as change agents
- administrative support for the project
- women's studies expertise and resources on campus
- resources to support faculty development activities
- an impetus for reform or specific opportunity for faculty development
- a reward mechanism for participating faculty
- a legitimate home base for the project within the institutional power structure
- salary or released time for a project director to oversee the effort for a specific period of time.

If these conditions can be met, the results can be impressive, even astonishing. At a Southwest regional conference hosted by the Western States Project on Women in the Curriculum in October 1984, we listened to project representatives report on their activities: workshops, conferences, and colloquia; library acquisitions; computer searches; development of bibliographies, syllabi, and handbooks. With very limited funds but boundless energy, project leaders had developed a variety of strategies in different settings and at different levels for drawing attention to the new scholarship on women and getting it taken seriously. We came away renewed by their lively determination. The work is vital. And it is being done.

Notes

1. The Project at Montana State University was supported by Grant No. G007901078, U.S. Department of Education. The original proposal was written by Peggy Leiterman-Stock, now of the University of Hartford.
2. The University of Arizona Project was supported by Grant No. ED 0237 81, National Endowment for the Humanities.
3. Janet T. Spence and Robert L. Helmreich, "The Attitudes Toward Women Scale: An Objective Instrument to Measure Attitudes Toward the Rights and Roles of Women in Contemporary Society," *Journal Supplement Abstract Service Catalog of Selected Documents in Psychology* 2 (1972): 66.

4. For a complete discussion, see Betty Schmitz and Anne S. Williams, "Seeking Women's Equity through Curricular Reform: Faculty Perceptions of an Experimental Project," *Journal of Higher Education* 54, no. 5 (September/October 1983): 556–65.

5. The Northern Rockies Program was supported by Grant No. G008102311, U.S. Department of Education.

6. The Western States Project on Women in the Curriculum was supported by Grant No. 830-0761, The Ford Foundation.

10

Out of Necessity: National Summer Institute in Women's Studies, the Great Lakes Colleges Association

Barbara Caruso and Katherine Loring

In 1979, the members of the Great Lakes Colleges Association Women's Studies Committee identified a problem. On each of our member campuses were one or two faculty members, administrators, and librarians who were interested in women's studies, but who in most cases could point to little systematic study in the area, and who, because of time and energy constraints typical of small campuses, were unable to pursue this interest. Although the Women's Studies Committee in some ways provided support and an opportunity for faculty development, it did not address in a systematic way the questions of feminist theory and pedagogy that many of our members were trying to explore. Our concerns led us to wonder what other predominantly small, predominantly liberal arts colleges found to be the greatest obstacle in the path of women's studies on their campuses. We applied for and received a grant from the Ford Foundation to conduct a study of small liberal arts colleges to determine those perceived needs.

The results of that study varied from campus to campus. Student involvement, administrative commitment, and community support were all concerns; the most consistently voiced need, however, was for faculty development. The Ford study confirmed our consortial understandings and, in the process, suggested a further project: to design a faculty development program that would be accessible to faculty members burdened with all the constraints of small liberal arts college teaching, yet that would, at the same time, provide an experience with women's studies that was intensive, generally applicable, and more than casually introductory. Out of this necessity, the National Summer Institute in Women's Studies was developed; it has been offered for three summers now.

Initial Planning: Working Toward Balance

From the first, the conception of the Institute required us to work toward balance. Faculty development in women's studies was a new endeavor, and traditional models of individuals engaged in private and isolated projects did not seem to mix readily with our conviction that working together as a community of scholars, exploring questions of feminism in a feminist context, was desirable. Since our work was interdisciplinary, the traditional model of a seminar linked to a particular field of study (with advanced and experienced participants) was not appropriate. Yet, there needed to be a clear sense of shared exploration to give the time together a focus and to help participants apply this experience in their home institution and in individual work. Further, we needed to examine both theory and the application of theory in a college environment; that is, we needed to concern ourselves with feminist pedagogy. These curricular demands for balance paralleled the need for balance in participant and staff selection. It was important that our community of persons involved in higher education be drawn from many areas of the college structure— faculty, administrators, librarians. And if our motive was to serve not only our own consortium but also the greater women's studies community, we had to balance participant and staff selection to reflect both commitments.

The final product—the Summer Institute—is a result of these and other attempts at achieving balance. It has not been an easy task, and each year finds us making adaptations that change the particulars of the Institute. We remain committed, however, to certain principles that undergird the enterprise. Attention to issues of race, class, and sexual preference infuses all parts of the institute. Establishing a learning environment that pays attention to the form of feminist community as well as to the content is essential. And feminist pedagogy as well as feminist theory is at the heart of our endeavor.

Creating a Community

The greatest successes sometimes spring from issues of expediency. One such fortuitous success for us was our choice of location and facilities. Each year the Summer Institute has been housed in a small and quaintly aging dormitory on the University of Michigan campus; for three weeks we are its sole inhabitants. The congenial relations between the university's Women's Studies Program and the consortial program offer advantages of finances and of facilities (libraries, recreational areas, computer center, media resources, guest scholars, food service). But equally important, the residency component of the Institute serves as a base for all the other enterprises. On one level, dormitory living offers a quick trip back to dimly but fondly remembered college days. Someone else makes the food, washes the dishes, and keeps the public space clean. For many participants and the staff, who are typically women (not planned, but a result of self-selection; three or four men have attended the Institute), the dormitory experience is also a return to a "community of women" that many have not experienced since college, and that others have never experienced. Participant evaluations do not fail to mention this as a plus.

The late-night talks indigenous to dormitory living are consistently related to course material. Here is a rich opportunity for the exploration of the private, personal, and political connections that so inform feminist theory. To encourage this intensive and constant stimulation, staff and participants live on the same halls; guest lecturers, special workshop leaders, and other visitors are also housed with participants. This reduces the tendency to elevate the "expert" and "teacher" above the "student," and ensures the widest exposure to new knowledge or interesting perspectives. Building on this principle, the Institute is administered by two women who spend the previous year involved with recruitment, arrangements, etc., and who are actively present during the Institute. The director also facilitates a teaching and curriculum group, and the associate director/manager of local arrangements supervises all the individual projects. This design, once again, encourages the conception of the Institute as a place of shared learning, where hierarchies are blurred, where administrators view themselves as enablers, and where the teachers are sometimes students and the students are often teachers.

Shared responsibility appears in another feature of the learning environment: small special interest groups. These groups are formed by the participants in an informal and ad hoc fashion, with staff participation but not leadership. In addition to small-group meetings (most recently on sexuality, Marxism, spirituality, and urban living), the dormitory houses a small women's studies library, a resources area, and all of the "classrooms." Twice a week, the living room becomes a theater for films in women's studies that come complete with program notes and ordering information. The close proximity of all this activity helps maintain the sense of shared purpose so essential to this Institute and further helps to shape the group. This attention to the forming of a group is consistent with principles of feminist pedagogy, which suggests that this sense of shared purpose also helps to distinguish the women's studies classroom from others.

To balance this three-week intensive experience and to guard against too much "community," participants must attend the Institute's public lecture series, which is available also to the larger community. The discussions following these lectures offer participants an opportunity to try out, on a new audience, insights and arguments learned at the Institute. Other events are also planned in cooperation with women's groups in the city, not only to provide participants with additional outlets, but also to model the principle that women's studies is not simply an academic and institution-bound activity. Here again the learning environment of the Institute addresses the form as well as the content of women's studies.

The Institute's Curriculum

The curriculum of the Institute is also designed to balance the desires to provide a common experience, to explore interdisciplinary study, and to keep our roles as "teachers" of Women's Studies—regardless of our particular duties—clearly before us. As a consequence, the weekly schedule is divided between two major commitments, each meeting three times a week for two hours. A theory seminar meets in groups of approximately ten to fifteen persons plus a seminar leader, and a teaching and curriculum workshop meets in groups of five plus a facilitator/teacher. This structure allows for a wide distribution of participants and staff, since the workshop groups are derived from a mixture of theory group participants. This arrangement also allows for the balancing of practice and theory that is central to a women's studies perspective that focuses on transforming not just a curriculum, but the way a curriculum is constructed and experienced.

Because we come together as a diverse group of persons from a variety of disciplines and with differing experience with women's studies (the hardest aspect of the Institute to monitor), the theory seminar has to approach "theory" in a way that will answer our collective needs. The result is a syllabus of readings designed to explore interdisciplinary study with an emphasis on feminist and women's studies concerns, and with attention to modes of explanation. More specifically, in the first week we explore some introductions to the "questions" a feminist might ask of her/his world. W.E.B. DuBois's "Of Our Spiritual Strivings" (*The Souls of Black Folk* [Greenwich, Conn.: Fawcett, 1961]), Evelyn Beck's "Why Is This Book Different From All Other Books" (*Nice Jewish Girls: A Lesbian Anthology* [Cambridge, Mass.: Persephone, 1982]), and Lillian Smith's "Custom and Conscience" and "The Women" (*Killers of the Dream* [New York: Anchor Books, 1963]), are part of the core reading for that section.

In the second and third meetings we explore what it means to explain something. For example, we ask the question "What makes a female or a woman?" In this section, representative readings from various disciplines are studied, and their "way in" to the question is discussed, for its method more than for its content. Readings by Linda Gordon, Nancy Chodorow, Miriam Shapiro,

Angela Davis, Judy Grahn, Evelyn Fox Keller, and Audre Lorde form a section of this core reading. In subsequent meetings we continue to use as many modes of analysis as possible to explore the following topics: "Gender Identity and the Politics of Sexuality," "National Minorities, Race and Racism," and "Class."

These are in some ways artificial divisions, and the readings in each area overlap with others. Cherrie Moraga's "La Guera" (*This Bridge Called My Back*, ed. Moraga and Anzaldúa [New York: Kitchen Table Press, 1983]), for example, appears in "Gender Identity," although it would be equally appropriate in the section on "Race and Racism." Similarly, John Gwaltney's "Nancy White" (*Drylongso: A Self-Portrait of Black America* [New York: Vintage Books, 1981]) appears in the section on "Race and Racism," although its attention to a working woman's life makes it a fine candidate for the section on "Class." This overlapping is, of course, intentional, for while each section provides us an opportunity to discuss a particular area intensely, the overlapping keeps before us the notions that women's lives defy rigid classification, and that women's studies cannot afford to compartmentalize or rank oppressions.

Of course, each syllabus section contains selections addressing that particular area of concern. In the section of "Gender Identity and the Politics of Sexuality," for example, we include McKenna and Kessler's "Toward a Theory of Gender" (*Gender: An Ethnomethodological Approach* [New York: John Wiley, 1978]) and Adrienne Rich's "Compulsory Heterosexuality and Lesbian Existence" (*Signs* 5, no. 4 [1980]). In the section "National Minorities, Race and Racism," the Combahee River Collective's "A Black Feminist Statement" in *This Bridge Called My Back*, and Hooks's "Introduction" to *Ain't I a Woman* (Boston: South End Press, 1981) both appear. And in the section on class we include Selma James's "The Working Woman" (*The Power of Women and the Subversion of the Community*, ed. Costa and James [Bristol, England: Falling Wall Press, 1975]) and Ellen Willis's "Economic Reality and the Limits of Feminism" (*MS*, June 1973).

To complement this extensive immersion in feminist theory, the teaching and curriculum workshops focus on more praxis-related concerns. How to change a syllabus to integrate a particular aspect of women's studies, as well as the politics of "mainstreaming" itself, become topics. The pursuit of appropriate faculty-student relations, the introduction of issues of race and racism to a white class by a white instructor, the value of self-disclosure, the methods of contract grading, the actual transformation of a department's curriculum, or the impact of Freire's principles on the design of a women's studies classroom are possible areas of discussion. The teaching and curriculum workshops take a shape determined by participant interest and to some extent by facilitator expertise. We have tried pursuing workshops that are topic-centered but have found that, in the end, the need for discussion based on individual experience and the growing intensity of the environment make participant-centered workshops more congruent with the Institute's aims.

The immersion in theory and the teaching and curriculum workshops are augmented by the public lecture series, which addresses many similar topics. A recent series included Evelyn Torton Beck on "Anti-semitism, Racism and Homophobia: Three Sides of the Same Coin," Alice Echols on "Mother Knows Best: Feminist Sexual Politics, 1968–1983," Barrie Thorne on "Language and Gender," and Bernice Sandler on "Women in Higher Education: These Are Times That Try Men's Souls." Lectures are most helpful when the public discussion session (mentioned earlier) is followed by a private discussion or workshop session that allows for a fuller exchange between the speaker and Institute participants. The Institute also offers special workshop sessions, instruction in bibliographical research and feminist research methodology, and other "special events." If a participant were to choose to do everything available, there would be little free time.

Going Home Again

It should be clear that the Summer Institute endeavors to keep participants busy, partially to ensure that the attendees get their money's worth, but more specifically to work toward building the kind of shared experience that can lead to breakthrough thinking. We also hope to build in a carry-over that makes support of Institute participation attractive to the home institution. Each participant (or group of participants, if from the same college or university) is asked to pursue an independent project. This may involve transforming an existing course, planning a new one, designing a lecture series in women's studies, or developing any sort of activity that can have an impact on the home campus. Not only does this make the faculty-development benefits apparent to the home institution, it also reinforces the notion that women's studies demands action as well as thought.

In the first year of the Institute, the independent project was emphasized strongly, but because of time constraints most participants accomplished less on the project than either we or they had hoped. In some cases, concern about completing the project interfered with participants' ability to benefit from other aspects of the Institute. In subsequent years, several adjustments have been made to ease this problem. The theory seminars, teaching and curriculum workshops, and special sessions are scheduled so as to allow the participant some blocks of time for work on their projects. In addition, our expectations and goals changed: in the three-week period we expect not to see the project completed, but to see it off to a good start, its problems and approaches defined and resources assembled.

Participants: Diversity and Balance

Part of what makes the Institute successful, of course, is the balance of individuals, both participants and staff, involved in the endeavor. In some respects this has been the hardest area to deal with. We want the Institute to support the GLCA consortial faculty development needs, yet participating women's studies scholars and teachers outside the consortium also have a real claim on the Institute: thus, we have had to be careful about issues of "ownership." To address this, the GLCA Women's Studies Committee has agreed that there should be a critical mass of GLCA representation among staff and participants, but that this group is flexible in number (not a majority) and in kind. So far we have managed to make this loosely defined system work.

Balancing inside and outside GLCA participation is only one criterion of selection for participants and staff. Variety of disciplines and roles on campus is another area of concern. We try to ensure that more than one person represents each constituency, so that dialogue in their particular area of expertise is possible. We are, of course, eager to maintain high recruitment and retention of participants and staff of color and of diverse national origins, ages, classes, and sexual preference. These types of balance are not always easy to achieve while still retaining the small size (twenty to twenty-five participants) that we are convinced is ideal for the task we propose.

Similarly difficult is to bring together persons at comparable levels of experience with women's studies. In the first year we were clear to advertise for people "already involved in women's studies," and we gave the impression that we were an "advanced" institute. In the third year we advertised for "people with an interest in women's studies," and this time gave the impression that we weren't so advanced. In fact, the makeup of each group was similarly diverse, with some participants clearly more experienced than others. The way feminists describe our awareness of women's studies and our involvement in it varies greatly. What for one person represents experience, for another indicates near ignorance. Fortunately, the curriculum of the Institute, with its attention to interdisciplinary theory and workshops based upon particular experience, is able to absorb these differences. And the growth of all participants, as recorded on Institute evaluations and as demonstrated by projects pursued with success on home campuses, seems to argue against a rigid profile of an ideal participant. A person with energy and curiosity seems to be essential.

Another difficulty the Institute faces, and that seems indigenous to all such endeavors, is the scarcity of monetary support. This is the greatest deterrent to participant recruitment. In the first two years the Institute was subsidized by a grant from the Lilly Endowment, which lowered participant fees and allowed for more liberal spending on food, entertainment, and special events. In the third year the Institute was supported almost entirely by the Great Lakes Colleges Association and by participant fees. Although the $1,300 for room, board, and tuition was well within reason, the frequently marginal nature of women's studies programs and the often low rank of faculty in the area made institutional faculty development funding hard to come by. Individuals did, with the help of the Institute director, find some funding from private and community agencies. And letters to deans from the president of the GLCA sometimes convinced administrations that money spent for faculty development in this area would come to a good end.

Certainly this has been the case. In the three years of the Institute, countless courses have been transformed, programs have begun, and individual faculty members have been revitalized by the community they discovered. This last is surely an important benefit, when one considers that persons on our campuses already engaged in women's studies often work is isolation and frustration and that the result of those conditions is burn-out and a consequent lessening of effectiveness. This is the necessity out of which the GLCA National Summer Institute was born and for which it continues.

11

Wheaton College Dissemination Conference: Sharing Resources

Bonnie B. Spanier

A Timely Effort

In June 1983, as the culmination of its three-year, FIPSE-funded project, "Toward a Balanced Curriculum: Integrating the Study of Women into the Liberal Arts," Wheaton College hosted a national conference. Attended by administrators and teachers from sixty postsecondary schools across the continental United States and one in Canada, the Balanced Curriculum Conference represented a timely effort to expand and strengthen the network of institutions involved in integration projects. It was timely in two ways. As a collegewide project, the conference galvanized the Wheaton faculty as we planned and implemented it. Coming at the end of the first, formal phase of our integration efforts, the conference enabled us to measure our own progress and to see more clearly how much work remained. The conference was also timely in the national context. Colleges and universities throughout the country are reviewing and redefining their curricula, and they need to understand why and how scholarship on women should be a part of new core curricula or distribution requirements. Also, by June 1983 many institutions had accumulated several years of experience in integration work and had developed a variety of models and strategies that were usefully shared with schools about to undertake projects.

As we planned the conference, participated in the panels and workshops, and observed the questions, problems, and discoveries of the teams from participating schools, we could understand more clearly our own experience of the preceding three years.

Wheaton's Balanced Curriculum Project

Wheaton's approach to moving women's studies scholarship into the body of mainstream teaching was ambitiously comprehensive in its goals. In 1980 Wheaton College began its organized integration efforts after it received a three-year grant from FIPSE to promote the incorporation of scholarship about women into introductory courses in all disciplines. For reasons pertaining to the size (about 100 faculty and 1200 students) and mission (quality liberal arts education for women) of the college and the strong support from the administration, the project was designed to reach as many faculty and affect as many disciplines as possible to promote voluntary curriculum revision starting at the introductory level.[1]

Based on a survey of the faculty, various components of the project were developed to promote self-assessment, faculty education in the scholarship about women and gender, and consequent course revision and evaluation. Incentives provided by the federal grant and additional college funds included release time from teaching, stipends for summer work, book allowances, and seminars of varying length. Funds were also available for lecturers, consultants, and visiting scholars.

As we began our project we made two assumptions that reflected the structure of our faculty and curriculum but that are also fairly typical of liberal arts colleges. First, we thought the introductory courses were the logical place to start because students would carry these questions with them throughout the rest of their education. As a result, our initial activities were defined by departmental and disciplinary boundaries. Second, although Wheaton had a women's studies minor at the time, we had neither a women's studies program nor many faculty members whose research focused on women's experience. We thought we could undertake integration without that base because we clearly had sufficient interest and support to do this work.

The need for interdisciplinary perspectives rooted in feminist theory was noted by our Outside Advisory Board of women's studies experts (Paula Goldsmid, Peggy McIntosh, and Elizabeth Minnich) after the first year of our grant. Serious attention to interdisciplinary feminist theory was a key development that moved us beyond a limited, discipline-based vision of integration as we learned more about the work we had undertaken. I point this out because schools lacking a well-developed women's studies program and a variety of women's studies scholars might easily overlook the interdisciplinary and theoretical perspectives from women's studies if the focus of integration work remains bounded by traditional disciplines. We therefore enhanced department-based activities with multidisciplinary programs such as workshops on the impact of women's studies across the disciplines, seminars devoted to new perspectives in literature and language, and a series of workshops to improve teaching methods and to promote active learning. The final critical addition to this program was the formation of faculty study groups on feminist theory.

Because the major goal of our project was outreach to faculty, a measure of our success is that by the third year of the project, more than half the faculty had been involved in some aspect of the project, and many of them continue both their education and course revision without financial compensation. Another important outcome—particularly since Wheaton did not have a women's studies program—is the transformation of a number of faculty members into teachers who are knowledgeable in women's studies scholarship and feminist theory, capable of teaching women's studies courses, and committed to women's studies scholarship and teaching as the essential foundation for enlightened integration. Above all, we came to recognize that integration is a long-term and monumental task. Therefore, the Balanced Curriculum project is being institutionalized at Wheaton as an ongoing part of regular faculty and curriculum development. The internal advisory committee composed of faculty, administrators, and students will continue to oversee integration efforts, with a faculty member appointed by the Provost to act as Coordinator.

Among the written products of the early stages of our project are enriched or transformed syllabi, bibliographies and related materials for different stages of faculty education and course revision, and a case study of the process of curricular change at

Wheaton.[2] The conference at the end of the three-year grant period was intended as an important dissemination vehicle to foster integration efforts nationwide by sharing our experience and case study.

Although the initial intent of the conference had been to stimulate integration efforts elsewhere, we found that it was equally important in its impact on the Wheaton participants, both resource people who had been involved in the Balanced Curriculum project and others who had not been active. Involvement in planning and facilitating the conference fostered individual and group commitment to the project. Of course, the conference gave us an opportunity to compare ourselves to other schools and projects. It helped us appreciate how far we had come in three short years and how much farther we needed to go. Some participants who were less familiar with women's studies and integration were very impressed with the quality of the presentations and the scholarship represented and also the eagerness of our guests to learn from our and others' experiences. In that way, the conference served to legitimize women's studies and integration at home. Legitimizing integration remained an issue even after three years. The conference itself, the positive feedback from it, the publication of the sourcebook, and the collection of follow-up reports from participating schools all served as an impetus to the Wheaton community to continue its own work and to sustain its responsibility to the schools that attended to develop connections within the network. The conference, thus, served to strengthen our institution's commitment to long-term integration work.

The Conference Goals and Design

The overall goals of the conference were (a) to initiate or stimulate the integration of the study of women into curricula at postsecondary schools across the country, and (b) to expand and strengthen the network of institutions involved in integration, thereby to facilitate mutual support, exchange of resources, and assessment of progress. Two key strategies for assisting institutions in developing integration projects were to require participating schools to send teams and to make each team submit an integration project proposal as part of the application process.

The purpose of requiring teams of two or three educators rather than allowing individuals to represent institutions was made explicit: to strengthen (or establish) an appropriate base of support to develop integration efforts at the home institution. We suggested in the "Registration Materials" booklet that the team consist of one faculty member with knowledge of recent scholarship on women or issues in educational equity and two other educators who were interested in integration and carried enough weight in the community to tap resources and broaden campus support, such as a faculty member involved in educational policy and an academic administrator with responsibility and resources for curriculum and faculty development. Thus, although many women's studies faculty were interested in attending, we suggested that the team itself be a mixture of veterans and relative newcomers to women's studies.

Our own experience, and the guidance of our Outside Advisory Board, told us that to develop an institutional commitment to integration, a team of administrators and faculty members would need to attend at an early stage to a number of practical and political issues, and to set feasible short- and long-range goals. They should assess internal and external resources available, gauge potential obstacles, target specific aspects of the curriculum for initial integration efforts, and set a reasonable time schedule for short- and long-term goals. We hoped that the conference would enable them to initiate projects and also to understand the comprehensive nature of effective integration.

Applicants to the conference were asked to include information about the needs and interests of their institution, to make an assessment of their own (and regional) resources and potential, and to design an appropriate project to begin in 1983–84. At the conclusion of the conference, each team was asked to submit a final description of their project, allowing for revisions during the conference. Follow-up forms were sent six months and one year after the conference to team leaders, asking them to assess their project's development and, when necessary, to adjust the short- and long-term goals.

When we started our own three-year project we had conceived of the final conference as a vehicle for sharing the experience and resources of the Wheaton project, of telling others what we had accomplished. But through contact with other colleges and universities who had designed and implemented other curriculum integration projects, we came to appreciate many models and realized that each institution must tailor its integration efforts to its particular resources, interests, and needs within the political realities of its situation. Therefore, we expanded the purpose and scope of our dissemination conference beyond the Wheaton experience to utilize the growing resources of many different schools and projects.[3] We also wanted to address the complex and evolving relationship that we now recognized between integration efforts and women's studies and the need to include multicultural perspectives in both integration and women's studies work.[4] At the conference itself we became aware of the need to address more explicitly other, even more controversial issues, such as class and sexuality.

Registration Procedure:
Motivating Self-Assessment, Initiating Change

In the application process we tried to initiate self-assessment that would enable each institution to recognize and adopt the model most suited to its needs. A booklet of "Registration Materials" described the purpose and scope of the conference and the application procedure for institutions.[5] Since we envisioned many interested institutions to be just starting or at early stages in integration projects, the booklet included a summary of the background and philosophy of women's studies and the related transformation of the curriculum. We also referred the readers who did not know how to begin considering appropriate strategies for their campus to the working paper from the Southwest Institute for Research on Women: "How to Integrate Women's Studies into the Traditional Curriculum."[6]

To help applicants formulate projects appropriate to their institutions, we provided the following series of questions:

A. Significance of the needs and source of concern of the institution.

Describe the needs and interests in the local context: In what ways have issues of concern to women affected the interests of the institution? What is the special impetus for taking action at this time? Have any actions addressing integration been undertaken in the past? How does the tentative proposal build on those efforts? Who will benefit from the integration activities, and in what ways?

B. Resources available.

Who are the on-campus and local resources in women's studies and equity issues? How and where (disciplines, departments, special programs) are faculty already incorporating information about women and gender into the curriculum? What courses or programs are offered in women's studies? Describe the institutional resources (regularly scheduled luncheon discussions or informal reading groups, funds for faculty or curriculum development or guest speakers) which could be applied to integration efforts in relation to the institution's current commitment to this area. Where in the administration is the potential or actual support for integration of women's studies? What role do students play in addressing these issues? What are the major barriers or sources of resistance which inhibit interest or work in integration?

C. Feasible approach to initiate or stimulate integration efforts.

Given the structure of the curriculum, the interest and resources available, and the current needs, describe one (or more) project(s) that would initiate or foster integration efforts in the coming academic year at your institution. Why is this project the most feasible approach at this time? If successful, what might this project lead to as a further step toward a gender-balanced curriculum?

We wanted to encourage applications and also make the procedure itself a worthwhile experience not only to prepare the teams for the conference, but also in the event that we could not accept all applicants. We found that many schools took the registration process very seriously and were anxious about being chosen to attend.

The possibility of obtaining travel funds, which we requested as part of the extra dissemination money from FIPSE, set up a competition among schools for that assistance. We required some financial commitment from the institutions to qualify for travel aid. When we received extra FIPSE money, we distributed the travel funds to broaden the geographical representation and diversity of participating schools.

After receiving the applications, Wheaton's Balanced Curriculum Advisory Committee decided to include as many institutional teams as possible. With the aid of FIPSE's dissemination competition award, coordination with another major outreach project, the Leadership for Educational Equity Program centered at the University of Maine at Orono and funded by WEEA, and a contribution from Northeastern University's Women's Studies Program, we could make it possible for nearly sixty colleges and universities to attend the conference (more than twice as many as originally anticipated). Of the sixty participating institutions, ten were all-women's colleges and fifty coeducational. Small (fewer than 2500 students) and large schools were about equally represented. A majority (thirty-five) were located in the Northeast, twelve in the South, seven in the Midwest, five in the Far West, and one in Canada (Ontario). Only one school, Howard, was a predominantly black institution.

The Event: Building Coalitions for Change

The conference took place on Wheaton's campus in June 1983, over two and a half days. The keynote address and panel presentations were given in a large lecture hall for all participants (about 250 people, including Wheaton faculty, administrators, and a few students). At three points in the schedule, the large group divided up into small discussion sessions of about ten to twenty members.

With our choice of speakers and topics, we wanted to acquaint participants with three major aspects of curriculum integration: (a) the vision of transformation in light of the wealth of material on women and gender, including the significance of race, class, and culture; (b) the politics and process of changing the curriculum using a variety of approaches; and (c) locating the resources within and beyond institutions.

The topics addressed at the conference reflected our concern for both the relative newcomer to women's studies scholarship and integration and the educator more experienced in these areas. The conference was designed to persuade key faculty and administrators of the national significance of this work and the potential benefits to their institutions. We hoped that the position of faculty members engaged in integration and women's studies efforts would be strengthened as they became recognized, by their own and other institutions, as valuable resource personnel in this regard. The structure of the teams brought administrators and teachers, newcomers and veterans, together for the kinds of coalitions essential for productive and lasting integration work.

The opening panel, "Taking Women and Gender Seriously," provided the rationale and vision of curriculum transformation as well as examples of the impact of the new perspectives in the disciplines. Catharine Stimpson's keynote address traced the intellectual development of women's studies and set integration in context as a timely outgrowth of more than a decade of new questions and strong scholarship. Speakers stressed the comprehensive, inclusive nature of women's studies and integration. In a later panel, Betty Schmitz of Montana State University identified the need to attend to the full range of human experience, to study "*all* women, women of color, lesbian women, women of all classes and ethnic heritages. It means confronting not only androcentric bias in the curriculum, but racist, heterosexist, and classist bias and dealing with *all* women *on their own terms.*" She articulated the challenge of integration work:

> Can you in your projects raise precisely those issues which the mainstream has the most difficulty confronting and acknowledge and support the presence of those women who cannot be "added and stirred"? If you cannot ask *when* and *how* you'll raise these, maybe your question is in fact *whether* to initiate a project of this nature.

Discussion of the impact of women's studies scholarship within the disciplines took place in the small-group sessions. We scheduled two occasions for discipline-based working sessions, each geared to different audiences. The first session was to be attended by participants with expertise in that discipline, the second by those outside that discipline. Our rationale was to provide a critical perspective on a discipline other than one's own and to promote outreach in those areas not represented by the team members of each institution. This strategy was effective in some cases. In the second session in the natural sciences, for example, many non-science people were eager for suggestions how to overcome their science colleagues' belief that gender and women are irrelevant to science and math teaching.

The emphasis on practical planning of integration efforts was intended to help committed faculty and administrators with the political and strategic dimensions of building coalitions, widening the circle of support and interest, identifying internal and external resources, and becoming part of the institutional structure so that integration and women's studies work becomes a regular part of faculty and curriculum development. To that end, our invited panelists discussed models developed at schools throughout the country, political issues such as affirmative action and the academic reward system within traditional structures, and appropriate teaching methods for integrating women and gender; concurrently held small-group sessions allowed participants to meet with some of the speakers to pursue the concerns they raised, such as transforming the conventional syllabus, taking women's studies seriously, and developing an effective faculty workshop. The speakers also enumerated the dangers of inadequate integration projects and warned against reinforcing white, Western, middle-class solipsism, superficial teaching about women and gender, and dilution of women's studies scholarship to avoid difficult topics such as racism, classism, and heterosexism.

While many participants came with an interest in learning how to garner grants, much of the advice they received suggested ways of making integration part of existing programs (the "piggy-back" model described in Chap. 7) and utilizing current internal and external resources. That perspective on integration shifts it from a separate concern to an essential part of institutional programs, such as core curriculum reform, student development, or a project on writing across the curriculum.

Assessing the Event: Process and Product

The diversity of the participants and presenters, in terms of their background (or lack of it) in women's studies and of their position in their home institutions, led to a diversity of expectations about what integration entails, how it can be achieved, what it should look like, and how the conference would answer those questions. Consequently, assessment of the conference varied. People who came to the conference with a background in women's studies thought there should have been more focus on the hard issues of race, ethnicity, class, and sexuality, as well as on problems such as sexual harassment and violence against women. Frequently, participants who were just beginning to think about integration wanted more concrete products to take home: model syllabi, textbooks, grant proposals, or transformed syllabi in the natural sciences. In this desire for a product that could be added on to or plugged into current curricula we recognized some of our own early expectations, before we had really undertaken our own project, that effective integration could be accomplished in a time-limited period by discovering and adopting modules, syllabi, or selected readings that would correct the imbalance of the traditional curriculum.

After our three years of concerted hard work we recognized that integration starts the process of fundamental transformation of the curriculum through extensive faculty development plans and an in-depth critique of the disciplines. In other words, although we need to share resources and develop networks to make programs more efficient, integration requires engagement in a process, not adoption of a product developed by someone else. The ultimate consequence of successful integration work may be transformation of every aspect of education: teaching, disciplinary questions and assumptions, departmental structures, the relationship between the classroom and the rest of the institution. Integration cannot be accomplished without a thorough understanding of twenty years of feminist scholarship and commitment to ongoing feminist inquiry.

What were the participants' most significant gains from the conference? In their evaluations they repeatedly cited:

• the far-reaching vision of curriculum transformation and the importance of doing it;
• a realistic grasp of the process of change—learning to set manageable goals and take small steps, "not to expect too much" at first;
• how to expand the circle of involved faculty and to take academic and institutional politics into account;
• knowledge of the essential place of multicultural perspectives in integration and women's studies;

• getting "persuasive material" for their colleagues and administrators; and

• acquaintance with the fine scholarship being done in women's studies and its effect in the disciplines.

Most participants commented on the inspiration and exhilaration they experienced in the supportive and congenial atmosphere of the conference, which generated new or revitalized energy and excitement about this work. One participant wrote: "Most valuable was the realization that the effort is so widespread, serious, and a powerful force in other institutions." Faculty already experienced in women's studies and integration, some of whom found little that was new to them in some of the introductory talks, nonetheless expressed satisfaction about the strong affirmation they received for the kind of work they had been doing. Thus, the conference seemed successful in motivating different constituencies among the participants, including people from Wheaton.

NEXT STEPS: INITIATING INTEGRATION PROJECTS ELSEWHERE

The projects proposed by the teams ranged from developing a women's studies course to reach many students, to organizing faculty education in women's studies with unspecified course revisions to follow later. Most projects included several components to foster faculty and curriculum development. The following summary indicates the range of activities across the projects.

A majority of the projects specified starting a faculty seminar on integration and women's studies, stressing faculty development and education as a first step. The next most frequently cited activity was the intended use of outside consultants to address faculty on integration and the impact of women's studies scholarship on the curriculum and disciplines. Nearly one-third of the projects included a focus on developing a specific course in women's studies as a necessary prelude to influencing the rest of the curriculum, and an equal proportion were aimed at changing the core curriculum at their schools. Also frequently proposed were faculty discussion groups, as a less structured and more flexible alternative to faculty seminars. In a few cases, planned projects included the development of bibliographies, the establishment of a consortium of schools, surveying the faculty on current integration efforts, bringing in speakers, fostering team-teaching of new material, and evaluating texts for sexist content.

FOLLOW UP

Six-month reports were sent by half of the participating institutions, describing what had been accomplished thus far, what problems were encountered, whether any changes were anticipated in the project plan, and what kinds of network activities would be useful. Only a few schools cited problems: some resistance to women's issues by faculty or students, lack of interest from faculty, and underlying anxiety. More often the reports stated, some with surprise, that their efforts were meeting with support from the administration, cooperation and enthusiasm from faculty, and large audiences for women's studies speakers. Two schools said that they had instituted a minor in women's studies.

It is clear that many schools across the country are making progress in organizing and defining the objectives of their integration efforts. Now conferences, newsletters, and other publications are needed for faculty engaged in integration work to communicate about what is happening or could be happening in the classroom as more time and energy are spent on transforming the curriculum with women's studies.

* * * *

The Wheaton College project, "Toward a Balanced Curriculum: Integrating the Study of Women into the Liberal Arts," was made possible by grant #G008004262 from the Fund for the Improvement of Postsecondary Education. I would like to thank Darlene Boroviak for her help preparing this essay.

Notes

1. For the origin and early stages of the project, see Bonnie B. Spanier, "'Toward a Balanced Curriculum'–The Study of Women at Wheaton College," *Change*, April 1982, pp. 31–34.
2. Bonnie Spanier, Alexander Bloom, and Darlene Boroviak, eds., *Toward a Balanced Curriculum: A Sourcebook for Initiating Gender Integration Projects* (Cambridge, Mass.: Schenkman Publishing Co., 1984).

3. Outside resource people for the conference included Kathleen Adams, Johnnella Butler, Mary Childers, Nancy Cott, Margo Culley, JoAnn Fritsche, Paula Goldsmid, Beverly Guy-Sheftall, Paul Lauter, Judy Lensink, Felicia Lynch, Peggy McIntosh, Elizabeth Kamarck Minnich, Deborah Pearlman, David Savage, Ruth Schmidt, Betty Schmitz, Marilyn Schuster, Janet Sims-Wood, Catharine Stimpson, Ines Talamantez, Martha Tolpin, and Susan Van Dyne.
4. Bonnie B. Spanier, "Inside an Integration Project: A Case Study of the Relationship Between Balancing the Curriculum and Women's Studies," *Women's Studies International Forum* 7, no. 3 (June 1984): 153–60.
5. Betty Schmitz provided invaluable assistance from her experience with the Montana State University "Women in the Curriculum Project" and the Northern Rockies Institute.
6. "How to Integrate Women's Studies into the Traditional Curriculum," SIROW Working Paper #9, August 1981; available for $3.00 from the Southwest Institute for Research of Women, Women's Studies Program, Modern Languages 269, The University of Arizona, Tucson, AR 85721.

Appendix

MOVING TOWARD A BALANCED CURRICULUM

A NATIONAL CONFERENCE SPONSORED BY WHEATON COLLEGE
June 22–24, 1983

<u>Wednesday, June 22</u>

9:00   **Opening Remarks**

Bonnie Spanier, Wheaton College
President Alice Emerson, Wheaton College
Alexander Bloom, Wheaton College

Panel: TAKING WOMEN AND GENDER SERIOUSLY

Interactive Phases of Curricular Re-Vision
Peggy McIntosh, Wellesley College, Moderator

The Difference It Makes In The Humanities
Johnnella Butler, Smith College

The Difference It Makes In The Social Sciences
Darlene Boroviak, Wheaton College

The Difference It Makes In The Natural Sciences
Bonnie Spanier, Wheaton College

11:15   **Keynote Address:**
THE DEVELOPMENT OF WOMEN'S STUDIES

Catharine Stimpson, Douglass College
Founding Editor of *Signs*

1:30   **Panel: MOVING TOWARD A BALANCED
CURRICULUM: INSTITUTIONAL MODELS**

Alexander Bloom, Wheaton College, Moderator
The Smith College Model
Marilyn Schuster and Susan Van Dyne
The Montana State University Model
Betty Schmitz

The Wheaton College Model
Bonnie Spanier
The Yale University Model
Nancy Cott

3:30   **Concurrent Working Sessions: THE IMPACT OF WOMEN'S STUDIES SCHOLARSHIP IN THE DISCIPLINES I**

Participants attend small-group sessions in their own disciplines. Administrators meet separately.

5:00   REFRESHMENTS
Free time to look at exhibits in the
Science Center Reading Room
and/or to organize participant generated sessions for
Thursday evening.

6:00   **Dinner**
Dinner with Wheaton Contact Person.

8:00   **Lecture-Recital: ANOTHER VOICE**

Barbara Winchester, Soprano – Dinosaur Annex Music Ensemble
Maria Benatti, Violin – Artistic Director
Music at Eden's Edge
Ann Sears, Piano – Wheaton College

Thursday, June 23

9:30   **Panel: STRATEGIES FOR THE INSTITUTION AND THE CLASSROOM**

Alexander Bloom, Wheaton College, Moderator

Appropriate Teaching Methods for Integrating Women
Frances Maher, Wheaton College

Black Studies and Women's Studies: An Overdue Partnership
Margo Culley, University of Massachusetts, Amherst
Johnnella Butler, Smith College

Moving Beyond the Curriculum:
The 'Political' Value of an Integration Strategy
JoAnn Fritsche, University of Maine, Orono

11:00   **Concurrent Working Sessions:**
INTEGRATION APPROACHES AND STRATEGIES

Participants attend small-group sessions.

1:30   **Concurrent Working Sessions:**
**THE IMPACT OF WOMEN'S STUDIES SCHOLARSHIP
IN THE DISCIPLINES II**

Participants, including administrators, attend small-group
sessions in a discipline *other than their own.*
Resource people attend in their own discipline.

3:15 **Panel: THE WEALTH OF MATERIAL ABOUT WOMEN:
LOCATING RESOURCES**

Bonnie Spanier, Wheaton College, Moderator

Reconstructing American Literature
Paul Lauter, SUNY, Old Westbury and The Feminist Press

Black Women's History
Janet Sims-Wood, Howard University

Library Resources on Women
Sherrie Bergman, Wheaton College

4:45   **Library Reception**
Reference materials will be on display.
Journals and other materials about women will be on display in
the Women's Information Center of the Library.
Cash bar.

SPECIAL MEETINGS

a. Leadership for Educational Equity Project (participating institutions)
b. Ad hoc regional gathers to discuss local networks, pooling resources

8:00   **Film: "ROSIE THE RIVETER" or**
              PARTICIPANT-GENERATED SESSIONS
              Optional; sign-up lists in Science Center Lobby.

Friday, June 24

9:30   **Presentation: ASSESSING PROGRESS:**
              A CASE STUDY APPROACH

              Martha Tolpin, Bentley College

10:15   **Panel and Discussion: THE NEXT STEP**

              Alexander Bloom, Wheaton College, Moderator

              A View From The Funding Agencies
              Felicia Lynch, FIPSE

              In-House Resources
              Paula Goldsmid, Scripps College

              The Small Liberal Arts College
              David Savage, Lewis and Clark College

              From Issue to Action
              Betty Schmitz, Montana State

11:45   **Closing Remarks:**
              WOMEN, GENDER AND THE CURRICULUM

              President Ruth Schmidt, Agnes Scott College

This conference has been supported with funds from The Fund
for the Improvement of Postsecondary Education; the University
of Maine at Orono's Leadership in Educational Equity Project
(WEEAP); and Northeastern University's Women's Studies Program.

III

Classroom Consequences

12

The Changing Classroom

Marilyn R. Schuster and Susan R. Van Dyne

As the essays in the first two sections illustrate, rising expectations and diminishing resources define the context in which curriculum transformation must take place. Our women students certainly have rising expectations about the value of higher education to prepare them for high-paying, high-status employment. Most women students have faith that the values and skills of a traditional liberal education will fit them for a productive adult life; they expect, on graduation, to succeed in the culture as it's now constructed. They expect to match the culture's paradigms of worth and achievement rather than to change them. At the same time that they expect liberal arts study to widen for them the career paths once traveled mostly by men, women have given up none of their faith in personal fulfillment through affinity relationships and caretaking networks, in whatever forms these are structured.

A crucial irony exists here. Women students' rising expectations expose a fundamental conflict between our culture's ideology of the liberally educated person and the actual possibilities in that culture for a liberally educated woman. Women students in the last decade, for the most part, did not question the values of their traditional education as much as the profound lack of fit between their education and what they expected to achieve by virtue of it. The current college generation of women students feels entitled, largely as the legacy of the women's movement, to a new image of themselves innately valuable, intellectually competent, and socially equal to men. Yet they must confront during and after college a culture still shaped by and serving primarily the needs of men. Their traditional education gives them no adequate means of bridging this gap, nor of adequately understanding their own experience in the context of this culture.

The woman-focused classroom serves as an invaluable laboratory for examining the changing expectations of women students and for uncovering the causes of conflict and sources for change in transforming liberal education. What we call a woman-focused classroom is one in which women students are acknowledged as important members of the class and in which the professor exposes the class to a reflection of human experience that not only explicitly includes women, but also draws attention to racial, cultural, and class diversity.

Our advances in transforming the traditional curriculum began in women's studies with a process of negative definition: we identified what is needed by cataloging what was missing or marginalized. Reimagining the core of the liberal arts curriculum, then, means exposing the conflict between opposing worldviews: an exclusive, white, male, Western European view of human experience that calls itself humanist, in contrast to a much more inclusive vision of critical differences in gender, ethnicity, and socioeconomic background. As the essays on classroom experience in this section illustrate, we've moved beyond negative definition to positive strategies: first in women's studies classes such as Elaine Marks describes, then in pilot efforts to transform courses throughout the curriculum, from philosophy to the sciences.

The Woman-Focused Classroom: Multiple Transgressions

Whenever women enter the classroom, there's sure to be trouble. The primary difference between a woman-focused course and others involves multiple transgressions that create discomfort for many students, and often their teachers as well. If not addressed, these heightened tensions can lead to disappointment and confusion. Instead, they can become a productive part of the teaching process if the teacher is willing to draw attention to them. We want to analyze the inclusion of women in the classroom in at least three dimensions: as the subject of study on the syllabus, as an important focus of the teacher's attention, and as women students. Although we intend to identify why and how women's presence in any of these guises is inherently disruptive of old certainties and civilities, and thus a cause of conflict, our goal is to demonstrate how making women visible in the classroom in these three ways is potentially transformative of higher education's entire shape and substance.

A woman-focused classroom brings previously invisible paradigms and unspoken contracts into sharp relief. The invisible paradigms shape the content and organization of our syllabus. The unspoken contracts govern our responsibility to our discipline and our institution and also the way we claim and exercise authority in the classroom. They include unarticulated clauses about what students expect to get from us as teachers and for themselves by becoming educated.

The syllabus, the teacher, the classroom—what happens to each when women are not marginal but appear instead as conspicuously central? What may be surprising is that such a radical alteration of familiar patterns may never forget nor exclude the world of men in the ways that the traditional classroom often forgets and excludes the presence of women. The male-defined world intrudes and colors experience even here. Nonetheless, the ultimate goal of such a fresh configuration is to transform the vision of men as much as of women.

THE SHAPE OF THE SYLLABUS

Women are extremely problematic when they appear on the conventional syllabus. Elaine Marks in Chapter 13 demonstrates how a syllabus devoted exclusively to women's cultural production sharpens our understanding of difference and of problems of interpretation. How the example of women refuses to confirm our inherited criteria for judgment is explored in each of the essays in this section. We see the shapes that formerly structured our knowledge most clearly when we try to study something that distorts them.

Attempting to be attentive to differences not only between genders, but for ethnic groups, socioeconomic backgrounds, and chosen lifestyles, we are forcibly reminded how often traditional syllabi are founded on the demonstration of sameness. We've called this the "fountainhead" paradigm of syllabus design or "reproduction by analogy." In teaching courses shaped by this paradigm, we've conventionally agreed we know where to start: ·we start at the fountainhead, or with the first instance of greatness. The hidden power of this paradigm lies in what we agree to call the first instance, for this primary example often serves to define how everything that follows on the syllabus will be perceived. As Helen Longino and John Schilb show in their transformation of philosophy and literature courses, whether we begin with Aristotle or Henry James, the framework derived from these fountainheads becomes the lens through which we see the rest. Unless we devise strategies for complicating the framework, such as pairing familiar and unfamiliar texts, other phenomena or other angles of vision will be valued according to the degree they can be accommodated to the initial perspective, that is, to the extent they are analogous to the original.

The order of items on the syllabus is always value-laden and is never perceived as merely random. Whatever form it takes, the syllabus whose invisible paradigm is the fountainhead or which reproduces greatness by analogy with the primary example can never do full justice to difference. Instead these paradigms exist to demonstrate likeness. When differences are multiple rather than simply dualistic, such paradigms of syllabus design serve us even less. Longino's philosopher's progress makes this very clear.

Historically, our first attempts to transform the conventional syllabus by being more inclusive of the lives of women, minority groups, and different classes revealed extensive subcultures, vast strata of experience previously invisible. Yet simple inclusion of the new knowledge within the inherited framework was problematic, because the invisible paradigms continued to control our interpretation of the fresh data. As long as we agreed to view women through the lens of the dominant group or gender, the most noticeable characteristic of their experience was oppression. Fortunately, the example of black studies offers alternatives to this analysis. If we adopt an insider's view, rather than the exclusionary perspective of the conventionally designed syllabus, we realize that the identities of women are richly diverse and can be defined independent of the dominant group.

How much power these paradigms still hold, even after we know their failings, may be unintentionally confirmed in our designs for women-focused courses. We've been more successful so far in developing courses that treat women's history or women's literature in its own terms, apart from men's. We are beginning to learn, in courses like those described in this section, how to make women central and then how to put the world of women's and men's experience back together again; that re-vision demands reconceiving the entire paradigm. In the process of genuine transformation we must be willing to create a syllabus whose outer boundaries are in constant flux, in which terms that seemed familiar become problematic. The list of lexical items on Marks's syllabus signals that teachers and students must pay close attention to shifting meanings and to the ways meaning is conditioned by specific cultural contexts as women's lives and cultural production become central concerns.

What belongs on the syllabus will be a matter for open and almost constant debate. At times it seems nothing can be omitted. The discipline of being rigorously interdisciplinary yields a syllabus that is unwieldy and impure by the conventional standards of most departments. Sue Rosser's inclusion of materials from the history of science in a biology course, for example, or Greta Salem and Stephen Sharkey's attention to urban architecture in social science courses, demonstrate creative means to enrich and transform conventions that become constricting when we pay attention to women.

In our analysis, the process of curriculum transformation is marked by the conflict between our attempts to order knowledge more inclusively and the stubborn structures of these invisible paradigms. The very process of trying to replace them serves to remind us how intransigent they are. Yet we are ready to claim significant progress has been made by bringing these invisible, unspoken assumptions into the light of critical scrutiny where their power can be self-consciously articulated and, with care, combated.

THE TEACHER'S DILEMMA: CHANGING THE TERMS OF AUTHORITY

What unspoken power relations surface when women appear at the head of the classroom, or when a woman teacher occupies one of the chairs in a circle of students? How does this relation change when the teacher is a man or a woman team-teaching with a man? The experience of women teachers, particularly in women-focused courses, shows that we need to move beyond an analysis that identifies women teachers as unambiguous role models and mentors to be emulated. In practice, as Marks's analysis bears out, what women teachers represent to women students is often highly conflicted and may provoke as much denial from students as desire. As Jean Baker Miller suggests, the teacher/student relationship is founded on an assumption of temporary inequality in which the goal of the participant with more power or knowledge is to end or reduce that inequality by sharing these resources.[1] Yet the temporary inequality of the teacher/ student relationship is enmeshed in a cultural context of more permanent inequalities, in which dominant groups, such as men and whites, inhibit access to their power by subordinate groups, such as women and non-whites.

Who is the woman teacher to her students? She possesses the power attributed to her institutionally as teacher, and yet her explicit goal is often to empower her students by sharing her authority. She holds the keys to mastery of a subject, yet her concern for students' growth is often described as nurturing. In claiming her own personal authority in the classroom, the woman teacher cannot fully shed the patriarchal culture's definition of her gender. Because her status for students remains embedded in a social context of male/female permanent inequalities, their prior cultural conditioning is an omnipresent invisible paradigm even in a woman-focused classroom.[2] The team-teaching experience of Judith Anderson and Stephen Grubman taught them how all-determining gender socialization can be even when the explicit goal of a course is to examine it critically.

In her powerful role as teacher, a woman may be perceived as having the conflicting attributes of mother and father at once and therefore may provoke deeply ambivalent responses. As analogous to the mother figure, the woman teacher is seen as a source of comfort, sustenance and possible identification. Yet she may be feared as encouraging dependency. She also resembles a father figure to students in her enviable authority, imagined autonomy, and in the occupational necessity she has to judge, evaluate, and possibly reject them.[3]

A further complication is added when the woman teacher, whose explicit goal is to empower women students by sharing her authority with them, attempts to present an inclusive picture of human experience, part of which is the discomforting recognition of women's history of subordination. We find that the initial reaction of women students to having women on the syllabus is grief at the loss of earlier illusions. To avoid perceiving themselves as losers according to the dominant culture's definition, they may struggle to assert behavior and values that correspond more nearly to the dominant group. Or they may cling to a faith in an individual solution, believing that the picture of women as a group may be representative of another historical time or place, but that their own merit and discernment will allow a different and superior fate for themselves.

As the essays in this section suggest, men and women have encountered these conflicts very differently. Women teachers, more visibly linked to "women's issues," are frequently identified as the source of the discomfort experienced in these classrooms. Role-modeling, in other words, is far from simple or certain. Rooted in the larger culture and complicated both by the student's personal hopes and internalized assumptions, it can take several forms. Initially a woman student may think (consciously or not), "I want to be like this person." Eventually she may think (unconsciously), "I want this person to be like what I want to become." The result is usually disappointment, even resentment, because the teacher won't conform to this desire. We don't mean to suggest that the greater presence of women teachers on women's college campuses, in women-focused courses and in curriculum transformation efforts elsewhere, is not a significant advantage to women students.[4] Only by appearing in significant numbers can we mirror for students the range of possibilities of being adult and female. Yet we should recognize that in this mirror the woman student is likely to project images of women that the culture has drawn for her, including self-doubt and low self-esteem, as well as to see reflected in her teacher attributes of power and possibility that she might claim for herself.

Because male authority is validated in the larger culture, men may use that cultural expectation to legitimate the study of women. At the same time, as the essays in this volume by men and by mixed teams demonstrate, changing the terms of authority in the classroom may be more problematic for male teachers. In other words, the discomfort experienced in the woman-focused classroom is not one-sided. When we present women's experience, we must also confess our ignorance and awkwardness. Teaching about women is, in Peggy McIntosh's phrase, "hazardous to the ego."[5] We frequently appear both passionately political and puzzlingly tentative in our presentations of this material. We candidly identify our biases because we intend not to deceive our students with the old myth that humanistic learning is value-free and objective. Moreover, because we're aware that knowledge and modes of understanding are historical by nature, we carefully qualify our assertions and resist global, eternal claims for our new truths. Students who are used to directive, authoritative teaching often interpret this as weakness.

WOMEN LEARNING: A PEDAGOGY OF EMPOWERMENT

Power relationships, we've been arguing, are at the root of these invisible paradigms. How is power felt in the woman-focused classroom? Frequently our pedagogy departs intentionally from conventional models. The same critique that transforms the traditional syllabus in order to take women seriously as a legitimate subject of study, and that strives to examine women's experience in its own terms, reminds the teacher to respect an individual student's right to report her own experience. Aware that power may have been hoarded by dominant groups to the disadvantage of women in the past, the woman-focused teacher is self-conscious about broadening the authority group in the classroom, including students as significant sources of approval and intellectual validation for their peers. Wary of the pitfalls of competitive hierarchical modes of evaluation and judgment, she or he is likely to foster collaborative learning and shared reponsibility for measuring achievement. Schilb's essay proposes useful exercises for achieving these goals. Intellectually rigorous about uncovering the cultural biases that may mar our generalizations, the woman-focused teacher will try to illuminate differences among students as much as promote a sense of community in the classroom. All these essays assume student-centered education as a high priority.

Ideally, students learn to value the authority of their own experience as they become critical of the forces that have defined it. The shift in authority is part of a larger structure that is also shaken. The classroom situation usually provides safety zones for students. Although being a student always implies being at some intellectual risk, and usually involves exposure to information in conflict with comfortable convictions, distance is usually maintained between the intellectual content of the course, the task at hand, and the student's personal feelings and choices in life. When we study politics, emotions, or psychological development, we rarely allow them to become part of the teaching process itself. For example, it is one thing to analyze the *Brown* v. *Board of Education* decision; it is quite another to confront racism when it's expressed in the classroom. One can maintain a comfortable distance studying the history of the Equal Rights Amendment, but drawing attention to misogyny in the classroom, in ourselves, or in our dealings with each other breaks down that distance.[6]

Teachers whose regular departmental courses have an important focus on women have reported another significant source of conflict. Often these courses (such as women's fiction, women and philosophy) will attract two distinct groups of students with conflicting agendas for the course. One group is there because it is a literature, philosophy, biology or social science course, and they come with the same expectations they bring to other courses in that discipline. The other group is there because it is a course that gives significant authority to women's experience; these students may not particularly care about the discipline or have much experience in it. The first group will resent the "politics" of the second group who, in turn, will be impatient with the lack of feminist consciousness of the first. The teacher is frequently caught in a crossfire, alternately disappointing one group and then the other. The only solution, not easily arrived at, is again, to bring the conflict to the surface and try to help each group understand how it might profit from the perspective of the other.

Changing the terms of authority, acknowledging conflict, and bringing it to the surface are gestures that point to what is perhaps our largest single assumption about the college classroom: that in this privileged space we can suspend, the better to examine, cultural assumptions that are so pervasive they seem natural and inevitable. This has always been a goal of higher education; women-focused teachers refine that goal by attempting to unmask and undo the consequences of our culture's differential socialization of men and women. Women and other subordinate groups have so fully internalized the dominant group's definition of their being, however, that the process of becoming self-conscious initially can seem to be denying what they know as their identity. As Anderson and Grubman discovered in their efforts to transform courses in communications, students may be extremely fearful of relinquishing the invisible paradigms of personal definition and gender they have absorbed in their educational socialization, because these seem, quite literally, all that they know about themselves.

Resistance can often block empowerment, because we've underestimated how profoundly radical an undertaking curriculum transformation truly is and the deep psychological investment we all have, even against our will, in the old invisible paradigms. When we try to implement new modes of learning that are congruent with our analysis of the necessarily inclusive shape of knowledge on the transformed syllabus, we must again confront how the same powers that shaped the syllabus have shaped us and our expectations of the educational process.

CONFLICT AS AN AGENT FOR CHANGE

What's to be done with the important recognitions gained in the last decade of teaching in women-focused classrooms? To name and thus make available for transformation what goes on in the classroom we need to examine the experience and transformative strategies of the women's studies classroom, as Marks does in Chapter 13, to reshape non-women's studies offerings such as the philosophy, literature, communications, social science, and biology courses described in the other essays. As we employ new strategies for organizing knowledge on our syllabus, for exercising our authority, or when we ask students to take a self-conscious stance toward their socialization, we must be more candid about the conflict we produce. To repeat our earlier axiom, when women enter the classroom, whether on the syllabus, as a central concern of the teacher, or as students, there's sure to be trouble. If we identify conflict, as Jean Baker Miller suggests, with process, with the potential for change,[7] fewer students—men as well as women—will fear it. Openly acknowledged conflict is the expression of movement, the outward sign of the necessary condition for re-vision of the status quo.

In naming the opposing forces that make up the process of change, we may give our students access to the sources of their own resistance. Further, we may become more self-conscious about our own, often unwitting, collusion in clinging to these paradigms.

Notes

1. Jean Baker Miller, *Toward a New Psychology of Women* (Boston: Beacon Press, 1976), pp. 3–12.
2. For the differential treatment of women and men in the classroom, see Bernice R. Sandler, "The Classroom Climate: A Chilly One for Women?" compiled by the Project on the Status and Education of Women in 1981 and available from the Association of American Colleges.
3. For an extended analysis of this phenomenon, see "The Politics of Nurturance" by Margo Culley, Arlyn Diamond, Lee Edwards, Sarah Lennox, and Cathy Portuges of the University of Massachusetts, Amherst. This essay will appear in *Gendered Subjects: The Dynamics of Difference in the Classroom*, a forthcoming anthology edited by Culley and Portuges (London: Routledge & Kegan Paul, 1985).
4. See Elizabeth Tidball's important essays in *Educational Record* 54 (Spring 1973): 130–35, and in *Signs* 5, no. 3 (Spring 1980): 504–17. She confirmed at a conference at Skidmore College ("Towards an Equitable Education for Women and Men") that a significant positive statistical correlation continues to exist between the presence of women faculty at women's colleges and the high production of women achievers among their graduates.
5. See her article by this title in the special issue (Spring 1982) of *Women's Studies Quarterly* devoted to curriculum transformation, pp. 28–31.
6. Vicky Spelman develops sources of anger in the classroom and strategies for engaging emotions productively in "Combatting the Marginalization of Black Women in the Classroom," *Women's Studies Quarterly* (Summer 1982): 15–16.
7. Miller, *Toward a New Psychology*, p. 126.

13

Deconstructing in Women's Studies to Reconstructing the Humanities

Elaine Marks

The Intersection of Women's Studies and Post-Structuralism

"Women as knower(s)" is the center of our concern.[1] Of all the many exclusions that have, until now, defined women's relation to culture, the most serious are the exclusions that keep us outside the desire for theory and the theory of desire. To be a knower at this point in the history of women's studies means to push thought as far as it will go.

I came to women's studies from U.S. feminism and from French studies. I am marked by both—as a teacher of French literature and of comparative U.S. and French feminist theory and practice, and as a scholar interested in the intersections between feminist and post-structuralist theorizing. Under the label of post-structuralist, I include that body of interdisciplinary texts by Jacques Lacan, Louis Althuser, Roland Barthes, Jacques Derrida, and Michel Foucault, among others, that has had a significant effect on the development of "feminist" inquiry. We read this effect in the work of certain contemporary French women writers: Hélène Cixous, Luce Irigaray, Julia Kristeva, and more recently in the work of American university women in French: Jane Gallop, Peggy Kamuf, Naomi Schor, Alice Jardine, Nancy Miller, Mary Lydon . . . the list grows longer.

Both women's studies and post-structuralism developed against and in spite of the traditional humanities in their respective cultures. They have proposed other texts to be interpreted, other ways of interpreting them and, more important, other reasons for interpretation. In France, the rebellion came from within the academy against the notion of the unity of the controlling subject in favor of the decentered subject and the *primary structuring role of language*; in the United States, the rebellion came from outside the academy, from the women's liberation movement. It was (and is) a rebellion against the authority of the father(s), an attempt to decenter man.

Women's studies was generated by the women's liberation movement. Its ideology, its structures, and its energy reflect this genealogy. The women's liberation movement did not begin in 1968; but in 1968, as we look back, the forces on the left of the political spectrum that produced the movement seemed to coalesce. On the American scene, 1968 brought together elements of the civil rights movement, of student unrest and desire for curricular reform, of protest against the Vietnam War, and of the gay liberation movement's basic demand for the recognition of difference. All these groups shared a dissatisfaction with the quality of life in the United States and a belief that the cause of their dissatisfaction was oppression: oppression by a ruling elite—white, occidental, managerial, and male—that sought to exclude what was different and by so doing was responsible for colonialism, racism, and sexism, and their continued reproduction. 1968 was the year when it became clear to many of us that if the human condition was immutable, the human situation was in large part man-made and could be changed . . . by us.

Women's studies, imbued with this *Weltanschauung*, carries out within the academy, through curricular and pedagogical reform and through research, a very particular mission: it locates in the traditional disciplines those points at which the universal and the man-made are confused; it seeks for theories that will explain the oppression and the repression of women within culture; it deconstructs and reformulates traditional academic inquiries. Women's studies shares certain perspectives with French post-structuralist practice: an awareness of the discrepancy between words and that to which they refer; a belief in the primacy of the cultural over the natural. Both women's studies and post-structuralism add yet another wounding blow to the list established by Sigmund Freud in his "General Theory of the Neurosis" (1917). In the wake of

Copernicus (the earth is not the center of the universe), Darwin (human beings do not occupy a privileged place in creation), and Freud (the ego is not master in its own house), women's studies and post-structuralism reiterate, as a ruling assumption, that man is not the measure of all things, and that androcentrism, phallocentrism, and heterosexism deserve the same critical attention as ethnocentrism and logocentrism.

The principal methodology of post-structuralism is deconstruction: to split the binary pair (masculine/feminine; active/passive; sun/moon) and show one term inhabiting the other; to show inconsistencies in major arguments through attention to detail; to locate the inevitable blind spot hiding within crucial metaphors; to contextualize both within the individual texts and by placing the individual text in relation to other texts of the same period but of different genres, or in relation to intertexts that both precede and follow.

The qualifying adjectives "feminist," "collaborative," and "interdisciplinary" differentiate women's studies from other academic divisions. A fundamental conviction directing women's studies instructional and research programs is that those of us who are engaged in these activities do not merely add more data to an existing corpus of knowledge, but rather revise paradigms in all fields of study—from medicine to linguistics, from religion to sexuality, from history to communication. To be involved in women's studies is thus to rethink all the hypotheses that have been made about human beings and their relation to the world. It is not an easy task. It implies a thorough understanding of traditional assumptions and their consequences.

Transforming the Core

How does a women's studies curriculum deconstruct traditional humanities courses? What curricular and classroom insights and strategies have women's studies programs and teachers developed that might be applied to departments and courses throughout the curriculum? The University of Wisconsin introductory humanities core course in Women's Studies and a course I teach in rotation with other French Department colleagues, *French Women Writers Today*, provide some clues.

The title of our introductory humanities core course has recently and significantly changed from "Images of Women in a Historical and Cross-Cultural Perspective" to "Meanings of Woman in Western Culture." The title change involved considerable discussion about why some of us felt that "images of women"—a phrase used extensively in the early 1970s (the Madison program began in 1975)—was no longer appropriate. To us, "images" suggested a fixed and static outcome, whereas we were interested in processes of representation, requiring the active participation of the reader in determining meaning. The course is not always taught by the same instructor, and the conceptualization varies between the more empirical and positivist orientation of my colleagues in American and British literature, obsessed by the notion of women's "experience," and the more theoretical and speculative orientation of my colleagues in European literatures, obsessed by the notion of "language" and the "unconscious." The following rather lengthy example is taken from the description of the course proposed by Biddy Martin, now an Assistant Professor of German and Women's Studies at Cornell University:

> Women's economic, social and cultural movement over the past ten years has begun to transform our society's structures and values as it profoundly affects our personal lives and choices. Women's Studies 101 reinterprets the traditional cultural representations of women in their various forms from women's point(s) of view in light of perspectives and changes brought about by the Women's Movement.
>
> This course will begin by establishing a conceptual framework for considering the question of women and cultures; after an introduction to key concepts, we will analyze traditional religious, philosophical, scientific and literary representations of women for underlying patterns of sexual differences and power. A large portion of the remainder of the course will be devoted to examining the ideological and material constraints on what it means to be a woman in contemporary American society; we will consider concretely the socioeconomic, psycho-sexual and racial dynamics of our culture from the perspective of our own experience as women and men of various ages, races, classes and sexual preferences. Our study will include different forms of social organization and control, from the less apparent such as language, to more brutal expression of power in rape and violence. We will conclude with the history and the impact of the women's movement(s) in this country and around the world.

Biddy Martin's course description raises five crucial points about the ways in which women's studies transforms the traditional curriculum. The first is that women's studies is conceived, in this course description, as part of the women's movement, and its sources in that movement are not forgotten in the classroom. Activism and analysis are not collapsed, but they are brought together. The second point is that the reinterpreting is carried out from the point of view of women writers, critics and analysts, women in the position of subjects and knowers. The third point involves the importance of the conceptual framework. Key concepts such as sexual difference and how it is constructed, social organization and control, power and ideology are introduced during the first week and reiterated throughout the semester so that the students, as well as the teacher, possess the appropriate analytic tools. The fourth point involves the transformation of the traditional humanities course and corpus into an interdisciplinary course that includes readings in religion, philosophy, science, literature, psychoanalysis, and sociology. The emphasis is on reading and interpretation as is customary in the humanities, but the range of readings is considerably broadened. The fifth and last point is that this women's studies course considers not only the oppression and repression of women, but also insists on differences of race, of class, and of sexual preference as these are present in our "experience" and in our language. This course could not have been conceived without the context of the women's movement, of a feminist analysis, of a post-structuralist perspective, and of a women's studies program.

Lessons from a Women's Studies Classroom: Deconstructing Masterpieces

The women's studies classroom, and the process of learning experienced in the women's studies classroom, provide a further model for restructuring the traditional classroom. As an example I will describe a course I teach, "French Women Writers Today," and how it deconstructs a traditional course, "Masterpieces of French Literature."

The course has been taught each semester since fall 1975 with an enrollment of between thirty-five to fifty students, 90 percent of whom are female. Before this course existed there was (and still is), each semester, a "Masterpieces of French Literature" course, in translation, in which one or two texts by women writers who figure as part of the canon of French literature are included: *The Princess of Cleves* by Madame de LaFayette from the seventeenth century and, from the twentieth century, a single text, usually by Marguerite Duras. In the undergraduate and graduate literature courses conducted entirely in French, women writers rarely have a place in the syllabus. They do, however, and again since 1975, have a place in courses devoted entirely to them and taught exclusively by women faculty to a student group that is again about 90 percent female. These courses on women writers have included French women poets from Marie de France to Andrée Chédid; *Ecriture féminine* and *Discours féministe* (Women's Writing and Feminist Discourse); French women prose writers of the twentieth century. In general, the students, preponderantly female, ask for and take these courses with pleasure.

What happens in these courses that does not happen in the regular courses taught, for the most part, by men? On the one hand, the question is constantly raised about what it means to write and read as a woman. And this question, in turn, obliges the class to confront the existing theories about the relationship of author-text-reader. On the other hand, the coming together of a group of women reproduces the harem ghetto of girls' schools and colleges in which desire circulates differently than in the more blatantly heterosexual classroom. Here the texts we read by Colette, Simone de Beauvoir, Violette Leduc, Marguerite Yourcenar, Nathalie Sarraute, Marguerite Duras, Monique Wittig, and Hélène Cixous participate in this circulation of desire, raising important questions about the unconscious and its effects, about the possibilities for political organization and social change.

I would like to insist on the melange of the intellectual, the affective, and the political as fundamental to the women's studies classroom and, at the same time, as subversive in relation to the institution and the institutionalization of literature, literary studies, and the humanities. This is the place where deconstruction and reconstruction come together or, rather, where we can move from one strategy to the other, back and forth, undoing and putting together and undoing. Here we are supplementing the literature program by bringing in material from the margins, here we are adding to the corpus of canonical texts, correcting the canon. But here, too, we are contesting the canon and the very concept of canons and masterpieces; we are putting into question all the unexamined theories that have allowed literary studies to flourish in the academy. And because we are paying attention to the circulation of desire, we are also allowing for the possibility of conflict. Battles and betrothals can take place in the women's studies classroom. This will not be to everyone's liking. It will be particularly difficult for those who do not teach in a women's studies classroom to engage those students who have been involved in such a classroom and who look forward to repeating what they have learned and felt there.

I will illustrate how I teach this course by going through what might take place in the classroom on the first day of the semester. Like most women's studies instructors, I prefer a circular seating arrangement to row seating. This is rarely possible in classrooms that accommodate more than forty students in which the seats are fixed. I mention this to the class in passing. I spend a significant amount of time presenting myself, explaining my intellectual and political formation, and situating my ideology, by which I mean my unconscious assumptions and blind spots (I have figured some of them out) in a historical and socio-cultural context, insisting on the inevitable differences between students who are in the late teens and early twenties (there are exceptions) and myself. I present myself as strongly influenced in my approaches to the reading of texts by existentialism, marxism, psychoanalysis, linguistics, and feminism. I sometimes (not always) suggest that there is a credo for a feminist intellectual, and that a feminist intellectual "must" always put into question: (a) the authority of the fathers, symbolic and real, in the world and in texts; (b) the tendency to accept social and cultural constructs as natural; and (c) the belief in the unity and coherence of a conscious subject without taking into account the unconscious and its effects.[2]

These three points of the credo bring together what I consider to be both feminist and post-structuralist concerns. They have the advantage of involving the students immediately in the problematics of the course. Student participation is further encouraged by dividing the class into groups for the presentations they will give during the semester. The use of small groups, as well as other pedagogical devices used in progressive education, are common the women's studies classroom.

The syllabus for "French Women Writers Today" usually has an epigraph. Last year, the epigraph was taken from Hélène Cixous's 1975 essay "The Laugh of the Medusa": "Let the priests tremble, we're going to show them our sexts with pride!" If there is time on the first day of class, I explicate this sentence after we have discussed the two major topics: (a) Why French Women Writers Today? and (b) The Complexities of Reading.

In answering the question "Why French Women Writers Today?" I go through the title of the course word by word. In relation to "French," I emphasize the substantial, exciting, literary and intellectual tradition in France from the Middle Ages on that includes women, and I recite the litany of well-known names: Marie de France and Christine de Pisan in the Middle Ages; Louise Labé and Marie de Gournay in the sixteenth century; Mademoiselle de Scudéry, Madame de LaFayette and Madame de Sévigné in the seventeenth century; Madame du Deffand and Mademoiselle de Lespinasse in the eighteenth century; Madame de Staël, George Sand, and Flora Tristan in the nineteenth century; and a long list, which includes the women writers we will be reading, in the twentieth. The adjective "French" also evokes a significant series of cultural stereotypes as well as important and revealing cultural differences with the United States, differences that allow us to view our own culture at a critical distance. (Again, if there is time, I might read a passage from Gertrude Stein's *Paris, France*, in which Paris is represented through books and the odor of woman.)

The second word in the title is "Women," and here I emphasize the new ways of thinking about women, of reading and writing women, the new scholarship on women, and the centrality of the women's movement, one of the most important political, social, and cultural movements of the twentieth century, which has changed mentalities, relations of power, and the literary canon. Feminist analysis provides a critique of the status quo, of things as they are, from those who are on the margins. Feminist analysis posits the oppression and the repression of women as a structuring factor that our language and our culture reproduce. Feminist

analysis attempts to understand this oppression and repression
and works toward social change. Feminist "deconstructionists,"
for example Hélène Cixous in France (and the word "feminist" is
a misnomer), bring together under the label *"écriture féminine"*
(feminine or woman's writing) the repression of the feminine and
feminine desire (in women and in men) and the repression of
writing (as opposed to speech) in the Western philosophical tradition. I also insist on the differences between the words *female*
(referring to a biological construct), *woman* (referring to a mytho-
logical construct), and *women* (referring to an historical construct).

The third word, "Writers," occupies center stage and invites a
pun with "righters." I ask the students the questions Jean-Paul
Sartre asked in *What Is Literature?* Who writes? Why? For
whom? Under what conditions? I stress the importance for all
women writers of "the coming to writing," the process of becoming a writer in a culture whose institutions dictate what is acceptable writing. I stress, too, that writers write with words, and that
in both written and spoken language, words are present, and that
to which they refer, the referents, are absent. I usually show the
class Magritte's famous painting, "Ceci n'est pas une pipe" in
which a realistic representation of a pipe is relegated to the world
of re-presentation. I also introduce Ferdinand de Saussure's
definition of the *sign* as a single word, constituted by an insepar-
able union of *signifier* (the speech sounds or written marks com-
posing the sign) and the *signified* (the conceptual meaning of the
sign).

I suggest that one of the ways in which theories of reading have
changed in the course of the twentieth century is by attributing
greater importance, indeed subversive and revolutionary meaning,
to the signifier as a means of shattering the coherent, closed text.
This "playing with the signifier" has been important in post-
structuralist and "feminist" theorizing in France. Another word I
define with care is "text," a word that has replaced the more familiar "book," "novel," "play," or "poem." Text, from the Latin
textus (weaving) is woven with words from other texts. Every text
is an *intertext* with vague boundaries. The concept of "text"
weakens the traditional concept of "author" and "authority," and
this is very important for the consideration of women writers. It
both opens the field of writing and textuality and closes down the

question of gender-specificity. (There is always the nagging question, are post-structuralist theories in some measure the last stand of phallocentrism against the women's liberation movements and their assertion of a specific historical and social difference?)

The word "writer" also leads to such topics as (a) the importance of the writer's intentions and how the significance of these intentions is undermined by concepts of text and intertextuality and by attention to and playing with the signifier; and (b) the prestigious role accorded the writer and writing in French culture, in which the male writers function as "holy men" and as "priests." Here I would reinsert Hélène Cixous's line: "Let the priests tremble, we're going to show them our sexts!"

The last word of the title is "today." The word leads to the question of historical context and dating. The reader's position in 1984, for example, and the writer's position at the time the text was published: 1929, *Sido* (Colette); 1939, *Coup de Grâce* (Marguerite Yourcenar) and *Tropisms* (Nathalie Sarraute); 1958, *Memoirs of a Dutiful Daughter* (Simone de Beauvoir) and *Moderato Cantabile* (Marguerite Duras); 1964, *La Bâtarde* (Violette Leduc); 1969, *Les Guérillères* (Monique Wittig); 1975, "The Laugh of the Medusa" (Hélène Cixous). The date introduces history, time, change, and death. The date also obliges me to provide information about the differences between the French and the U.S. experiences since World War I in relation to the status and the representation of women, as well as the socioeconomic and cultural-intellectual scenes.

I conclude this opening class with a few words about the complexities of reading (they have been alluded to all along) and the ties between these complexities and the feminist inquiry. I usually put on the board a simple outline that contrasts a deconstructive practice to what is construed as "commonsense" as shaped by decades of "New Criticism." For example, I would contrast the following binary pairs: the "opaque" text of the deconstructive practice and the "transparent" text of the commonsense approach; the notion that meanings are produced in the reading of a text and the notion that meanings are given by the author; the emphasis on signifiers and the emphasis on signifieds; the emphasis on indeterminacy and contraditions and the emphasis on coherence. I insist on the obvious: that we read, decode and interpret all the time, not only books, but also pictures, people, nature, the universe. We read our culture and we reproduce it. I insist, too, that in the classroom, we will engage in both the commonsense approach and the deconstructive practice. It is essential to have a construction to deconstruct.

I end, then, by reintroducing the concept of "l'écriture féminine" and working with Hélène Cixous's quotation. The concept of "l'écriture féminine" was developed in the early and mid-1970s and is only now beginning to be understood as very different from the older and deceptively similar concept of "littérature féminine." "L'écriture féminine" made its debut in "The Laugh of the Medusa," a poetic manifesto included in the 1975 issue of L'ARC, *Simone de Beauvoir et la lutte des femmes* (Simone de Beauvoir and the women's struggle). "The Laugh of the Medusa" has become the *locus classicus* for presenting those discourses—psychoanalytic, deconstructionist, anthropological, marxist, and surrealist—that traverse the concept of "l'écriture féminine."

"The Laugh of the Medusa" is an attempt to deconstruct phallocentrism (the primacy attributed by Freud and Lacan to the phallus) by ridiculing men's fear of not having it or losing it, by dramatizing the anxiety it provokes in them and ways in which this anxiety colors everything they do, including their writing, their speech, and their exchanges with women. "L'écriture féminine" emerges as the antagonist to phallocentrism. On a theoretical level, "écriture" involves a materialist concept of writing, as opposed to the institutionalized and heavy-with-sacred-meaning "littérature." "Ecriture," according to Jacques Derrida, has been repressed in Western culture, along with death, absence, and the feminine. "L'écriture féminine" claims to disrupt the repression of the feminine—in both women and men—and sets up against the phallocentric law of castration (of tale-cutting and closure) the flying, stealing, returning, arriving, perpetual body movements of the orgasmic medusa.

As an example of what is involved in the writing and the reading of "l'écriture féminine," I return to the course's epigraph, the most famous line of "The Laugh of the Medusa," a line that occurs at about midpoint in the text. The narrator, in her exploration of the dark continent, comes upon the Medusa and finds that she is not a monster, not deadly, and has not been decapitated, but that she is, on the contrary, laughing and beautiful. "Let the priests tremble, we're going to show them our sexts!" The sentence falls conveniently into the most blatant binary opposition. On the one side are the priests, etymologically the old men (the dirty old men) representing the law and the authority of the fathers, the symbolic order of language; the priests who derive their patriarchal power from a masculine god; the priests who interpret the sacred books and the holy texts, the priests for whom women are polluted, excluded, secondary, but also feared and desired. The imperative "Let the priests tremble" gives us the effect before the cause. The trembling, whether in fear of castration or with desire, suggests the uncontrollable body movements of the hysteric. The priests have been displaced and put in the position of the woman. Their bodies speak. They have no words.

A collective feminine "we," a sect of young writing women, flashes their "sexts," shamelessly and proudly exhibits their "sexts." The traditional representation of writing women as spinsters and bluestockings with their inferior texts and sexes, their missing parts signifying their inferiority, is disrupted by the portmanteau word that brings together sexuality, the female body, and writing. The play on words shows the reader how an innovative, subversive women's writing might look and sound. The showing of the sexts takes us back to the title, to a joyful medusa, and reverses the traditional killing and decapitation of women and female power; the power has been restored and is manifested in provocative, assertive sounds and gestures. "The Laugh of the Medusa" is also a programmatic text: we should look at women's texts as sexts, as the unconscious writing itself through the body, inscribing its repressed contents. Sexuality and textuality are inextricably engaged.

The strength of women's studies in language and literature has been to reaffirm the ties between textuality and sexuality at the same time as it displays, persistently and sometimes aggressively, women's texts. This has been true in both France and the United States. French manuals for the study of literature since 1968 have already asserted: "In the years following 1968, the explosion of

women's movements constitutes on many levels, political, cultural, medical, sexual, and professional, the determining element of what is news (*d'actualité*) in our period."[3]
The coming together of U.S. feminism and French post-structuralism in women's studies courses in the humanities provides both theoretical guidelines and pedagogical practice that test and transform the traditional curriculum. The sometimes-violent reactions against women's movements in France and the United States and the intense resistance to women's studies in some colleges and universities acknowledge the emergence of a new form of power that upsets conventional expectations. It is essential that independent women's studies programs *offer* and *control* their own courses to provide a basis for transforming courses throughout the curriculum. It is through discussion of curricular development among scholars from different disciplines, but committed to the concept of women's studies, that significant multidisciplinary and interdisciplinary work may be produced and the overall curriculum not only transformed, but infused with new life and the best of the new scholarship.

Notes

1. Dorothy E. Smith, a Canadian educator and sociologist, has written: "We are confronted virtually with the problem of reinventing the world of knowledge, of thought, of symbols and images. Not of course by repudiating everything that has been done but by subjecting it to exact scrutiny and criticism from the position of women as subjects . . . or knower(s)." "Ideological Structure and How Women Are Excluded," *Canadian Review of Sociology and Anthropology* 12, no. 4 (November 1975): 367.
2. As the course progresses we try to develop ways of working on and in the text, to do a symptomatic reading of the text with special attention to what Terry Eagleton calls, in *Literary Theory: An Introduction* (Minneapolis: University of Minnesota Press, 1983), "evasions, ambivalences, and points of intensity in the narrative—words which do not get spoken, words which are spoken with unusual frequency, doublings and slidings of language . . . . Literary criticism can attend not only to what the text says, but how it works" (p. 182).
3. Bruno Vercier and Lacques Lacarme, eds., *La Littérature en France depuis 1968* (Paris: Bordas, 1982) p. 233.

Appendix

Spring 1983
FRENCH LITERATURE IN TRANSLATION 251
French Women Writers of Today

DEPARTMENT OF FRENCH AND ITALIAN
& WOMEN'S STUDIES PROGRAM

"Let the priests tremble, we're going to show them our sexts!"
Hélène Cixous, *The Laugh of the Medusa*

What we read and how we read structures our point of view and our actions. We will study 8 representative prose texts written between 1930 and 1975 by French women writers usually excluded from "masterprices in translation." We will situate each writer and each text in their appropriate historical, social, and cultural contexts; we will analyze different strategies for reading texts; we will explore the problematic relationship between "lived experience" and language; we will consider how women and men are represented and constructed in "life" and in "literature."

Work Requirements

All participants will be expected to prepare the reading assignments, to take part in classroom exchanges, to write one paper (5–7 pages), and to pass a mid-term and a final examination.

Required Texts

1. Simone de Beauvoir, *Memoirs of a Dutiful Daughter* (Harper)
2. Violette Leduc, *La Bâtarde* (Farrar, Straus & Giroux)
3. Colette, *My Mother's House and Sido* (Farrar, Straus & Giroux)
4. Marguerite Yourcenar, *Coup de Grâce* (Farrar, Straus & Giroux)
5. Nathalie Sarraute, *Tropisms* (George Braziller)
6. Marguerite Duras, *Moderato Cantabile* (Grove Press)
7. Monique Wittig, *Les Guérillères* (Avon)
8. Hélène Cixous, "The Laugh of the Medusa" in *New French Feminisms* (Schocken)

Books on Reserve (Helen C. White Library)
Simone de Beauvoir, *The Second Sex*
Germaine Brée, *Women Writers in France*
Margaret Crosland, *Women of Iron and Velvet*
Mary Ellman, *Thinking About Women*
Jane Gallop, *The Daughter's Seduction*
Elaine Marks and Isabelle de Courtivron, eds., *New French Feminisms*
Virginia Woolf, *A Room of One's Own*

Reading and rereading of the required texts and excursions into related material are encouraged. There will be occasional distributions of *critical* material.

Midterm: March 2
Term Paper Due: April 25
Final Exam: May

I. Essential Lexical Items

the absurd	gender	psychoanalysis
analysis	imagination	reading
avant-garde	ideology	rhetoric
binary opposition	interpretation	semiotics
body	intertextuality	sign
code	language	signified
context	logocentrism	signifier
death	marxism	social organization
deconstruction	meaning	and control
desire	modernism	structuralism
difference	post-modernism	post-structuralism
discourse	mortality	text
diachronic/	paradigmatic/	theory
synchronic	syntagmatic	tropes (metaphor,
epistemology	phallocentrism	metonymy, synecdoche,
experience	political	etc.)
feminism	power	the unconscious
fiction	problematic	work writing
formalism	process	

II. Essential Dates:

1900	Freud, *the Interpretation of Dreams*, Colette, *Claudine at School*, the death of Nietzsche
1900–1913	The Belle Epoque
1914–1918	The First World War
1917	The Russian Revolution
1939–1945	The Second World War
1949	The Chinese Revolution
1946–1954	The Indochinese War
1954–1962	The Algerian War
May 1968	
1982	Election of a Socialist president

14

Rethinking Philosophy

Helen E. Longino

Ten years ago, I could not have imagined how the intellectual discipline of philosophy might respond to distinctively women's issues. Even when my own research changed its focus to include such questions as the relevance of the feminist critique of science to the philosophy of science, my philosophy teaching remained absolutely traditional in content. Some courses eventually came to include some components, like abortion and affirmative action, that reflected women's concerns, but courses like the "Introduction to Philosophy," or "Metaphysics," or "Philosophy of Mind" remained impervious to the social and intellectual turmoil surrounding our activities in the classroom.[1]

The changes in women's economic and cultural conditions in this period range from the increased, if still token, representation of women in positions of authority and public responsibility to the feminization of poverty. These changes have been matched in contemporary scholarship by changes in our understanding of women's past and women's "nature." While we started, in this wave of the women's movement, by thinking of women as affected by the (masculine) activity of the public sphere, i.e., as objects or victims of action, a more recent focus by historians and anthropologists on women's activities in their own spheres of action reveals them as strong, powerful, creative, and adaptive.

The new visibility of women in our cultural and social history is accompanied by a reorientation in our conceptions of gender differences and their significance. This reorientation has been sparked most recently by the work of educational psychologist Carol Gilligan, whose research on women's moral development suggests that women's patterns of moral judgment express an ethic of caring distinct from the ethic of rights expressed in men's moral judgments.[2]

The changes in our understanding of women are mirrored in changes in our thinking about the meaning of women's entry into public life. For a long time women have been tolerated in public life to the degree they learned to "think like a man," to act like men. Women's education has, for the most part, been governed by this fact. The new research suggests another vision. One can see the integration of women into public life as an opportunity to expand the values governing that life.[3] Such an expansion will be required for our students to realize their dreams. They must themselves build the future that can accommodate them. One lesson we have learned from the post-suffrage era is that this will not occur without related changes in women's education.

I began thinking in a systematic way about the curricular implications of such reflections when writing a paper for a Mills faculty conference, specifically for a session on what it means to be educating women in the 1980s. In writing the paper I finally settled on recounting the transformation of my "Introduction to Philosophy" course as a way of communicating to my colleagues what I thought important in women's education. In the course of writing that paper, what had previously been piecemeal, ad hoc improvements and additions took on some theoretical justification. The account that follows describes the gradual development of the course and student response to it in the spring of 1984.

Philosopher's Progress

My aim in teaching philosophy is to help students develop their analytical and critical abilities as well as to make available to them the Western philosophical tradition. To my admittedly prejudiced eye the study of philosophy in the context of a liberal education is intellectual empowerment par exellence. I firmly believe that the skills acquired in the study of philosophy equip students to live richer and more meaningful lives than they would otherwise.

Women, as we well know, are still on the whole persuaded that
their reasoning skills are inadequate or inferior to those of men.[4]
The single-sex classroom is an excellent place in which to disa-
buse women students of this idea. Here, they come to have
respect for themselves and for one another as thinkers that I have
seldom seen in mixed-sex classrooms. My hope is that they will
eventually see themselves not, or not primarily, as receivers of
knowledge, but as agents of knowledge, as shapers of their culture
and society, as builders of the future. Teaching philosophy with
these aims at a women's college has forced me to bring the social
and intellectual ferment of the contemporary women's movement
into contact with the business of the classroom. It has had a profound and at times unsettling impact on what I have chosen to
teach.

The "Introduction to Philosophy" course is one of several
introductory-level courses, but it is not a prerequisite for any
other philosophy course. Thus, it doubles as a service course and
as a disciplinary entry course. Typically, in a class of twenty-four,
about twelve are satisfying their own or their academic advisors'
conceptions of the requirements of a liberal education and have
no intention of taking any more philosophy. Of the rest, about
three or four are thinking of majoring in philosophy, and the
other eight or nine expect to take more philosophy without
majoring.

My task as instructor is to develop a syllabus that acquaints the
students with some major figures and central questions in the philosophical tradition and with methods of philosophical analysis
and argument. In addition, I wish to convey to students that philosophical inquiry is a living intellectual activity in which they themselves may continue to engage long after the final examination.
Over the years I have experimented with various syllabi intended
to satisfy these aims. Initially, I tried the Great Books approach:
relatively short works by Plato, Aristotle, Descartes, Berkeley,
Russell, and so on. This quite excited that one-sixth of the class
thinking of majoring in philosophy and frustrated those unwilling
to parse sentences produced before 1960. Five years ago I decided I
could best reach students by organizing the course around questions relating to the nature of the self. One of the points of the
course is to show how different and competing conceptions of

human nature underlie different and competing analyses of the life of the self in the world. Thus, after some initial readings on the Socratic enterprise, we spend several weeks on these subjects: human nature, education and work, personal relations (friendship and love), religious belief, death and the meaning of life.

CRITIQUING THE CANON

The anthology I use includes more women authors than most philosophical anthologies not devoted either to "the woman question" or to contemporary moral and social issues: three out of forty-two.[5] Interestingly, they are included only in the sections on friendship and sex, and they are quite traditional in style and content. They employ standard methods of argument and analysis and strive for universality, a universality that transcends (by ignoring) sexual difference.

Our attempts at universality are undermined by passages such as this one from Hobbes's *Leviathan*, discussing human nature:

> So that in the nature of man, we find three principal causes of quarrel. First, competition; secondly, diffidence; thirdly, glory.
> The first maketh men invade for gain; the second, for safety; and the third for reputation. The first use violence; to make themselves the masters of other men's persons, wives, children, and cattle; the second, to defend them; the third for trifles.[6]

How can I ask students to see themselves in this description? Or how can they take seriously Aristotle's wonderful remarks on friendship when Aristotle asserts the inferiority of women as friends? How is it possible to ignore the fact that in the readings in the section on love, women and female pronouns appear as beloved and not as lovers? Or to ignore the fact that the analyses of education are clearly addressed to white men, who will never experience barriers based on sex or race, and who will learn about the lives of these others through the texts they are assigned to read in their liberal educations? The list continues. Simply to use non-sexist language in my lectures cannot redress the balance, for the issue is not one of imbalance, but of judgment and perception. Playing "what's wrong with this picture?"—that is, acknowledging or even criticizing the misogyny and androcentrism of the texts of the philosophical tradition—may engage advanced students, but it discourages and alienates beginning students. They have not come to this course to find out what philosophy *cannot* do for them. Once I have brought a critical eye to my text, I find I cannot continue teaching it without radically transforming it.

EXPANDING THE DISCOURSE

This place of paradox has dissolved only slowly. Each year, I have introduced changes which, when put into practice, make clear the need for even further change. For instance, in the first year of trying this approach, the class and I talked about the implications of Hobbes's unthinking assignment of male and female roles in the discussion of human nature. This led me to add Adrienne Rich's essay "Claiming an Education" to the readings on education.[7] As I thought through the questions Rich addresses in that essay, as well as in the essays "Taking Women Students Seriously" and "Towards a Woman-Centered University,"[8] I found it necessary to add Simone de Beauvoir's reflections on women as "the other" to the selection of readings on human nature.[9] And after students asked for a selection on personal love by a woman, I have added not just Sharon Bishop's essay on "Love and Dependency" to their list, but essays on the obligations of parents and on altruism and self-respect.[10] I am still searching for satisfactory readings on religious belief that do not assume that that belief is in a larger than life father-figure. For the moment St. Teresa of Avila provides an example of Christian mystical writing and a selection about satori gives some introduction to non-European conceptions of religious experience.[11]

Course transformation is limited by what is available. It generally takes time before a philosophical perspective has articulations suitable for introductory level courses. I have, for instance, included selections from Hannah Arendt's *The Human Condition* at several stages in the course.[12] Her work, however, presupposes so much familiarity with the European intellectual tradition that it is difficult for students to get much from these selections. Not until the literature develops further will positive analyses of human nature that do not equate "male" with "human" and reconsiderations of the concept of rationality that do not divorce that capacity from human emotionality become available for inclusion. The materials are not presented as supplanting the traditional selections, nor do I intend to stop teaching Plato, Aristotle, Hobbes, Descartes, Hume, and the others. Students are never required to commit themselves to a philosophical position, but to understand the boundaries, interconnections, and incompatibilities of philosophical ideas; that is, they are required to reason and analyze. Not all the students share the values of the women-focused materials, nor do I expect them to. In fact, to my dismay, I received a paper on the problem of evil that explained the presence of evil in the world as resulting from Eve's choice to disobey God. The point of including the materials is both to provide a balance to the overwhelmingly male perspective of the anthology and to give the students a way of entering into dialogue with these authors who, even by their language shut them out.

To present philosophy as something more than a gleaming knick-knack in the cabinet of Western civilization has pedagogical consequences as well as consequences for course content. I have often used classroom discussion as a way of making sure that the students "really understand" a particular text or argument. In the introductory course, I am learning instead to initiate group reflection on a subject, using the readings as a touchstone (or as the anthology's title suggests, an "occasion"). If a reading is particularly difficult, I just say so and outline the central points. Rather than get them to recite an author's position or arguments, I ask, for instance, for their own views about the subject and then how those are similar to or different from what they've read. I encourage them to ask each other questions and to probe one another's reasons.

The intention to have them use philosophical work to organize their thinking about daily life carries over into their paper assignments as well. I assign four essays in addition to a final essay. The first is an exercise in paraphrasing an argument. The second, on the selections about human nature, asks them, among other things, to reflect on what it would be like to treat themselves and others as if we really were Platonic reasoners, Hobbesian competitors, Sartrian (or de Beauvoirian) choosers, or Skinnerian response systems. The other two sets of essay topics, in addition to standard "compare and contrast" or "analyze the argument" questions, always include several suggestions for applying the readings to their own experiences (of education, friendship, religious faith). This year, for the first time, students read their papers to one another on the day they were due. The class was broken down into groups of three or four so they could also discuss the papers they heard. I believe that this practice is responsible for the very high level of participation in regular discussion and for its high quality—markedly better than in earlier years.

All this is designed to help my students take themselves and one another seriously, as people and as thinkers. Do they think of their identity as women? The older students are the most attuned to questions of sex and gender; the younger ones tend to pay less attention. Some even claim that they don't notice an author's gender! When asked about particularly flagrant abuses of the falsely generic masculine pronoun in the readings, however, the class as a whole indicated instant recognition. And in the papers on personal relations, they were quite sensitive to the ways an author's gender might have affected the content of what s/he said. My feeling is that while at some level they notice the drama of intersexual tensions and the absence of women, they need a great deal of encouragement to articulate what they notice and to think themselves as women into the texts.

The students have differed in interesting ways when questioned about the impact of the women-focused and women-authored material on their experience of the course. While all were positive, they ranged from "it is good to have a woman's point of view" to "I felt after reading the selection by Arendt [on work] that I could be myself and that my own thoughts on the subject were valid." Some students saw the readings as expressing a point of view they would not have found in a text by a male author: "It made my understanding more well-rounded." Others felt it corrected their image of philosophy as a masculine preserve, and thus enabled them to think of themselves as doing philosophy. I think the difference in response is due both to how willing students are to think of themselves as women in a still-sexist society and how ready they are to take responsibility for their own "mental hygiene." Surely, my fundamentalist student was at some level refusing to engage thoroughly with the ideas of the course. Just as surely, the student who totally altered her conception of faith lived them deeply.

Models for Educating Women: Remedial or Empowering

The choppy, piecemeal transformation I've described exemplifies the difficulties of taking women students seriously (to borrow a phrase from Adrienne Rich), that is, as agents of knowledge in the context of scholarship of the sort I was reared on as a graduate student and a beginning instructor in philosophy. It also roughly exemplifies the pattern others have discerned in the process of taking women seriously in the curriculum. My initial goal in teaching women was to prepare them to function and compete successfully in a world structured by and around values and traits they are not likely to have developed. The skill I could transmit to them was that of logical analysis. In addition, I could teach them to use this skill in connection with certain dominant cultural themes, such as rights, or truth. I have come to characterize this ideal of education as the ideal of "remedial masculinity."

"Remedial masculinity" is, I think what Bryn Mawr's M. Carey Thomas was calling for when she urged the "men's curriculum" for her female students.[13] This was a progressive notion at a time when most people thought that what women needed to know was how to cook and sew and possibly manage a household. But transmitting a body of knowledge to a group that is, at best, marginal to that knowledge is tricky and can facilitate the conflation of two distinct ambitions. One is the hope to create informed onlookers, at best transmitters of the culture, as traditionally understood mothers and elementary school teachers and volunteers who support the musical and arts institutions. Alternatively, one can hope to transform one's students from marginal onlookers into participants.

My ambition to transform the students forced a reconstruction of the syllabus and ultimately a modification of the original ambition. The challenge is not to remedy our students' weaknesses, but to provide them with an education that values their strengths and prepares them to deploy them in their future lives, an education that includes them and their interests in our understanding of human life. And, for female instructors, one that includes us and our interests. This is not to say that we should cease to remedy deficiencies, but that we take a closer look at those qualities labeled as deficiencies and that we not limit ourselves to shaping students to fit into a fixed, unchanging world. This means, in philosophy teaching, attempting not only to rally against the sexism of authors like Aristotle, Hobbes, and others, but also to think about what a particular issue looks like from a woman's point of view. There may be many such points of view, but as long as women and men continue to occupy such different social positions, those perspectives identified as women's will be different from those identified as men's.

If, in the remedial model, differences between women and men are minimized and such as remain are seen as impediments to be shed by women, in an inclusive or empowering model, differences are perceived as providing an opportunity for cultural expansion and transformation. A woman's education would not teach her only how to overcome her dependency and lack of competitiveness, but to value her concern for others, her sense of responsibility and cooperativeness as qualities which, if properly developed, can help bring about positive changes in the world she is about to enter. Such an education would prepare her to meet resistance both to her person and to her ideas and would teach her how to flourish as a person, as a professional, as a member of society. Such an education would develop her resiliency rather than hardening her. The philosophy classroom is an excellent place in which to begin.

Notes

1. Parts of this essay appeared originally in "Building the Future: Reflections on Teaching at a College for Women," *Liberal Education* 70, no. 3 (Fall 1984): 209–22.
2. Carol Gilligan, *In a Different Voice* (Cambridge, Mass.: Harvard University Press, 1982).
3. These contrasting conceptions are apparent in contemporary career guidebooks for women. See Barbara Bate and Lois S. Self, "The Rhetoric of Career Success Books for Women," *Journal of Communication* 33, no. 2 (Spring 1983): 149–65.
4. That this is still the case is dramatically revealed in a study of freshmen intending to major in science at Radcliffe/Harvard. See Norma Ware and Nicole Steckler, "Choosing a Science Major: The Experience of Women and Men," *Women's Studies Quarterly* 11, no. 2 (Summer 1983): 12–15.

5. James Edwards and Douglas MacDonald, eds., *Occasions for Philosophy* (Englewood Cliffs, N.J.: Prentice-Hall, 1979).

6. Ibid., p. 74.

7. Adrienne Rich, "Claiming an Education," in Rich, *On Lies, Secrets and Silences* (New York: W.W. Norton, 1979), pp. 231–45.

8. Rich, "Taking Women Students Seriously" and "Towards a Woman-Centered University," in Rich, *On Lies, Secrets and Silences.*

9. Simone de Beauvoir, *The Second Sex* (New York: Random House, 1952, repr. 1968), pp. xiii–xxix, 53–60.

10. Sharon Bishop, "Love and Dependency," *Philosophy and Women*, ed. Sharon Bishop and Marjorie Weinzweig (Belmont, Calif.: Wadsworth, 1979), pp. 147–54; Virginia Held, "The Equal Obligations of Mothers and Fathers," in *Having Children*, ed. Onora O'Neill and William Ruddick (New York, Oxford University Press, 1979), pp. 227–39, and reprinted in *Mothering: Essays in Feminist Theory*, ed. Joyce Trebilcot (Totowa, N.J.: Rowman & Allanheld, 1984), pp. 7–20; Larry Blum, Marcia Homiak, Judy Housman, and Naomi Scheman, "Altruism and Woman's Oppression" in *Women and Philosophy*, ed. Carol Gould and Marx Wartofsky (New York: G.P. Putnam's Sons, 1976), pp. 222–47, also reprinted in Bishop and Weinzweig, *Philosophy and Women*.

11. St. Teresa of Avila, *The Way of Perfection*, ed. E. Allison Peers (Garden City, N.Y.: Image Books, 1964); and D.T. Suzuki, *Essays in Zen Buddhism Second Series* (New York: Samuel Weiser, 1971).

12. Hannah Arendt, *The Human Condition* (Chicago: University of Chicago Press, 1958), pp. 7–21, 79–83, 153–59, and 313–25.

13. A faculty member from its founding in 1885, M. Carey Thomas was president of Bryn Mawr College from 1894 to 1922.

Appendix

Philosophy 9
INTRODUCTION TO PHILOSOPHY   Helen Longino
Spring, 1984   Mills College

We will be exploring some of the central questions regarding human existence that have traditionally been the concern of philosophical inquiry. We will read the work of both classical and contemporary philosophers (primarily European and American) and use the class period to discuss the readings. Assignments are from the anthology *Occasions for Philosophy*, in the bookstore, and from books on reserve in the library. Many of you will also wish to purchase *A Preface to Philosophy* from the bookstore. This is a handbook with helpful chapters on reading and writing philosophy.

Written work includes 4 short papers and a final examination. The final grade will be determined according to these percentages (approximately): 10% class participation; 5% first paper; 15% each, second and third papers; 20% fourth paper, 35% final exam. Late papers will be marked down.

Texts in bookstore:
Occasions for Philosophy, Edwards and MacDonald (Prentice-Hall)
A Preface to Philosophy, Woodhouse (Wadsworth)

Books on reserve:
The Human Condition, Hannah Arendt (University of Chicago Press)
The Second Sex, Simone de Beauvoir (Random House)
Philosophy and Women, Bishop and Weinzweig, eds. (Wadsworth)
Having Children, O'Neill and Ruddick (Oxford University Press)
On Lies, Secrets, and Silence, Adrienne Rich (Norton)
Introduction to Zen Buddhism, D.T. Suzuki (Grove Press)
The Way of Perfection, St. Teresa of Avila (Doubleday)

Weekly Schedule

WHAT IS PHILOSOPHY?

Jan. 27 Plato, "Euthyphro" (*Occasions*, p. 4)
Jan. 30 Plato, "Apology" (*Occasions*, p. 19)
Feb. 6   Vlastos, "The Paradox of Socrates" (*Occasions*, p. 40)
Nietzsche, "The Problem of Socrates" (*Occasions*, p. 54)
First paper due February 8

HUMAN NATURE

Feb. 13 Plato, "Persons as Rational" (*Occasions*, p. 61)
Hobbes, "Persons as Creatures of Appetite and Aversion" (*Occasions*, p. 72)
Skinner, "Persons as Products of Conditioning" (*Occasions*, p. 76)
Feb. 22 Sartre, "Persons as Self-Creators" (*Occasions*, p. 85)
de Beauvoir, *The Second Sex*, Introduction and pp. 53–60.

EDUCATION AND WORK

Feb. 27 Arendt, *The Human Condition*, ch. 1. sec. 1; ch. 4, secs. 20–21
Peters, "The Justification of Education" (*Occasions*)
Second Paper Outline due Feb. 27
Mar. 5   Herbst, "Work, Labor, and University Education" (*Occasions*)
Rich, "Claiming an Education"
_____. "Taking Women Students Seriously" (*On Lies, Secrets, and Silence*)
Second Paper due Mar. 7

INTERPERSONAL RELATIONS

Mar. 12 Aristotle, "Friendship and Its Forms" (*Occasions*)
Simone Weil, "Friendship" (*Occasions*)
Mar. 26 Ehman, "Personal Love" (*Occasions*)
Bishop, "Love and Dependency" (*Philosophy and Women*)

April 2   Held, "The Equal Obligations of Mothers and Fathers"
           (*Having Children*)
           Blum et al., "Altruism and Women's Oppression"
           (*Philosophy and Women*)
           Third Paper due April 6

                          BELIEF IN GOD

Apr. 9   St. Anselm, "The Ontological Argument" (*Occasions*)
           St. Thomas Aquinas, "The Five Ways" (*Occasions*)
           Hume, "Is The World Intelligently Designed?" (*Occasions*)
Apr. 16   St. Thomas Aquinas, "Reason and Revelation" (*Occasions*)
           Kierkegaard, "Truth as Subjectivity" (*Occasions*)
           Dostoyevsky, "Evil and the Final Harmony" (*Occasions*)
           St. Teresa, *The Way of Perfection*, chs. 22, 28, 29
           Suzuki, "Satori" (*Introduction to Zen Buddhism*)

                        THE MEANING OF LIFE

Apr. 23   Arendt, *The Human Condition*, ch. 1, sec. 3
           Tolstoy, "My Confession" (*Occasions*)
           Nagel, "Death" (*Occasions*) optional
           Fourth Paper due April 27
Apr. 30   Slote, "Existentialism and the Fear of Dying" (*Occasions*)
           Lachs, "To Have and To Be" (*Occasions*)
           Arendt, *The Human Condition*, ch. 6, sec. 44–45
May 7   Nagel, "The Absurd" (*Occasions*)
May 11   Final Examination

15

Transforming a Course in American Literary Realism

John Schilb

Although women's studies now spans a wide range of disciplines, it may have begun mainly in English, for at least three reasons: English departments have long included a significant number of women faculty, English majors have often been women, and it is hard to study literature without noticing how it can illuminate the role of gender in human life. Yet it is fair to say that many English courses still reflect traditional paradigms. They still focus overwhelmingly on male authors; they still operate as if the new scholarship on women had never existed. Although specific traits of English faculty might explain this phenomenon, we should view it in the context of the academy as a whole. While feminists have achieved degrees of influence in various disciplines, they have failed to transform any of them much.[1] The basic resistance of the English curriculum to feminist change parallels the inertia of other fields.

Rather than sketch a chronological account of developing a course in American Realism that expressed my commitment to women's studies, I want to emphasize certain issues I had to confront that must be considered by all of us who would try to change our own courses and encourage colleagues to change theirs. I taught the course on American Realism during the Spring 1984 semester at the University of North Carolina-Wilmington. The catalog description of the course I inherited read: "Realism and naturalism in literature from 1855–1900, emphasizing Dickinson's poetry and fiction by Howells, James,

and Crane." This was not the complete list of prescribed authors,
and it did have the virtue of recognizing the existence of at least
one woman writer. But like most courses, this one defined American Realism through a narrow canon occupied almost exclusively
by male writers.[2] Even now, most English majors probably graduate believing that the only American woman writer of the
nineteenth century was, in fact, Emily Dickinson. Teachers who
would alter this situation by including more women writers in
American Realism probably need to acquire new knowledge
themselves.

Beyond Emily Dickinson: Who Are American Women Writers?

Many teachers in English and other disciplines are, indeed, willing to consider how they might include more material about
women in their courses. Yet their efforts often turn out to be limited. Several English instructors, for example, have reacted to
women's studies by adding a single woman author to their
otherwise male-dominated syllabi. Despite their conviction that
they have thereby fulfilled their duty, the results constitute mere
tokenism. An instructor of American Realism might decide to
add, say, Kate Chopin's *The Awakening* to a list that continues to
exalt male authors, and then congratulate himself or herself for a
feminist job well-done. But the students could still emerge from
the course with the traditional impression that American literature was created mostly by men.

One way to confront token inclusion of women is to acquaint
faculty with texts they might not have encountered before. Unless
they have attended women's studies conferences, subscribed to
women's studies periodicals, or received the book lists of feminist
publishers, they might not have learned of works that teachers of
women's studies have long cherished. For instance, I did not
know about Rebecca Harding Davis's *Life in the Iron Mills* and
Maimie Pinzer's *The Maimie Papers*, which I was to use in my
American Realism course, until I met Florence Howe, their pub-
lisher and a visiting colleague of mine at Denison University.[3]
When she heard I was preparing an American literature survey
course, she strolled into my office, dumped copies of the books on

my desk, and told me they would move me to tears. I read them
in the next few days and found she was right; they enthralled me.
Since then, I have practiced "the Howe approach" and bestowed
texts on friends when they were planning their courses.

Reconceiving the Syllabus, Questioning the Canon

Nevertheless, acquainting faculty with texts can accomplish only
so much. Rarely do instructors quickly proceed to overhaul their
syllabi. More often, they simply brood with greater intensity
about the problem of "squeezing some women" into their courses.
Before much significant change can occur, they need to sense the
importance of entirely reconceptualizing those courses. They need
to feel that, instead of trying to cram more material about women
into courses that remain otherwise intact, they should reconsider
the whole experience from a women's studies perspective.

Such radical rethinking does not come easily to most teachers.
Whatever the course, they tend to believe that a fixed, definite
body of knowledge exists and must be conveyed during the
semester. English faculty are passionately devoted to the idea of a
literary canon—an eternally durable set of indisputable masterpieces. Indeed, I think it hard to underestimate the tenacious grip
of the canon on the minds of even those English teachers most
sympathetic to feminism. I felt guilty just contemplating the
exclusion of certain authors from my American Realism course.
Would it be madness to drop Howells? Could I look people in the
eye and inform them that I had not "done" Norris? Would
someone note the string of non-canonical authors I planned to
include on my syllabus and consider me hopelessly eccentric?
Although I eventually designed a course that I consider
transformed, I was struck by how psychological obstacles of this
sort could still afflict me after I had taught women's studies for six
years. My own anxiety about subverting the canon helps me
understand, if not endorse, the reluctance of colleagues to
challenge it.

Faculty must, however, overcome their dedication to "coverage" if they are to transform their courses instead of merely to
tinker with them. It would be useful for teachers to study how

their disciplines came to establish certain assumptions, principles, insights, and methods as professionally legitimate. The research could lead them to acknowledge a crucial truth: the systems of values that teachers now esteem evolved from imperfect humans influenced by time and place, and, since particular conditions did affect how fields developed, the present state of those fields should not be declared sacred.

Only in the past few years have people in various disciplines thoroughly reviewed this matter of origins. Barbara Herrnstein Smith, for instance, laments the dearth of research into why the discipline of English has valued certain works and neglected others:

> It is clear that, with respect to central pragmatic as well as theoretical problems of literary value and evaluation, American critical theory has simply painted itself out of the picture. Beguiled by the humanist's fantasy of transcendence, endurance, and universality, it has been unable to acknowledge the most fundamental character of literary value, which is its mutability and diversity. And, at the same time,...it has foreclosed from its own domain the possibility of investigating the dynamics of that mutability and understanding the nature of that diversity.[4]

Paul Lauter makes a similar charge, on a more specific level, in his account of how the American literary canon took shape during the 1920s. With an impressive array of evidence, he claims that "processes were set in motion that virtually eliminated black, white female, and working-class writers from the canon. Institutional as well as theoretical and historiographic factors were involved in that exclusion."[5]

In planning my American Realism course, I was encouraged by the kind of scholarship that Smith calls for and Lauter demonstrates. They sustained me in my hope of keeping my integrity even as I questioned the repertoire of authors traditionally linked with such a course. Nevertheless, I felt a need to justify all the writers I eventually chose. Even when teachers grow skeptical of the literary canon, we ought to provide rationales for the course selections we come to make. But we need to remember that these rationales can actually be of our own devising, rather than involuntary precepts bequeathed by our professional guilds.

Proposing New Criteria for Inclusion

The Lauter article gave me support, too, for the particular criteria I invoked when I chose the authors for my course. By reminding me about the kind of writers banished from American literature as recently as the 1920s, it increased my determination to restore them. I felt a renewed belief that my students would get a distorted view of American literary realism if I perpetuated the slighting of black, white female, and working-class authors. As I attempted to develop the course from a consciously held women's studies perspective, I tried to reconceive the era of realism by asking myself a question that faculty in all disciplines should ponder: How might a course reflect the fact that women have been half of humanity? One answer for the teacher of literature: allow roughly half the authors in a course to be female. (In my particular course, five out of twelve were.) I am not suggesting that when faculty choose texts, they should adhere to rigid quotas; however, a gender-balanced selection of writers can help the course give women a regard commensurate with their numbers.

English faculty might believe they can correct the imbalance by including male-authored works featuring women as central characters, such as, in a course on American Realism, Henry James's *Daisy Miller* and Theodore Dreiser's *Sister Carrie*. But a work may pay attention to women and still give signs of male authorship. Readers never really encounter Daisy Miller directly; they must see her more or less through Frederick Winterbourne's point of view. While they probably grow to distrust him, they must still occupy themselves with his thinking more than hers. I suspect that James, at least in this stage of his career, was readier to screen Daisy through a male consciousness because he could more easily imagine what a male consciousness might want to report about her. Dreiser, on the other hand, discloses Carrie's inner thoughts, yet his descriptions of her as a sexual object seem to reflect his own notorious libido. Also, a significant chunk of his novel dwells on the mind and actions of George Hurstwood. I value these two books for the psychological nuances and sociological observations they do indeed yield, and I included them both in my course. But even though their male authorship does not discredit them, they fail to provide insights that distinguish particular works by women.

Reading Women Writers: Speaking Subjects Tell Their Stories

Addressing the import of women as half of humanity should involve deeper issues than the appropriate balance of writers. The teacher of American Realism ought to consider how texts and class sessions might draw out the contrasts in male and female existence during the period. For example, in our discussions of Harriet Wilson's *Our Nig*, Kate Chopin's *The Awakening*, and the group of letters called *The Maimie Papers*, my students and I analyzed the politics of sexuality operating at the time—how women had to contemplate bodily appearance, motherhood, marriage, and codes of sexual behavior from a perspective that men simply could not share. Admittedly, the James and Dreiser novels broach these subjects, but not with the same degree of immersion in a particular woman's consciousness nor with the same acute sensitivity to life as a woman herself experiences it. Harriet Wilson's autobiographical fiction registers with vivid agony the problems a northern, lower-class black women faces in raising her child alone. Kate Chopin's Edna Pontellier mediates the claims of selfhood and marriage with a sense of dilemma that did not burden men of the time. Maimie Pinzer, the pseudonymous author of letters to Boston socialite Fanny Quincy Howe, uses the correspondence to explore several distinctly female issues: among them, the relationship of feminine beauty to a woman's economic survival.

THE ROLE OF "SENTIMENTAL" FICTION: REDEFINING REALISM

By studying *Our Nig* and Rebecca Harding Davis's short story *Life in the Iron Mills*, the students and I attempted to discern the underlying purposes of a female literary tradition in nineteenth-century America. Associating the age of realism almost entirely with men becomes downright ludicrous when one considers that throughout the century, most of the published writers and most of the reading public were women. Unfortunately, the novels that women produced by the thousands during these years have largely been dismissed in the twentieth century as "sentimental." Because the language and plot stress the vicissitudes of the heart rather than the torments of the intellect, scenes of domestic life rather than the wilds of nature, and the daily lives of heroines rather than the exploits of heroes, they have been falsely accorded a marginal role in the development of the American literary aesthetic. Recently several feminist scholars have sought to discover and, for the first time, seriously examine these neglected works.[6]

Although *Our Nig* and *Life in the Iron Mills* often flaunt highly emotional rhetoric, with blatant appeals to the reader's sympathy, I tried to help the students understand their fictional techniques in light of what the authors were trying to accomplish. More specifically, these works and others of the so-called "sentimental" tradition could be said to represent protest against various social injustices, couched in the language of extreme feeling because women thought the men in charge of society wrongly excluded feeling from their operations. Harriet Wilson wrote an autobiographical novel soliciting pity for its heroine not only because she herself desperately needed funds, but also because she wanted to reveal a northern culture marked by sexual, racial, and class oppression. True, the worst villains in the book are women, and certain of the men come across as sympathetic. But it can be argued that her female ogres lash out at Wilson's heroine because society denies them any constructive way of exercising power. If they emerge as petty tyrants of the hearth, their cruelty may be seen as a response to their exclusion from the public world of men. Their acts of egotism can be regarded as helplessly warped parodies of a more important phenomenon: the amorality of the men who established an oppressive social system in the first place and sustain it now. At any rate, as Wilson's narrative proceeds, it increasingly suggests the possibility of female friendship as a force that can mitigate social ills. Davis quite explicitly indicts a male-run system in *Iron Mills*: those responsible for industrial exploitation in Wheeling are clearly male capitalists, who thrive on a gospel of Social Darwinism instead of Christian charity. Even though the chief victim in the story is a man, Davis's narrator is a woman, and again the message is that society has to be infused with the compassion usually relegated to the female sphere. The relationship between "sentimental" fiction and such ideas would not, of course, have appeared for my students if I had continued male critics' traditional practice of disdaining the genre or ignoring it altogether.

RECONCEIVING THE GENRES OF GENDER

Issues of genre loom in another respect when one resolves to give women writers their due. Traditionally, literature courses of any sort emphasize three kinds of writing—fiction, poetry, and drama—and sometimes autobiography as well. But several women have turned to other types of writing, feeling barred from more public forms. A determined effort to rediscover women authors should involve attention to other genres, such as journals, diaries, letters, and even oral testimonies. As my students read *The Maimie Papers*, they realized that many women have created literature outside the small range of genres officially recognized by the English curriculum. Maimie's letters to Fanny demonstrate that even "ordinary" women have produced verbal art, if in forms not originally meant for public consumption. Wracked by sexism, poverty, syphilis, morphine addiction, her family's harsh treatment of her, and her past career as a prostitute, Maimie did not begin the correspondence hoping she might someday enter the halls of literary immortals. At certain points in her letters, she rejects the prospect of publishing an autobiography. Yet her correspondence shimmers with evocative accounts of her daily life and her struggles to achieve self-awareness and stability. Most readers of *The Maimie Papers* believe they have found a lost genius, and they wonder if other Maimies existed—with *their* writing hidden away, ready to be discovered by scholars willing to look outside the confines of the canon.

Competent Critic and Worthwhile Subject: The Role of the Student

One advantage of studying works like Maimie's in a literature course is that students may feel their own private writing might have more worth than they suspected. Also, they might come to recognize that writing by members of their own families might interest literary researchers.[7] When we finished our discussion of *The Maimie Papers*, one student noted how much she had become interested in her great-aunt's diary, and how reading Maimie's letters had led her to analyze its aesthetic features. The class left with the notion that some engaging texts might well lie in their own families' "archives." I was pleased that the traditional distance between the subject being learned and the person doing the learning had considerably narrowed.

Teachers of women's studies have, in fact, generally tried to make students feel they have a strong personal stake in learning the material of the course. Resolved to stay attentive to students' needs, women's studies faculty have geared their courses mainly to the empowerment of the people enrolled. While other instructors might also keep their audience in mind, those who teach women's studies tend to forefront the imperative of serving that audience. When deciding what they should include in their courses, they reject the traditional inclination to find certain content *intrinsically* valuable. Admitting that value is always a function of group interest, they hold that all curriculum materials should be chosen to benefit the most important group in the classroom, the students. Teachers who would transform their traditional courses from a women's studies perspective often have to grow more attuned to the lives of those who will sit in their classrooms. When they consider how their courses might reflect the fact that women have been half of humanity, they should consider what it means that female students now are half the college population. Given demographic trends, most faculty can expect women to predominate in their colleges for a long time to come. How might their courses be truly responsive to the majority of the student population?

Of the twelve students in my American Realism course, eight were female. Statistical reality, therefore, compelled me to teach it with a heightened consciousness of women's lives. At my particular institution, the University of North Carolina at Wilmington, additional facts about the general student body are worth noting. Some members are re-entry women, self-consciously returning to college after years away. Two of my students belonged to this category. Many of the students, women and men, are from the working class or the lower middle class. They worry, therefore, about the part that social stratification might eventually play in their lives. Moreover, a great many students are unsure how to cope with the changes in sex roles occurring around them. Since they come from a southern culture that still pines for the image of the "lady"—a term several of my male students habitually used— they are bewildered by the success feminism has apparently managed to achieve. At the same time, they want the South to be a truly modern society, recognized as such. This ambition renders their attachment to sexual stereotypes especially dysfunctional.

SETTING THE SYLLABUS IN CONTEXT:
LITERARY VALUES AND LIVING IN THE WORLD

Yet another fact about the world of UNC-W students is crucial; striving for a modern southern society means confronting the long-standing problem of racial inequality. The recent past of Wilmington is a vivid reminder of the continuing struggle for civil rights in this part of the country. On an album, the feminist singers Sweet Honey in the Rock protest the false arrest a decade ago of the Wilmington 10, an integrated group working for black progress. I experience chills when I play the album nowadays, asking myself what connections I need to make between my work at school and the lyrics of the songs. Most people at UNC-W are keenly aware, too, that their institution and other parts of the University of North Carolina system are under a federal court order to raise the number of black students within the next few years. It is also important to mention that even as I write this essay, members of the Ku Klux Klan are crowing over a legal victory in Greensboro, North Carolina, not very far away. Found innocent on charges that they violated civil rights when they killed Communist demonstrators at a rally, they clearly feel affirmed in their historic opposition to black freedom.

Therefore, even though I suspected the students in my American Realism course might be all white, which turned out to be the case, I resolved that the course would address the issue of race. I hope that by now I have made it clear, in fact, that to take a women's studies perspective involves more than just focusing on gender. Especially during the past few years, teachers of women's studies have made a determined effort not to lump all women together or focus merely on white, middle-class women. Instead, they have drawn attention to differences among women related to class, race, age, historical period, and sexual preference, among others. But my decision to include these other issues did not stem merely from a desire to keep up with the latest trends in feminism. If my selection of particular texts reflected the lines between gender and other variables, it did so largely as a response to the profile I constructed of my students. Attention to them and attention to developments in feminist theory dovetailed nicely.

In the first unit of my course we focused on a traditional theme—the passage from innocence to experience—and we studied three canonical works: *Adventures of Huckleberry Finn*, *The Red Badge of Courage*, and *Daisy Miller*. But our readings were transformative—to contrast male and female maturation. The second unit would concern the period after Reconstruction, focusing in particular on how black leaders deliberated the means to achieve equality for their people, and involved more daring non-canonical choices. Although Booker T. Washington's autobiography *Up From Slavery* and W.E.B. DuBois's collection of essays *The Souls of Black Folk* are not usually taught in literature courses, I had decided they were of sufficient literary merit, and of sufficient cultural interest, to be included. I had also decided to give out copies of poems by Paul Laurence Dunbar, whose work has been unfairly ignored by white critics.

I was tempted to begin this unit with *Our Nig*. Since it dealt with the North just prior to the Civil War, it offered a prophecy of the difficulties that would preoccupy blacks in the post-Reconstruction South. *Our Nig* would, in a sense, be a fitting non-canonical finish to the themes of the first unit, since the young heroine strains to acquire survival skills in a society of hostile northerners. Moreover, it would be delightfully timely to include *Our Nig*, for this 1859 work had just been discovered to have been the first novel published by a black writer in the United States. Finally, it was pertinent to the lives of the students, dwelling on the subjects of gender, race, and battle for education.

Enabling Texts and Enlarging Contexts: Disloyal to the Canon

Why, then, did I hesitate to enter *Our Nig* on my textbook order form? Because I considered it poorly written. As I have noted, its language is more blatantly emotional, more persistently didactic, than I had been trained to think was aesthetically proper. Having done my dissertation on Henry James, I had been relentlessly exposed to a theory that showing, not telling, was the crucial rule in the writing of fiction. I feared, too, that my students would share my doubts about the book's merits and resist my attempt to whip up discussion about it. Yet I eventually decided to include it.

Our Nig roused the students in ways I had not expected. They found it moving and instructive. Even though I had to help them relate it to the rhetoric of other nineteenth-century novels by women, they were readier than I had been to concede that its language had a legitimate function. Furthermore, they marveled at Harriet Wilson's vocabulary, for they had underestimated the powers of literacy that nineteenth-century black women could possess. In a way, I liked their surprise at her ability to write; it reflected their awareness that most black people had been denied literacy. Nevertheless, I was glad they now realized that the oppressed are not always helpless victims—that they have often developed, somehow or another, the resources to survive. It is historically inaccurate and paralytically depressing to present women only as passive tools of men, blacks as passive tools of whites. In putting aside the traditional values of my discipline and choosing to do *Our Nig*, I provided my students, whatever their own gender or race, with a text that gave them a crucial sense of black female potential.

The American Realism students also found *The Awakening* relevant. This novel struck them as amazingly contemporary in its depiction of a woman's quest for individual fulfillment, as opposed to mere acquiescence in marriage and motherhood. I stressed the book's challenge to conventions of femininity by bracketing it with *Sister Carrie* in a third unit entitled "Scandalous Novels." Both works gained notoriety when they first appeared because of their treatment of women as more than complacent angels. Admittedly, a feminist teacher can feel nervous about doing *The Awakening*, because its ending suggests the hopelessness of a woman ever being able to effect much change in her life. Edna Pontellier's suicide can be taken to reinforce the idea of Woman as Victim. Still, the novel raises such important questions about female dilemmas, and probes its heroine's psyche with such wonderful exactitude, that I consider it a necessary text in an American Realism course.

Moreover, the ending generated spirited discussions about how to evaluate Edna's last act. My students launched into an impassioned debate over how much they could judge her according to the standards of present-day feminism. One of the re-entry women declared that since Edna had been so nonconformist until that point, she should have been able to pull herself together and assert her independence in the midst of society. Another woman student, on the other hand, argued with equal fervor that no matter how much Edna resembled contemporary women, she had few constructive alternatives to suicide, given the demands imposed upon her by her cultural milieu and social class. Clearly, the whole group had to mull the various parallels Edna's story did and did not have with their personal lives, and clearly they felt energized by the process of juxtaposition.

READING LITERATURE TO READ OUR LIVES:
CRITICAL DIFFERENCES

It is worth underscoring here that even those inclined to view Edna through present-day lenses had to defend their perspective, with those lenses eventually cracking at least a bit. In other words, to choose texts largely for their relevance does not mean the class then blindly assimilates them to current experiences. Women's studies courses have often been accused of naive consciousness-raising, uncritical "touchy-feely" analysis of the subject matter. But the charge strikes me as grossly unfair, neglecting the amount of intellectual rigor that often distinguishes courses influenced by feminism. Although I wanted the students to recognize that literature could help them clarify their lives, I also wanted them to notice possible differences between themselves and the characters or authors. I insisted on their remaining sensitive to contrast as well as similarity.

I warned against glib identification even throughout the last unit, "Thwarted Artist," which focused on women writers whose perseverance could inspire the students. Although Emily Dickinson has become an immediately familiar name, hardly any of her poems were published during her lifetime, so she was especially courageous in the eccentricity of her own verse. But the students needed to understand her life and art in the specific context of New England Puritanism, even if they were tempted to construe her as a contemporary role model. Rebecca Harding Davis, the now largely unknown author of *Life in the Iron Mills*, also presented an image of encouragement, because without any previous literary training she was able to write a story that took the American culture of her day by storm. Still, as Tillie Olsen's extensive afterward to the Feminist Press edition makes plain, the student of her works needs to place them in the context of a woman's frustrated life in Wheeling during the second half of the nineteenth century. In reading *Life in the Iron Mills*, my students were encountering, too, a phase of industrial capitalism which they barely knew about, so I had to supply them with historical background for that economic fact. *The Maimie Papers* seemed a good work to end the course, since Maimie's last extant letter announces her decision to go to college—as a "re-entry woman" of 1922. And throughout the work, Maimie evoked a compelling narrative about a woman's attempt to "educate" herself, in the sense of obtaining insight into herself and her social conditions. Again, understanding Maimie required understanding the world of lower-class Americans in the early twentieth century—a social class well explained by Ruth Rosen in her introduction to the Feminist Press collection of the letters.

Changed Content in a Changed Context: The Transformed Course

I hope my course syllabus makes clear that in transforming a traditional course in American Literary Realism, I did not conjure up a wildly distorted vision of the subject. For one thing, I retained canonical authors like Twain, Crane, James, Dreiser, and Dickinson. I did drop Howells and Norris, but even the most tradition-minded teacher of American Realism would admit their reputations have sagged. Of the relatively few non-canonical authors I added, Kate Chopin has actually managed to achieve semi-canonical status. Because of time constraints, I resisted the temptation to include other works by women, such as Charlotte Perkins Gilman's short story "The Yellow Wallpaper." It is true that my categories for texts were somewhat unusual; American Realism courses often proceed chronologically or use groupings like "Naturalism." Yet my method of organization merely emphasized certain preexistent commonalities among writers. It is true as well that by including *The Maimie Papers*, I extended the period of the course to World War I, yet many American Realism teachers are doing the same.

Since the word "transformation" might suggest vaster, more frightening changes than I implemented, perhaps a better word would be "revision," particularly as it has been used by Adrienne Rich. In a classic essay, this feminist poet and theorist spells the word as "re-vision," and defines it as "the act of looking back, of seeing with fresh eyes, of entering an old text from a new critical direction." I looked back at this era in American literary history from what I deemed a feminist viewpoint, emphasizing things that are not usually emphasized. Rich defines a feminist viewpoint in the following way:

> A radical critique of literature, feminist in its impulse, would take the work first of all as a clue to how we live, how we have been living, how we have been led to imagine ourselves, how our language has trapped as well as liberated us, how the very act of naming has been till now a male prerogative, and how we can begin to see and name— therefore live—afresh.[8]

I tried to develop a course that would leave students with the impression that literature has the significance Rich assigns to it— in other words, that it can teach men and women how to understand their gender and their life as a whole. Unfortunately, portraying literature in this way requires at least something of a departure from the tradition of American Realism courses. Trained and nurtured in an academic world hostile to the feminist critique Rich values, faculty in all disciplines need to "see and name—therefore live—afresh." If they do not have to discard all their previous concepts, they will probably have to replace several of them—beginning with the notion that women belong at the margins of intellectual activity.

The Transformed Teacher—Becoming a Student, Again

As I have intimated, getting ready to teach a course like mine involves more than just a cognitive reorientation; it takes active learning. Ever since I became interested in women's studies, I have found myself needing to read material I never encountered in graduate school. I have had to study genres never thought of as literary; I have had to look at texts from other disciplines so that I could, for example, grasp the nature of the class struggle in Maimie's day. Most of all, I have had to consult other faculty, imploring them to supply me with their knowledge. Of course, it can be delightful to sit and talk with colleagues. Hence, a good way of prompting feminist change is the faculty seminar.

My institution has not reached the stage of sponsoring an all-faculty convocation on the role of women's studies in the curriculum. Nonetheless, I do see a chance to advance women's studies on the level of my department. We are reconsidering all our courses, trying to determine how the department can attract more students in an age of declining support for the liberal arts. Because women's studies emphasizes students in general and women students in particular, it might prove an effective tool for recruiting new students to the serious study of literature. Rich describes feminist re-vision as "an act of survival."[9] She is thinking especially of how women might endure, but adoption of a feminist view might help a discipline survive as well.

Of course, no curricular alteration will signify much unless it is accompanied by reflection on teaching. Is there such a thing as "feminist pedagogy?" In the past few years, advocates of women's studies have pondered the term a great deal, trying to settle on a definition. They may never succeed to everyone's satisfaction, yet they have repeatedly identified one central strand of the concept: feminist pedagogy emphasizes student participation. Throughout the course, I encouraged students to discuss the texts and attempted to stifle my own impulse to lecture. Since the class had only twelve students, I could easily draw people into the conversation; with a larger class, I would have set up small groups. One of my main techniques for starting talk was freewriting. For each class session, students had to write one and a half pages of spontaneous thoughts about the literature; then, I began class by having a few students present their ideas. I also stressed the students' contribution to their own learning by letting them devise their own take-home tests. More specifically, at the end of almost every unit they decided as a group what had emerged as important questions, and then they answered these questions in essays written outside of class.

I do not wish to prescribe all my techniques for all other teachers. Indeed, I think it far more profitable for a group of faculty members to analyze the practice of "feminist pedagogy" together. They could do so at the same time they consider feminist transformation of the curriculum; both topics can be part of one intellectual adventure. And in fact, that is what my work in women's studies has been for me, a multidimensional adventure. Ultimately, I respond to women's studies not because it is right (although I think it is) and not because it is wise (although I think it is), but because it is exciting. Teachers and administrators concerned about burn-out should take note: transforming courses can entail a stirring transformation of the self.

Notes

1. Perhaps historians will claim, with some justice, that their discipline has seen considerable progress insofar as the influence of feminism is concerned. Nevertheless, I suspect that many historians have yet to take women much into account.

2. When I refer to transformation, I refer to departures from how American Realism has generally been taught at *most* institutions. As a newcomer to my institution, I have only vague knowledge about the teaching of American Literature there.

3. Rebecca Harding Davis, *Life in the Iron Mills* (Old Westbury, N.Y.: The Feminist Press, 1972), and Ruth Rosen and Sue Davidson, eds. *The Maimie Papers* (Old Westbury, N.Y.: The Feminist Press, 1977). Florence Howe and Paul Lauter cofounded the Feminist Press in 1972. Their Reprints Series has subsequently featured several works by women.

4. Barbara Herrnstein Smith, "Contingencies of Value," *Critical Inquiry* 10, no. 1 (1983): 10.

5. Paul Lauter, "Race and Gender in the Shaping of the American Literary Canon: A Case Study From the Twenties," *Feminist Studies* 9 (Fall 1983): 435. Lauter is currently directing a Feminist Press project entitled "Reconstructing American Literature," funded by the Fund for the Improvement of Post-Secondary Education. The project has produced an anthology of syllabi for transformed American Literature courses. See Paul Lauter, ed., *Reconstructing American Literature: Courses, Syllabi, Issues* (Old Westbury, N.Y.: Feminist Press, 1983), pp. 25–32, for my model for an American Literature Survey.

6. See, for example, Nina Baym, *Woman's Fiction: A Guide to Novels by and about Women in American Fiction 1820–1870* (Ithaca: Cornell University Press, 1978); and Alfred Habegger, *Gender, Fantasy and Realism in American Literature* (New York: Columbia University Press, 1982).

7. These ideas were emphasized in the Modern Language Association-National Endowment for Humanities Institute on Women's Non-traditional Literature, which I attended at the University of Alabama in the summer of 1979.

8. Adrienne Rich, "When We Dead Awaken: Writing as Re-vision," in *On Lies, Secrets and Silence* (New York: W.W. Norton, 1979), p. 35.

9. Ibid.

Appendix

English 322—AMERICAN REALISM—Spring 1984
University of North Carolina at Wilmington
Instructor: John Schilb

GENERAL OBJECTIVES

to gain an understanding of the period often characterized as American literary realism, spanning roughly the years between the Civil War and World War I

to explore in general the relationship of literature to society, with emphasis on how literature, through form and content, expresses particular ideologies

to develop skills of critical thinking about literature, through discussion and writing

to develop a sense of community as a class

REQUIRED READING

I. From Innocence to Experience in the Age of Realism.
   Adventures of Hickleberry Finn (Twain)
   The Red Badge of Courage (Crane)
   Daisy Miller (James)

II. Transition: *Our Nig* (Wilson)

III. Reconstruction and the Future of Blacks: To What Extent the Mask?
   Up From Slavery (Washington)
   The Souls of Black Folk (DuBois)
   Selected poems of Paul Lawrence Dunbar on handouts

IV. Scandalous Novels
   The Awakening (Chopin)
   Sister Carrie (Dreiser)

V. Thwarted Artists
   Selected poems of Emily Dickinson on handouts
   Life in the Iron Mills (Davis)
   The Maimie Papers—excerpts (Pinzer)

REQUIRED WRITING

To facilitate class discussion and clarify our thinking about the works, we will do one and a half pages of freewriting for each time we meet. These entries will get a check if you simply do them. There will also be three major take-home examinations.

16

Communicating Difference: Forms of Resistance

Judith Anderson and Stephen Grubman

Our experience teaching several courses that focus specifically on how gender differences influence interpersonal communication demonstrated to us how volatile such material inevitably is, how unconscious most of our gender expectations are, and how force-fully these shape our behavior in the classroom as well as outside it. Our courses made central and starkly visible the dynamics that may impede communication, and thus effective teaching, in any course that attempts to incorporate material on differences between genders (or social, class, or cultural differences, we expect). But in other courses these obstacles to communication may be regarded as peripheral—a matter of personal teaching style, student interest or indifference. To the extent that our unconventional syllabus (i.e., focusing on gender differences in communication as our central concern) provoked responses that seem likely to be reproduced in other integration attempts, what we learned about our students and ourselves could provide an outline of sources and forms of resistance in understanding this material and inhabiting these classrooms.

Gender and Interpersonal Communication: Course Design

Our observations represent an experimental course repeated under several titles in slightly different contexts at the University

of Rhode Island. We chose to team-teach these courses for political as well as personal reasons. We were excited about teaching
together since we had been close personal friends for several
years, and we both eagerly looked forward to the opportunity to
share our own interpersonal relationship in a classroom setting.
But we were also aware of the political value of teaching these
courses together: for a woman and a man, both ardent believers
and active participants in feminist causes, to teach a course from
a feminist perspective should provide a loud and clear message
that women *and* men have much to gain from feminism. We
chose to focus on "Gender and Interpersonal Communication"
because we believed it a general enough theme to allow us to
explore a wide variety of interpersonal relationships and issues
from a feminist perspective. We also believed our course could
offer a critique of patriarchal culture that establishes rigid gender
roles and relegates males to a superior position in the world at
large while relegating females to an inferior position restricted to
the home. In our course content and in our pedagogy we would
try to value all individuals as equals, to value choice and autonomy for all individuals, and to value respect and tolerance for
differences among individuals.

We designed each course around the following objectives: (a)
to examine interpersonal relationships between women and
women, men and men, and women and men through discussions
of issues which significantly affected these relationships; (b) to
teach the course from a feminist perspective; and (c) to provide
opportunities for experiential learning as well as for cognitive
learning. The syllabus for each course followed this outline:

Class One: "Definitions of Patriarchy and Feminism"
Classes Two and Three: "Masculinity, Femininity, Androgyny
  and Beyond"
Classes Four and Five: "Verbal and Nonverbal Communica-
  tion"
Classes Six and Seven: "Power"
Classes Eight and Nine: "Sexuality"
Classes Ten and Eleven: "Homophobia"
Classes Twelve and Thirteen: "Relationships"
Classes Fourteen and Fifteen: "Directions for the Future"

We used our disciplinary background in communication theory to analyze when and why students resisted our attempts to discuss these patterns of gender differences. We attempted in our pedagogy to utilize not only what we knew of strategies for successful communication, but what we believed our feminist perspective could add to overcome these obstacles. The most important outcomes from these experiments are a preliminary typology of

- key elements that trigger resistance
- forms of expressing resistance
- meanings associated with these expressions
- strategies for mediating these forms of resistance.

The composition of our classes usually fit this pattern: the class size varied from sixteen to thirty students; 60 percent of the class was female and 40 percent male; 98 percent was white and 2 percent minority (black and Portuguese); age ranged from 19 to 25 in our classes on the main campus and at the College of Continuing Education.

Early Assumptions and Hard Truths

Our expectations for the first class we taught can only be described as idealistic. We believed we had designed a model course that would focus sharply on the key issues that influence interpersonal relationships between women and women, men and men, and women and men. Moreover, we believed our selection of readings and our plans for both cognitive and experiential learning would clearly expose these issues in a manner easy to understand and digest. We envisioned our students becoming intrigued with the material, stimulated by class discussions, and ultimately empowered to depart from our class and enter the world with a new set of feminist values: valuing women, valuing women as much as men, and valuing autonomy and choice for both women and men. This essay attempts to identify our naive assumptions as these were revealed to us by our students' responses to our course content and our pedagogy.

No matter how many times you teach the same course it always emerges in different form with different results because of the changing make-up and mixture of individuals in each class. As teachers most of us take this challenge for granted and seldom explore its ramifications beyond mere acknowledgment of its existence. Nevertheless, if we are ever to understand the forms of resistance that emerge in a mainstream course taught from a feminist perspective, we believe it is imperative to examine thoroughly the differences represented by the students and the teachers who make up the class.

When we examined the individuals who made up our classes, three categories became apparent: individual differences, gender differences, and the differences in the roles of teachers and students. Looking at each of these categories separately and then as a whole provides a complex picture of classroom interaction. Of course, each individual, whether male or female, faculty or student, brings to the classroom a personal history, a set of experiences, assumptions, and knowledge, which will influence each individual's perception of self, of others, of the group as a whole, and of the content and direction of a course. For example, an individual who has spent several years interacting with feminists, has had substantial exposure to feminist material, and has developed positive assumptions regarding the feminist movement, will bring a very different perspective into the classroom than an individual for whom our course was the first exposure to these ideas and feelings.

Gender may or may not seem relevant to faculty and/or students in traditional courses. In a course taught from a feminist perspective, the gender of the teacher and each student becomes a highly relevant factor for understanding and confronting forms of resistance. In our class, for example, we discovered that gender and power were important variables that affected both the nature and outcome of the interaction: female faculty member with male faculty member, female faculty member with female students, female faculty member with male students, male faculty member with male students, male faculty member with female students, female students with female students, and male students with female students. Some examples of how the different socialization of each gender affects classroom interaction should amply illustrate how important this factor is in understanding and challenging forms of resistance: the female (male) faculty member disagreeing with the male (female) faculty member over how to structure an exercise because she (he) believes it is too male (female)-oriented; the male (female) faculty member being able to empathize with a male (female) student's explanation of male (female) behavior because it was part of his (her) own experience, whereas the female (male) faculty member finds it difficult to accept the explanation because it is alien to her (his) experience; female (male) students viewing a case study from the anguish of the victim's perspective, whereas the male (female) students view the case study from the discomfort of the victimizer's perspective.

Differences in gender intersect dramatically with the inherent imbalance of power in a classroom felt by students because faculty create the course, conduct the course, and evaluate student work in the course. The dynamics of how power is exercised and felt become even more complex when a man and woman are teaching together. If, in a traditional course, this imbalance of power is assumed, at least by the teacher, to be "natural" or "most efficient," we wanted in our course to question this imbalance explicitly, to exert effort to minimize it, and to provide a more egalitarian model of interaction between faculty and students. To illustrate the dynamics of gender, power, and feminist pedagogy in action, imagine how confusing it might become in challenging forms of resistance if one faculty member reinforced the imbalance of power while the other faculty member attempted to minimize it; or if both faculty members attempted to minimize the imbalance of power, but the very fact of there being two faculty members persuaded the students that an even greater imbalance existed. Whatever the type of difference between faculty and students, these differences create forms of resistance and must be recognized if resistance is to be overcome.

Forms of Resistance: In Self-Defense

Professors in the field of communication should be among those educators least surprised at resistance to change. After all, even the most traditionally trained are thoroughly exposed to theories of resistance and combat it daily when we teach courses in public speaking, persuasion, argumentation, and group dynamics, all of which explore forms of audience resistance and strategies for overcoming it. Yet both of us entered our first class idealistically believing that mere exposure to new information as professed by two informed "ideal" role models would be ample enough reason for both ourselves and our students to overcome years of thoroughly ingrained societal and personal forms of resistance. Our pedagogical naivete may reflect our own resistance to the long, arduous, and frustrating task of understanding the complexity of resistance we faced.

We identified six primary forms of resistance: *fear of change, loyalty, shame, ignorance, prejudice,* and *minimizing.* In addition, we also identified six types of internal processes that, we believe, interact with the forms of resistance in positive and negative ways: *sense of security, self-sufficiency, self-confidence, self-examination, self-disclosure,* and *open-mindedness.* These, we hope, are useful descriptive terms that are associated with a variety of student behaviors and our sense of their meanings.

Fear of change, loyalty and *shame* are all interrelated and are easier to understand in conjunction with each other. Because we have all been socialized in a patriarchal society that has carefully taught us traditional gender-appropriate behavior through the family, through the educational system, and through the mass media, we have more or less successfully learned these roles and come to believe these roles are "normal," "acceptable," and "natural" to a greater or lesser degree. Hence, when we began our classes with definitions of patriarchal and feminist perspectives followed by a discussion of masculinity, femininity, androgyny and beyond, we were directly challenging both the behavior commonly reinforced for each gender and the beliefs commonly held about that was "normal," "acceptable," and "natural" for each.

Fear of change became evident as a form of resistance through expressions of concern and anxiety about self-identity in an "unknown" egalitarian world of the "beyond" in which gender differences might not carry the values we are accustomed to. Students often raised these doubts: If you eliminated "masculine" or "feminine" from your self-vocabulary, how would you know who you were, or how you were to dress, or how you were to act, or how you were to interact with others? Moreover, wouldn't everyone else view you as abnormal or unacceptable or unnatural if you eliminated gender differences from your self-identity and, subsequently, from your behavior? In short, *fear of change* most often centered around questions involving self-concept and approval by others, both integral elements of interpersonal communication and highly resistant to change and risk-taking.

Loyalty emerged as a defense mechanism against the fear of losing self-identity and found expression through lists of all the ways students felt they benefited from traditional gender roles in the family, throughout school, in relationships, and in society at large. Students articulated their concerns negatively: But why would I want to become consumed with a job and get ulcers like men do? But why should I want to do the laundry, clean the house, or look after kids like women do, if I didn't have to? What would my parents or my girl/boyfriend think if I changed my beliefs and behaviors? In short, *loyalty* most often focused on questions surrounding advantages each gender role accrued and the approval one received from traditional role models one admired and trusted (and perhaps feared losing if they changed). Again, it is difficult to challenge a positive reward system that is deeply entrenched and that offers benefits and approval.

Shame was associated with questions about how individuals might be criticized or made to feel ashamed if they didn't behave in "normal," "acceptable," or "natural" ways appropriate for their gender: What if I, as a male, cried every time my feelings were hurt? How would other males—and females—react to me? In short, *shame* most often centered on questions of disapproval or rejection by significant others or people in general. Once more, it is difficult to overcome resistance to change when the perceived risks appear negatively weighted against the individual.

Ignorance, prejudice, and *minimizing* emerged as related responses when our classes focused attention on the subject of homophobia two-thirds of the way through the semester. We anticipated even more resistance than usual toward such a highly charged topic. By now we were realistic.

Ignorance manifested itself in at least two ways: lack of information on a cognitive level, and lack of information on any personal experiential level. These two kinds of ignorance were then played off each other as a form of resistance, as seen in such expressions as "I don't understand this since I am not a homosexual or lesbian," or "I don't need to understand this since I don't know anyone or choose to know anyone who is homosexual or lesbian." A third kind of ignorance probably existed in our classes, but was never overtly expressed: feigned ignorance by any individuals who were homosexuals or lesbians, but who feared rejection by other class members if they seemed to be informed. It is difficult to challenge resistance to learning information if the information appears personally irrelevant or threatening.

Prejudice was much more difficult to observe directly as a form of resistance while discussing homophobia, probably because of the "liberal" atmosphere usually prevailing in college classrooms which dictates "outward tolerance for differences." We faced almost absolute silence (perhaps a covert expression of prejudice) following any attempts to evoke responses. In no other class sessions had there occurred such apparent unwillingness to explore a topic. Popular wisdom argues that it is much easier to deal with a blatant bigot, because at least you know exactly who and what you are dealing with. Popular wisdom may continue to hold true for the classroom as well, unless covert prejudice involving learned stereotypes about issues, behaviors, individuals, and groups can be coaxed into the open and confronted.

Minimizing occurred throughout the courses, but perhaps more overtly on the topic of homophobia. Students found it easier to "dismiss" this topic as "unimportant" because they could personally distance themselves and claim, as "liberally educated" students, that they were not part of the problem. Regardless of what topic was being discussed, *minimizing* took the form of dismissing any information not considered of sufficient personal importance. Both male and female students tended to minimize the importance of language in shaping the gender expectations. They refused to treat seriously such issues as titles (Ms., chairperson), the feminization or masculinization of occupations (authoress, male nurse, female lawyer), or the use of sex-exclusive pronouns (he, she, him, her). Resistance to change is difficult to counter if the subject of change is considered personally irrelevant or insignificant.

Engaging Resistance: Strategies for Change

As each course progressed and as the forms of resistance became clearer, we also began to identify internal processes interacting with the forms of resistance in positive and negative ways. *Sense of security* appeared as an important internal process that tended to weaken resistance if the individual possessed a strong sense of personal security, and tended to reinforce resistance if the individual felt vulnerable. Such factors as older age, higher level of achievement, respected position in society, greater financial security, and wider variety of life experience seemed to be connected to a strong sense of security and a consequent willingness to consider change. Closely tied to *sense of security* was *self-sufficiency.* The more self-sufficient the individuals had become in the areas of economic and personal independence, the less resistant the individuals were to change. Similarly with *self-confidence*; the more self-assured the individuals, the less resistant they were to change. *Self-examination* and *self-disclosure* also emerged as significant processes. The more extensively individuals "knew" themselves and the more willing they were to disclose what they knew about themselves, the less resistant they were to change. *Open-mindedness* could almost be classified as a composite term since sense of security, self-sufficiency, self-confidence, self-examination, and self-disclosure all seemed to be prerequisites for being open-minded to the possibility of change.

A useful way to understand the complexity of resistance involved is to visualize the interaction between forms of resistance and types of internal processes. To aid this cause, we offer the model in Figure 16.1.

Where should we locate ourselves on this grid as gendered teachers, attempting to share power, no doubt experiencing resistance even as we advocated profound personal and institutional change? *Fear of change* for us often became fear of backward steps toward traditional gender roles, or fear of losing hard-fought political and social gains; *loyalty* for us often meant loyalty to feminist principles or loyalty to our own developed feminist lifestyles; *shame* often accompanied any suggestion that our behavior might be associated with traditional stereotypes or prejudices; *Ignorance* often emerged in moments of awkwardness or embarrassment when we realized we were personally unfamiliar with "traditional" experiences; *prejudice* often evinced itself against traditional positions or values and even sometimes against those who espoused them; and *minimizing* often took the form of discounting the significance of a traditional value or of insensi-

Figure 16.1
Interaction Between Resistance and Internal Processes

Forms of Resistance	Types of Internal Processes	Sense of Security	Self-sufficiency	Self-confidence	Self-examination	Self-disclosure	Open-mindedness
Fear of Change							
Loyalty							
Shame							
Ignorance							
Prejudice							
Minimizing							

tively responding to a traditionalist issue by dismissing it as trivial. As can be concluded from these examples, it is conceivable that forms of resistance experienced by faculty may be initially so different from those experienced by students that the classroom could become a battleground of "feminists" vs. "traditionalists." Because we initially discovered and explored our own forms of resistance while we encountered our students' forms of resistance, we were able to improvise strategies to combat both our own resistance and their resistance.

We found the following general strategies effective. They are arranged in an order that moves from the less explicit to the more self-consciously identified; as teachers we depended on the full range throughout every week of our course.

Role Modeling: interacting with each other and with students from an actively non-sexist, pro-feminist perspective emphasizing equality and respect.

Communication Behavior: establishing direct eye contact, genuinely listening as active listeners, avoiding interrupting, and establishing supportive communication climates rather than defensive-producing climates with each other and with students.

Facilitating: guiding ourselves and students through the process of critical listening and differentiating among facts, opinions and feelings.

Questioning: teaching ourselves and students how to direct questions that lead to self-discoveries and application of information.

Structuring: instructing ourselves and students how to frame arguments in a logical, persuasive order so that even disparate views can be admired for their substance and form.

Challenging: learning together how to probe false premises or distorted information and to discover all the diverse perspectives from which an issue can be viewed.

These general strategies are a tentative taxonomy of teacher-initiated behaviors. Our general strategies were developed out of necessity. Since our courses were among the first at our institution in which feminist values were mainstreamed, we were acutely aware of ourselves as models. The first step, and one which we used each time our classes met, was to teach positive interpersonal communication through example. All else evolved from that position.

17

Transforming the Social Sciences

Greta Salem and Stephen Sharkey

The Dimensions of Feminist Transformation

This essay describes our attempts to transform the teaching of social science at Alverno College by introducing feminist research and practice into our total curriculum. By "feminist" research and practice we mean, first, that which explicitly deals with the concrete life experience of women in society, in comparison with that of men, as an object of study. And second, we mean that which explicitly modifies the teaching-learning process to correct the tendency of traditional pedagogy to perpetuate institutional sexism.

As college teachers we move from the premise that such innovations are part and parcel of what is typically portrayed as liberal arts education, whose definitions tend to emphasize the development of critical thinking skills, on the one hand, and meaningful involvement in the life of society on the other. Feminist scholars now contribute strongly to energizing liberal education by reforming the content of what is studied. First, the new scholarship on women has expanded the picture of the social world made available to students, by revising history with herstory; second, feminist scholars have broken open old concepts—such as "power" or "mental health"—to reflect more meaningfully women's distinct experience and positive value.

But they do more. By having raised serious questions about the pattern of discrimination encouraged by traditional sex role socialization, they challenge educational institutions to revise their theories of how students learn and develop[1] and thus to rethink the teaching practices that implicitly or explicitly rest on those theories. The culture of the classroom comes to be transformed.

Politics and the Woman Student

Our department offers an interdisciplinary program integrating material primarily from sociology and political science. Within the liberal arts tradition we've described, our program is designed to help students critically interpret the social and political worlds they occupy, and also to develop the interests and skills they need to take on active citizen and community leadership roles. In creating a curriculum to achieve these goals, we've had to address not only the exclusion of women from the substantive data considered in traditional courses, but also the bias, embedded in so many secondary school and college course offerings, that elicits a passive stance from students toward political and social action.[2] Politics is still traditionally defined as a non-feminine vocation or avocation. If women are to be motivated to engage in political action, they need to see its particular relevance to their own lives. This special relevance is frequently masked by the gender-neutral discussion of political and social issues in traditional programs, which suggest that either women's experiences are not relevant to the issues at hand, or that their interests are incorporated with those of the so-called generic "man."

It is important for our female students to see the differential effects of social and political environments on their lives. They must also develop the capacity to do something concrete about the problems they identify. Combining these goals requires new classroom strategies that may be generally classified under the rubric of experiential learning. Although experiential learning strategies are increasingly considered an important component of feminist pedagogy, they have been adopted for years by college faculty members not necessarily committed to a feminist framework. These teachers looked to such strategies because they were dissatisfied with the educational results of an approach that focused primarily on the transmission of information—indeed, highly specialized information. They believed in learning-through-active-involvement. We share such a belief, and wish simply to highlight that this quality of experiential learning makes it particularly relevant to women, as an antidote to the socialization process that has taught them to be even more passive then men in social and political life.

We will analyze some of the specific feminist transformations we made in our particular curriculum, in both content and process terms. We'll also comment on some surprises we experienced—for better and for worse—as we worked through these changes. We will discuss what we observed in our students and also what we discovered about ourselves, personally and professionally, to identify how we think our experience might be useful to educators in other institutional settings; i.e., what might be "exportable" and under what conditions.

The "Quiet Feminism" of Alverno College

Alverno is a small, Catholic women's college in Milwaukee, characterized by what the most recent *New York Times Guide to Colleges* called a "quiet feminism." Its supportive environment (e.g., child care, support groups) has attracted a large number of returning women, as has its innovative Weekend College. The latter offers working women and parents a chance to pursue an education by attending classes on intensive weekends over a four-year period. We'll focus on the more classically organized Weekday College, in which social science operates as a discrete department.

The weekday student population is split almost evenly between the returning (24-years-old and up) and traditional (18–23) student. Although an aggressive effort in minority recruitment has increased that portion of the student body in the last couple of years, a little more than 90 percent of the current students are Caucasian. The vast majority are from southern Wisconsin; they reside in urban and suburban, as well as rural, areas. Most have some work experience, even those traditional-age students who enter Alverno from high school. Many are first-generation college students.[3]

Alverno's commitment to the education and empowerment of women is reflected both in its competence-based learning system, which focuses on using as well as transmitting information[4] and in the special programs that have marked Alverno's leadership in the identification of and response to the needs of women. Alverno was the first academic institution to publish the results of a study of women public officials[5] and the first to call a national meeting of women theologians in 1972. While there are a few women-focused courses in the curriculum ("The Psychology of Women," "Women and Health Care"), the administration's main focus has been to encourage the faculty to incorporate research on women in course offerings across the curriculum. Support from the Public Leadership Education Network (PLEN) has enabled us to work more systematically at this transformation within the Social Science Department in the past three years. PLEN consists of ten women's colleges (Goucher, Spelman, Carlow, Marymount, Manhattan, Stephens, Douglass, Alverno, Wells, St. Catherine's) and two national resource groups (The Center for the Study of Women and Politics at Rutgers, and the National Women's Education Fund, Washington, D.C.), who received funding from the Carnegie Corporation to develop pilot projects for the public leadership education of women. We have made significant revisions in courses at all levels, such as "Complex Organizations," "Social Policy Analysis," and "Social Theory." Because they set the stage for further development and thus are most crucial, we will concentrate on the two introductory courses that form the base of our program.

Introductory Social Science: The Social System

"Introductory Social Science: The Social System" provides an extended exercise in experiential learning. In the process of undertaking a class project, students organize a social system and take an active role within it.[6] Using a power-sharing model, students assume control of the class for several weeks, during which they are given a skeletal assignment requiring them to identify a social problem, organize themselves as a class to do the necessary research, and develop a set of proposals to address the concerns they have uncovered.

We train our students in participant observation and analysis and offer relevant readings to help them understand what they experience in this setting. We intend to provide opportunities for women to observe and experience concrete illustrations of the abstract sociological and political science concepts that make up the core of the traditional courses, to observe and try out a range of organizational structures and take on a number of organizational roles, and to identify and begin to develop the skills required for effective participation in community life.

Our feminist analysis enabled us to see new meanings for our women students in the skills and orientations most frequently highlighted in this course: (a) the ability to articulate one's view in both small and large groups, or more "public" settings; (b) a tolerance for the conflict, ambiguity and delay that naturally follow when many make decisions previously made by a few; (c) a willingness to take risks; and (d) a recognition of the interpersonal skills required to enable groups of individuals to work cooperatively on a common task.[7] The most important outcome of this experience, however, is the fact that a student begins to see the interrelationships endemic in any community and thus experiences first-hand the consequences of either acting on or ignoring her responsibility to the group. In other words, the concept of society or social system becomes much less an abstract term subject to reification.

GENDER, POWER, AND THE SOCIAL SYSTEM

A surprising and sobering outcome has been the consistent unwillingness of our students to debate, assume, or assign leadership positions when they are in control of the class. We frankly expected (or hoped) to see more concrete evidence of some change in basic gender attitudes, compared to what we knew from the experience of our own college days (the '50s and '60s). But in the past two and half years, students in this all-female class have consistently refused to assign leadership roles formally, and have had to face all the difficulties that emerge when a group's expectations about appropriate organizational behavior and responsibilities are unclear. Decisions and discussion are "backed into"; they often take place not in the public arena of the class, but in "safer" places, such as the halls or bathrooms, during breaks where no formal arguments need be presented or disagreements with potential opponents found. Entries in journals kept by the students about their daily activities and feelings consistently reveal apprehensions that "someone will become a dictator" or that " no one should be telling us what to do." In one situation, a student, totally frustrated with the disorganization of her leaderless group, called the class together to propose a working framework, which included some hierarchical distribution of roles and responsibilities. Although she was responding to a need that was universally felt and recognized by her fellow classmates, her stance was tentative and apologetic. When her peers offered her leadership positions in the new scheme "because she had brought the whole thing up," she refused.

The bathroom conferences are not signs of effective cloakroom politics, but rather, we must recognize, an avoidance of conflict. Nor is the pattern of fear merely a function of inexperience with group decision-making processes, a "freshman" phenomenon. (Many students take this course in their second year.) Even more important, Alverno students receive explicit training in social interaction skills all through their program, beginning with freshman orientation. Thus they come into our class with some background on this score. The unwillingness we observe contrasts dramatically with the classroom experiences of one of the authors in a coeducational institution, where leadership roles were *always*, without exception, designated, taken by, or assigned to male students. Clearly there is a gender issue here.

EMPOWERING WOMEN

As a response to this situation we decided to make a substantive change in the course material. Although we had always dealt with the issue of power, we had never focused specifically on the ways in which women handle it. We have now incorporated a unit dealing explicitly with women and power, in which we explore the dilemma underlying our students' very real uncertainty and pain. We schedule it *after* the students have struggled through their group experience, lived the limitations of their own socialization, and recognized the pattern in their collective behavior. We include in this section: (a) a comparison of the types of manipulation and coercion implicit in the traditional disciplinary definitions of power with feminist notions of empowerment and liberation; (b) a review of Jean Baker Miller's psychological explanation of the threat posed for women by the traditional conceptualization of power;[8] and (c) a consideration of the strategies that might help women acquire and exercise power in a way that is less personally threatening and more consistent with a feminist perspective.

Introductory Social Science: The Community

The second introductory course, "Introductory Social Science: The Community," takes students from the mini-society they created in the classroom to the local community in which they live, in order to demonstrate how the relationships "artificially" created in their previous course are, in fact, replications of those from the "real world." This course began as a more traditional introduction to urban sociology and politics with some added features designed to (a) help students see the differential impact of the urban environment and urban policies on women and other minority groups; (b) encourage students to examine their own relationship to their communities; (c) demystify the political system; and (d) encourage students to see political action as a viable strategy for dealing with problems that appear to be personal but are, in fact, structurally imposed.

USING GENDER AS A CATEGORY OF ANALYSIS

Initially we thought that the broad goals of this course could be achieved within the usual disciplinary paradigms. Yet the substantive modifications eventually required in the course were rather surprising. We had anticipated that the required changes would involve incorporating material on women and politics, as well as material on urban policies such as housing or transportation.[9] These policies appear to be gender-neutral but must, in fact, be considered in terms of their differential impact on the lives of women. Nevertheless, when we began to reconceptualize the course and moved from asking questions about the policies relevant to women's lives, to asking what it is like to *be* an elderly woman, a divorced woman, or a single parent, and to live in an urban or suburban environment, we found ourselves looking at material that we had never considered relevant. Thus, in addition to the literature we had planned to incorporate, we found ourselves looking at work in architecture, urban planning, and environmental psychology.[10] This change in questions engendered a more holistic approach to the study of urban life. Particularly striking was our finding, as we developed our materials, that the very design of the environment itself, the "built world," could so powerfully serve as an instrument of social control. For some it provides opportunities and openings; for others it imposes constraints and creates traps.

We make a strong effort to introduce this type of holistic, interdisciplinary analysis into regular class assignments by having students explore their own relationship to the community they live in. For example, we ask them to examine the census data for their community, which provide a quantitative characterization, and to contrast that image to their own experience within it. Thus they supplement the census data with a personal description and a personal delineation of community boundaries. To evaluate the quality of life in their community, they assess the ways in which it does or does not meet their needs, and how easy it is to get to places around the metropolitan area where their needs can be satisfied. This assignment is designed both to encourage students to think about their relationship to their context, and to understand that this is a built environment reflecting the decisions and assumptions of the power-holders who control it. The conceptual discussion of racial segregation is really enhanced when a black inner-city student contrasts the population data from her neighborhood tracts with that presented by a suburban white. And differences in the quality of life become more poignant when inner-city students repeatedly cite "coping with crime" as one of their biggest problems, while suburban dwellers complain of "not having enough to do."

We consider political power and decision-making structures in the second half of the course. In addition to the traditional material in urban politics, we include analyses of women as voters, as elected officials, and as community activists. The reading is supplemented by presentations by local officials and grassroots leaders. Equally important, however, are the assignments that we believe are critical to demystifying politics. Rather than reading material traditionally presented on the various models of local government, students are encouraged to go directly to their city or town halls and find out about their own. They are required to identify all the elected officials at the local, state, and national level with whom they have a constituent/representative relationship, and to select one for a personal interview. These interviews are used both to test the various theories of representation that have been discussed in class, and to allow students to acquire a sense of their respondent's identification of relevant issues and priorities.

The comparisons of student experiences in class are most instructive. They allow us to explore the range of political structures in the metropolitan areas, as well as variations in the styles and interests characterizing elected representatives. The most important outcome of this assignment, however, is the direct contact that students make with representatives from the political system. They begin to see public officials as human and accessible, and they see these positions as roles to which they might aspire. The political histories that constitute part of the interviews help illuminate the pathways to power and influence.

Transforming the Curriculum: Our Courses, Ourselves

In transforming these courses we found it impossible to merely "add on" units "about" women in relevant sections. On the contrary, we found ourselves changing the entire structure of the courses, reinterpreting basic concepts, creating new ones, asking questions not traditionally asked, and incorporating material that goes well beyond the disciplinary boundaries that have provided the traditional frameworks for these courses.

We have found it particularly difficult to introduce traditional conceptual language to new students at the same time that we point out the sexist bias in it. For example, we teach our students the meaning of the term "socioeconomic status," a concept thoroughly embedded in the social science literature. But then we need to point out that the traditional measures—income, education, and profession—do not always apply to women, who tend to take on the status of their husbands. Where does one place the divorced wife of a doctor who works as a secretary? Our feminist analysis must repeatedly undermine the conventional terms and assumptions of the discipline we purport to teach. How can we avoid the conflict in ourselves, and the genuine confusion of our students, produced when we teach them the language of the discipline and then reveal that it is ineffective in describing their own experience, or that of half the population?

We mediate this problem by using personal experiences, which students recall, as well as collective experiences, which we design, to illustrate the development and meaning of social science concepts. Our experience with exploring the meanings of power provides an apt illustration. Warren Paap recently analyzed how this concept is treated in fifty of the most popular sociology texts. He concludes that

> To the extent there is any developed and integrated model of power in an introductory text, it is a Weberian model. Further, it is presented in the context of macro-level phenomena, especially in the form of political institutions. This hinders the teaching process, in that forms of power more accessible to the experience of our students receive less attention, and the teaching of an applied sociology, useful for dealing with everyday life situations, is not facilitated.[11]

Paap goes on to complain of the general lack of a clear framework for integrating power at the macro and micro levels, the most common theme being that "power on the micro level is an epiphenomenon of factors operating on a macro level." The overall outcome of these biases is that, for the student, "power" becomes something "out there," associated mostly with large, established institutional settings like "government" or the "economy." Power may exist between individuals, but its connection to power in "the system" is vague. And if there is perceived to be only one kind of power, namely that which typically is observed in the traditional male-dominated institutions, then consideration of alternative definitions is impeded.

USING THE SELF AS A SOURCE OF AUTHORITY

In leading our students through the process of concept formulation, we move inductively, beginning with their daily lives to build concepts from the data of their experience. Thus we encourage them to *do* social science, not read about doing it from remote authorities. In studying power—and related concepts such as caste, class, and even socialization—we ask our students from the first day of the term to examine their own worlds. For example, we employ two autobiographical assignments in the social system course: one requires students to compose a brief essay on what high school was like; the other asks them to reflect how it felt to grow up as a girl. These essays generate poignant insights into gender-role socialization and stratification and into the experience of power structures in different types of settings. We ask students to share their essays to identify common patterns. They begin to develop typologies out of what their peers have set down.

The high school assignment, for example, says nothing about hierarchy or social structure. Yet repeatedly, in describing their high school experiences, students come up with their own typology of the high school "class/caste system" consisting of "jocks," "nerds," "dopeheads," "achievers," "preppies," and the like, ranked in terms of power and status. When we compare their typologies with the traditional hierarchal description of the school, they begin to see what the process of conceptualization is all about and how concepts relate to their personal experience. We can then discuss how power as a concept comes to be defined. They can witness how the definition of a concept reflects the perceptions of those who generate it, and indeed damages those whose reality is not reflected in that definition. If "jocks" are on the top of the student power structure in high schools, and the female students admire boys who are "jocks" and think they are powerful, and if there are no real athletic programs for girls to shine in, how can girls ever think of themselves as powerful, even in this very traditional sense? Is there a way for girls to feel good about themselves when what they do is seen as "second class" at best? And what can they do about the fact that they reproduce the class/caste system every day, at least in part, by "believing" it?

By grounding our introduction to disciplinary concepts in both the students' recalled experiences, coupled with those we create in the classroom, we realize we are utilizing, in teaching, what Reinharz has recommended as a paradigm for feminist research—namely, experiential analysis.[12] Furthermore, we find this nexus, this notion of teaching-as-guided-research, to be applicable also at intermediate and advanced stages of coursework in the program. Although we maintain a distinct survey course in research methods, there is no "research track" as is common in many programs. Instead, all courses include some investigative learning strategies as central pedagogical elements, so that students have repeated practice in the art of conceptualization and problem-solving. By involving students directly in the formulation of a disciplinary language, we demystify the process and encourage them from the start to view critically the material they read in the text. We are able to counter their previous socialization—that suggests women's experiences do not matter—by incorporating their experiences into the data on which learning is based.

In addition to changes in the way we present traditional concepts, and/or reconceptualize some of them, we discovered that the material we need readily transcends the more traditional disciplinary boundaries. Including work from urban planning, architecture, and environmental psychology in the community course, or ideas from social psychology, cultural anthropology, and global education in the consideration of power, are examples of the kinds of interdisciplinary extension we demand of ourselves. Last, we have found that by including action-oriented and self-reflective components in our program, we are forefronting issues rarely raised in such courses, but which are critical if we believe these courses should function as more than a passive vehicle for the transmission of the accumulated wisdom of the disciplines.

Transforming the Teacher: A Self-Assessment

While developing the changes in the specific courses outlined above, and as we became increasingly sensitive to how the dominant academic discourse had shaped our definitions of what was appropriate pedagogical form and content in the various areas, we necessarily came face to face with the roots of our own personal and professional identities. We came to ask why we considered what we had previously been doing to be "good" or "sound." We were forced to reevaluate our training and the types of analyses that seemed "natural" and "right." Adding new material was really not the problem. The real difficulty came in determining what to delete.

Most of us find, when we organize our courses, that we want to include more material than is possible given the constraints of time and student tolerance for assignments. For the most part, what is essential in any given course has been determined for us both by our training and the textbooks in our disciplines. Transforming the curriculum, however, requires us to question our previous training and to reject the traditional textbooks. This forces us to start from scratch to determine what is essential, as well as which of the materials that we had traditionally included might be deleted without damage to our students' disciplinary training.

Our own androcentric training and socialization make us uncomfortable about deleting material that *we* had to learn, that makes up the definition of "rigor." We end up confronting our own guilt about supposedly "softening" a course by removing certain content, as if retention of that canon were the only operant criterion for educational effectiveness. It is not. Time and time again we are forced to go to the roots of our disciplines to question what it is we need to know and how we can best understand it.

As a woman and a political scientist I (Salem) have been amazed at the blinders imposed by my disciplinary training. I had no difficulty in applying the more traditional approaches of my discipline to women, i.e., voting behavior, political socialization, and similar topics. I have been challenged, however, by the need to extend my interdisciplinary expertise when I shifted my focus from the approach that examines the political system from the perspective of the power-holder, to one that starts at the bottom and looks at the experiences of those who bear the consequences of the decisions made and the policies implemented.

As a man and a sociologist, I (Sharkey) came to realize how in my teaching (and probably my life as a whole) I was subtly playing out the distinction Gerda Lerner identified between "being humanitarian" and "being a humanist," a pedagogical version of the body/mind dichotomy. The former means acting well, being a good person, using knowledge to make life better for others. It is grounded in experience, and has been designated "the female sphere." Women nurture, care for, worry about, patch up, and weep for people. The latter explicates the *theory* of how best to do all these things. It is grounded in abstraction and academic expertise, and has been designated "the male sphere." Men debate the principles of caring, or design plans for others to be humanitarian. I viewed teaching as explaining well—or cleverly—the theories about how society works and how to be a good (non-alienated) person. I spoke *at* students, even as I spoke about how involved they were supposed to be in their own education. I was a wonderful humanist. My recent experience clearly challenges this whole notion; I suppose I am "feminized," but I am also more of a humanitarian, and my teaching is more worthwhile for me and more effective for the students.

The team-teaching approach has been as instructive for us as it has been for our students. We share with each other and with them particular behaviors that are rooted in our gender-role socialization. Thus Stephen must be constrained when he anxiously wants to tell the students what to do and how it should be done. Although he has an ideological commitment to empowering our students, he cannot rid himself of the fear of "losing control" of the class. Greta has been active as a teacher and a scholar in efforts to help women to take their own ideas and intellects seriously. Yet she must continually control her urge to laugh self-deprecatingly when she makes a strong point in front of the class.

By openly sharing these difficulties with our students, we model most effectively the consequences of our gender-role socialization as well as the personal effort and commitment required to transcend it. And by confronting together the challenges involved in changing both the substance of the curriculum and our behavior, we show that such changes need not necessarily be divisive, but in fact can enhance the intellectual development and personal horizons of both men and women.

We have seen, through their performance on assessments, work in on- and off-campus groups, and so forth, that our students have changed in several ways. They have been challenged to look into their own histories and experiences for insight, and have thus gained status for themselves as a source of knowledge and understanding. But most important, they have begun to see that society is not something out there, apart from them. In the beginning of our program students frequently talk about society or government as about some distant entity controlling them, but with which they have no connection and for which they have no responsibility. This empirically changes. And further, much of what we talk about allows our returning women students to put their personal problems into context. Because of the age mix in our classes, their articulation allows our traditional-age students to understand better the different ways in which groups of women experience their environment, and to recognize critical differences within gender.

We share with our students a basic orientation of questioning how knowledge is structured, and how knowledge is to be used. We expect, as we continue our work, to further revise our teaching approaches and conceptual paradigms, and to move beyond traditional disciplinary boundaries as the issues we are considering require.

The Dynamics of Change:
Key Elements in Curricular Transformation

We have adapted our program in three major ways. Substantively, we have incorporated women's experiences, issues, and perspectives into the content of the courses, by which we mean our behavior as teachers and students as well as our reading material. As a result, we have needed to reorganize the conceptual frameworks of our courses. Procedurally, we have included classroom experiences designed to help students develop a tolerance for ambiguity, as well as the interpersonal and intellectual skills necessary both to understand and to manage conflict. Finally, we have demystified the conceptualization process by helping our students participate in it on the basis of their own experience, and also, by opening our own professional development up to the students for scrutiny, to humanize it.

Although our strategies for changing the curriculum were developed within the particular context of a women's college with a strong commitment to experiential education, they would be very effective in any liberal arts institution—certainly coeducational ones—given several conditions. First, faculty need to be given the development time gradually to rethink their teaching approach, and be rewarded, or at least not punished, for doing so. Second, definitions of "the discipline" must be able to be questioned, and some institutional commitment must be given to helping interested faculty raise such questions. It helps if male faculty pursuing such questions are encouraged, and gender is not defined as only a women's interest or topic. Third, faculty-student ratios should ideally be kept low enough so that the kind of gender-role modeling we attempted may be effective inside and outside the classroom. Some of this modeling could be accomplished even in very large courses, as well, by redefining teaching assistant activities, or by encouraging the creation of male-female teaching partnerships for big sections.

We are convinced that all the changes we identify introduced a balance to the curriculum that was absent when the experiences of women were omitted—and their needs not addressed. Furthermore, because we now focus on the entire human experience rather than one half of it, we enrich the total educational process. This is a goal to be shared by good educators everywhere.

Notes

1. Carol Tavris and Carole Offir, *The Longest War: Sex Differences in Perspective* (New York: Harcourt Brace Jovanovich, 1977), especially chap. 6.
2. Greta Salem, "Participation and Education: Power Sharing in the Classroom," *Teaching Political Science* (April 1978): 307–17.
3. Marcia Mentkowski and Michael Strait, "A Longitudinal Study of Student Change in Cognitive Development, Learning Styles, and Generic Abilities in an Outcome-Centered Liberal Arts Curriculum," A final report to the National Institute of Education: Research Report No. 6 (Milwaukee, Wis.: Alverno Productions, 1983).
4. Alverno College Faculty, *Liberal Learning at Alverno College* (Milwaukee, Wis.: Alverno Productions, 1976; revised 1981).
5. Patricia Balch, *Women in Public life in Wisconsin* (Milwaukee: Alverno Productions, 1970; revised 1981).
6. Nancy Klein and Greta Salem, *Learning Through Problem Solving: An Introduction to Society*, 1976; a manual.
7. Salem, *Teaching Political Science*, p. 315.
8. Jean Baker Miller, *Toward a New Psychology of Women* (Boston: Beacon Press, 1976).
9. Jo Freeman, "Women and Urban Policy," in *Women and the American City*, edited by Catharine Stimpson, Elsa Dixler, M. Nelson, and Kathryn Yatrakis (Chicago: University of Chicago Press, 1981).

10. Gerda Wekerle, Rebecca Peterson, and David Morely, eds., *New Space For Women* (Boulder, Colo.: Westview Press, 1980).

11. Warren Paap, "The Concept of Power: Treatment in Fifty Introductory Sociology Textbooks," *Teaching Sociology* 9, no. 1 (October 1981): 57–58.

12. Shulamit Reinharz, *On Becoming a Social Scientist* (San Francisco: Josey-Bass, 1979).

Appendix: Syllabus 1

SPS 100
INTRODUCTORY SOCIAL SCIENCE: THE SOCIAL SYSTEM

Stephen Sharkey and Greta Salem
Social Science and Policy Studies/Behavioral Sciences
Alverno College

I. Purpose of the Course

To be human is to be social. To *understand* oneself and *act* meaningfully therefore involves studying the social context in which and through which we live out our lives. Social Science—defined as the systematic analysis of patterned social relationships—focuses on the ways we simultaneously *create* our social context from the premise that each of us both makes and is made by our social experience. The course seeks to help you develop an awareness of this complex press—that is, to introduce you to your relationship to the broader society—in two ways: first, by conducting research on a current social problem, and second, by analyzing the small-scale social system which emerges in the classroom as you carry out your research.

By organizing yourselves to perform a useful piece of social research, and by reflecting systematically on what happens when you do so, we hope that you will acquire both a basic understanding of contemporary social structure, as well as insight into the skills you need to take greater control of your own lives as members of this society.

II. Textbooks and Prerequisites

There are two required texts for this course:

- Nancy Klein and Greta Salem, *Learning Through Problem-Solving: An Introduction to Society* (a manual, attached to this syllabus)
- Barbara Ehrenreich and Deirdre English, *Complaints and Disorders: The Sexual Politics of Sickness* (Old Westbury: The Feminist Press, 1973)

III. Specific Course Objectives and Competences Offered

To reiterate, in this course you have the twin goals of organizing yourselves to perform social research, and reflecting analytically on that experience. Several specific objectives flow out of these goals, which will be pursued via the development of particular competences, or skills. These objectives, and the competences that they relate to, are as follows:

1. to develop your ability to make observations of and inferences about social phenomena;
2. to develop your ability to see *patterns* in social phenomena, and link such patterns to the broader historical context in which they occur;
3. to become aware of the effects of the existing political-economic structure on your values and behavior;
4. and finally, to develop your ability to formulate and communicate to others a convincing social scientific argument, by acquiring some basic research skills.

IV. The Course Structure

SPS 100 is divided into two main parts with a transition to link them. In Part One, members of the class are *introduced to a set of basic concepts and principles*, which can help you *organize as a group to choose and define a social problem for study*, and then *analyze some approaches for dealing with it.* Hopefully your analysis of approaches should lead to the formation of some concrete proposals.

After you build up your basic social scientific vocabulary, and practice some essential decision-making and interpersonal skills, the traditional role of the teacher will change, and so will yours. Decisions about which problem to study, how to organize the class to get the research done, what readings or other resources must be handled, and so forth, will be left to you. The instructor will provide some "external" feedback on how you're doing, via comments on checkpoint assignments, and in a one-to-one conference available for consultation on technical matters related to the discipline, when invited to provide it.

In Part Two of the course, we will concentrate on building a coherent general theory of how contemporary American society works, moving from issues that emerge from your experience during your life chances, as well as strategies that have been proposed for making our lives more humane. We will study a set of readings on three "central ideas," including the book by Ehrenreich and English. The instructor's role in this phase of the course will probably be more directive.

Since what actually occurs among you as a class group is a source of primary data which you'll be asked regularly to analyze, *attendance at scheduled sessions is required.*

V. A Topical Outline, Tentative Schedule, and Definition of Assignments

Part One   Introduction to Society Through Problem-Solving

Approximately 12 weeks, from August 24th to November 16th. Apart from readings and group discussion, the course goals and objectives will be pursued in this portion of the course through

- two brief autobiographical exercises
- an in-class short answer quiz
- a midpoint take-home essay
- an extensive journal kept on a regular basis
- two 1-page analytic papers
- a concluding take-home essay exam.

The autobiographical exercises are meant to help you see connections between your personal experience and that of others. There are *patterns* in your collective life which can be examined and understood, once they've been uncovered.

The in-class quiz is meant simply to test your knowledge of basic terms and concepts needed to analyze and speak intelligently about the patterns you observe directly or study in the readings.

The midpoint take-home essay serves essentially the same purpose, by giving you your first chance to lay out an interpretation of some of the patterns emerging in the classroom.

The journal provides a vehicle for you to develop observational skills. In it you should record all the activities related to the class project, including your own reactions to what happens, and keep track of information you gather as part of your contribution to the research process via interviews, library investigations, or whatever. the journal will be reviewed and critiqued on how well you're developing it as a source of meaningful data. Check the manual for more specific guidelines about what should go into it.

The two brief analytic papers will focus directly on material you gather in your journal, and are meant to give you practice in applying social scientific concepts to interpret what you systematically observe.

The last assignment for Part One, the take-home essay exam, will ask you to analyze the total problem-solving process and experience to date, and comment on the adequacy of any proposals that were developed to confront the social problem selected for investigation.

A tentative schedule and partial reading list appears below. Remember that you as a class may wish to add materials.

Week 1   Basic Introduction
8/24–   Readings: Klein and Salem manual, chs. 1 and 2
8/26   Syllabus
                 H. Gracey, "Learning the Student Role:
                     Kindergarten as Academic Boot Camp"
             Learning Experiences: lecture/discussion
                             Who Am I exercise
             Assignments: Autobiographical exercises

Week 2   Culture and Social Organization
8/31–   Readings: H. Bagish, "Confessions of a Former
9/2   Cultural Relativist"
                 C. Turnbull, "The Forest People"
                 W. Arens, "The Great American Football
                     Hero"
                 W. Chambliss and T. Ryther, "Varieties
                     of Human Experience"
             Learning Experiences: lecture/discussion
                             analysis of Who Am I and
                             one of the autobiographical
                             exercises

Week 3   The Nature of Social Problems
9/7–   Readings: Klein and Salem manual, ch. 3
  9/9   *Reread* the syllabus
                C.W. Mills, "The Sociological Imagination"
                Schneider, Stephan, Zurcher, and Ekland-Olson, "Social Problems: What They Are and How to Analyze Them"
        Learning Experiences: lecture/discussion
                film, "Equality vs. Social Class"
                Small and Large Group Interaction exercise
        Assignments: in-class quiz on Wed. 9/7
                begin keeping your journal after the Friday 9/9 class session

Week 4   Group Strategies for Studying a Social Problem
9/14–   Readings: to be designated
  9/16   Learning Experiences: lecture/discussion
                Brainstorming, Learning to Listen, Ugli Orange exercises
        Assignments: continue your journal . . . in fact keep it for the rest of Part One
                Midpoint take-home essay distributed Friday 9/16, due back *Wed. 9/21* in class

Week 5   Transition
9/21–   Readings: nothing new at this point; be sure to have
  9/23   completed everything assigned so far.
        Learning Experiences: On Wed. 9/21, we'll wrap up the discussion of basic concepts, so bring any questions you have. We'll also set up the schedule of one-to-one conferences with the instructor. Finally, we'll discuss some logistics for your takeover of the class.

**Friday, 9/23, you'll assume responsibility for the class.
You'll have responsibility for it until Friday, November 4th.**

Part Two The Nature of Community, Power, and Change
Approximately 5 weeks, from Nov. 10th to Dec. 10th.
In this part of the course, we try to summarize what you've
learned during Part One, and then build on it by refining your
grasp of how social systems in general—including your own mini-
system—work. We'll deal with this by studying three "central
ideas," those indicated in the title above. *There is only one assessment during Part Two: a take-home essay passed out on the last
day of the semester.* Below is a tentative schedule.

Week 12   What Do We Already Know?
11/10–   Is Every Group Like This!?
11/12   a film, "Lord of the Flies," is scheduled for 11/10.

Week 13   What is a Community? From Local to Global Visions
11/17–   Readings: "The Concept of Community" reprint
11/19   W.F. Whyte, "The Spatial Structure of
                        the Restaurant"
                        K. Erikson, "Trauma at Buffalo Creek"

Week 14   Power in the System

Week 15   Readings: Ehrenreich and English, *Complaints and*
11/24–   *Disorders*
12/3   Koen and Swaim, selection from *Ain't
                        Nowhere We Can Run: A Handbook for
                        Women on the Nuclear Mentality*

Week 16   Change for the Better
12/8–   Readings: E.F. Schumacher, "An Economics of Per-
12/10   manence"
                        R. Sennett, "Urban Peace through Dis-
                        order"

Syllabus 2

SPS 102
INTRODUCTORY SOCIAL SCIENCE: THE COMMUNITY

Greta Salem
Social Science Department/Behavioral Sciences
Alverno College

Purpose:

Although most of us spend very little time thinking about it, our day to day activities as well as our attitudes about them are to a large extent influenced by the quality of life available to us in the communities in which we live and work. We accept our local communities as givens. We enjoy the opportunities and resources and we adapt to the discomforts and inconveniences. Some accept the conditions of their lives without question. Others work to resolve what they define as the most pressing local problems. Few, however, ask the fundamental questions that lead us to explore the ideological, social, economic and political forces that shape the local community and our experience within it.

This course provides the opportunity for such an exploration. The local community that we will investigate is defined as a metropolitan area which consists of a central city and the adjacent suburbs and towns which appear to be integrated in one way or another with it. We will explore the metropolis both from the perspective of a range of disciplines that consider different aspects of urban life and from the perspective of the varying groups of urban residents whose experience is to a large extent determined by gender, socio-economic status, race, and ethnicity.

Thus, we will look at the metropolis as:

1. the product of a historical process—the historical perspective
2. the spatial distribution of homes, jobs, services, and cultural and recreational amenities—the ecological perspective
3. as the residential and work locale of varied socio-economic, ethnic and racial groups—the demographic perspective

4. as a locale of jobs, commercial transactions, services and products—the economic perspective
5. as the source of rules and regulations maintaining order in the environment and allocating resources—the political perspective, and,
6. as the locale of tensions, conflicts and disputes concerning the allocation of these resources to deal with the needs and desires of urban residents—the social problem perspective.

Each of these perspectives represents the work of a distinct disciplinary specialty and could easily provide material for a number of individual courses. We utilize them all in our introduction to the urban metropolis so that we can identify all the elements of the community's social and political fabric and begin to understand the nature of their interrelationship. This course then can be compared to the anatomy course with which medical students begin their professional training. It is designed to provide a somewhat superficial view of the whole "body"—the social, political, ecological, demographic and economic fabric of the urban metropolis.

The learning experiences in this course are designed:

1. to help students understand how these perspectives combine in the analysis of problems typically emerging in local communities;
2. to help students develop the technical skills required for learning about their own communities, and
3. to provide opportunities for direct contact with selected community leaders.

This course will be divided into **four major sections:**

In **section one,** we will briefly survey the historical development of the contemporary city. This will allow us to identify the social, economic and political forces involved in determining the shape of the communities in which we live.

In **section two,** we will analyze the problems associated with proposals for the racial integration of schools. This analysis will be used to illustrate both the multiple perspectives required to understand urban problems and to introduce the sociological concepts and theories used to explain how communities work. To conclude this section, each student will: 1) take an assessment on the application of these concepts and 2) produce an ecological analysis of her own community.

Section three will focus primarily on the political systems in the local community. This section will examine political institutions and political leaders. In addition, we will look at the political role of citizens with special attention given to those groups who tend to be least active—women and minorities. In this section each student will interview a public official who represents her and will observe a meeting of either the Milwaukee Common Council or a suburban council or Village Board of Trustees.

The **final section** will focus on the city and the economy. The focus here will be on the dynamics involved in urban economic growth and the particular economic concerns of the Milwaukee area. This section will conclude with a final interpretative essay which will provide an opportunity for each student to synthesize the material she has learned.

Outcomes

At the conclusion of this course students will be able to:

1. identify the environmental components in any metropolitan area
2. understand the ways in which they interrelate and shape the quality of the lives of the various population groupings living there and
3. most importantly, students should emerge with an enhanced ability to formulate educated questions about metropolitan problems and institutions and enhanced skills in diagnosing and developing strategies for dealing with them.

Text and Course Materials:

Lillian B. Rubin, *Busing and Backlash*
John J. Harrigan, *Political Change In the Metropolis*
Jane Jacobs, *The Economy and The City*
Virginia Sapiro, *Women, Political Action and Political Participation*

18

Integrating the Feminist Perspective into Courses in Introductory Biology

Sue V. Rosser

What is a feminist perspective in the sciences? How does it change the way we teach biology, even at the introductory level? Like all the other academic disciplines, science seeks to discover and explore the truth, in particular the laws of the physical and natural world. Biologists examine the realities and interrelationships among the living beings that inhabit the physical world. On our sexually dimorphic planet, an ineluctable aspect of that interrelationship has to do with the interrelationship between the sexes. The feminist perspective developed in recent years in the sciences reveals that what had seemed to be objective research actually reflected a masculine point of view. Building on Thomas Kuhn's work, which demonstrated that scientific theories are not objective and value-free but are paradigms reflecting the social and historical context in which they are conceived, feminist theorists are beginning to show how masculine assumptions have shaped scientific knowledge and theory.

Kuhn's work reveals the fallacy in thinking that, because scientists describe and interpret reality, i.e., facts that can be measured and compared, scientific work is "objective," operates independently of the culture in which it is located.[1] A feminist perspective also forefronts the fact that all investigations are carried out from some perspective. The decisions, either conscious or unconscious, regarding what questions to ask, who will ask them, what data will be collected, who will interpret the data, and what groups will be served by the research, all create a particular vantage point from which knowledge is perceived. In many disciplines perspective is acknowledged, such as a Marxist approach to sociology or a psychoanalytical approach to literature. The more consistent a perspective is with the dominant group in a culture, however, the less likely it is to be visible and acknowledged by members of that group. Science, like all forms of knowledge, is used to serve the dominant ideology; those who share those views or have a stake in their perpetuation act in their own self-interest when they maintain that they are observing objectivity.[2]

Feminist Perspectives and Scientific Objectivity

Evelyn Fox Keller has identified four levels in the various critiques that feminists have made of science.[3] All four claim that science is androcentric, shaped by masculine bias, but there are important distinctions. Beginning with a liberal position and moving toward the more radical, her argument may be summed up as follows:

1. The "liberal critique" charges unfair employment practices: almost all scientists are men.
2. The predominance of men in the sciences has distorted the choice and definition of problems to research, particularly in the health sciences.
3. The design and interpretation of experiments is gender-biased. For example, male rats are taken to represent the species in animal-learning research. Ordinary language is value-laden in ways that are not recognized; this creates bias in the interpretation of findings and in theoretical formulations, particularly in the behavioral and socially oriented sciences.
4. A more radical critique locates androcentric bias even in the "hard" sciences by examining the development of scientific thought in its historical, social, ideological context. Unicausal, hierarchical, competitive theories that reflect certain masculine values are construed as "objective" theories and shape the interpretation of scientific data.

In the same essay Keller demonstrates that the masculine, androcentric bias she and other feminists identify is rooted in a specific white, Western, culturally determined definition of what is masculine and what is feminine. This is important to note at the outset, because in science, as in other fields, feminists argue for a recovery of values conventionally considered feminine, values that have been overshadowed by attitudes conventionally considered masculine. This would mean, for example, a focus on interrelatedness rather than hierarchy, nurturance rather than domination. At the same time, feminists argue, by and large, that there is nothing intrinsically male or female about values that are identified as masculine and feminine in our culture.

The implications of this argument are twofold. First, it recognizes that subordinate groups in our culture have a different experience of the culture and its values than do powerful, white men. An outsider's perspective provides a vantage point from which to view the workings of the dominant ideology. Members of "outsider" groups, women and/or black scientists, for example, begin with a different perspective, whether they are consciously feminists or not and whether they ultimately assimilate into dominant values or not. Second, since values are seen to be culturally constructed rather than innate, both men and women, once aware of the distortions caused by androcentric bias, can contribute to a reconstruction of the scientific enterprise.

That the feminist perspective (a perspective that exposes the androcentric bias of most scientific research and that looks at female behavior and experience as well as male in developing models in biology, for example) has not been widely introduced into most areas of science at the present time is, perhaps, because women have been excluded or have excluded themselves from science. A natural outgrowth of reestablishing the importance of social and historical context in studying science is the recovery of the careers of women scientists. We need to unveil the stories of women scientists such as Rosalind Franklin and Barbara McClintock, to view what they have done, interpret the data, and reassess their role in the history of science. As in other fields, this will take a long time to accomplish, because women scientists have had to learn to view the world, and their discipline, from an androcentric bias in order to be considered successful scientists. The tendency to equate an androcentric perspective with objectivity in scientific fields makes the task of identifying and correcting for androcentric bias a monumental one. Fee, Haraway, Hein, and Keller have described the specific ways in which the very objectivity said to be characteristic of the production of scientific knowledge is in fact a masculine way of relating to the world.[4]

Rossiter has summed up the double difficulty faced by women in science: "as scientists they were atypical women; as women they were unusual scientists."[5]

Transforming Science Courses

As teachers of undergraduates, it is important for us to introduce students to the work of women scientists and to introduce a feminist perspective in science courses, both to make young women realize that science is open to them and to make both young men and women develop a more critical view of scientific method and its application. How does one incorporate the nascent scholarship on women and science into the biology curriculum? How can one integrate the four levels of feminist critique identified by Keller into the standard curriculum? When and where is such an integration appropriate?

The answer to these questions will vary depending on the subject matter and level of the course. For example, it is quite feasible to teach an upper level course on Human Reproduction or Biology of Women from a feminist science theoretical basis, since enough work has been done in this area to permit a transformation of traditional scientific thinking.[6] In contrast, the professor teaching an upper-level course in immunology might be able to integrate only the information of famous women scientists (Franklin, McClintock) who have made contributions to the field and to discuss the way in which the warlike terminology of immunology, which focuses on "competition," "inhibition," and "invasion" as major theories of how cells interact, reflects a militaristic world view.

INTRODUCTORY BIOLOGY

Since the degree to which feminist transformation has affected the fields within biology varies so drastically, how does one integrate this range of transformation into a basic biology course that attempts to introduce the student to all the fields in biology?

After an introduction to the scientific method, most introductory syllabi and textbooks attempt to cover the following five broad fields within biology: the cell, genetics, development, evolution, and ecology. I will indicate some issues that might be raised and an activity or reading that students might do to integrate scholarship on women and a feminist perspective in each of these areas. Many titles useful for teachers preparing courses in the sciences are included in the biology, psychology, and science sections of the *Selected Bibliography for Integrating Research on Women's Experience in the Liberal Arts Curriculum* in part IV, "Resources," at the end of this volume. In addition, specific titles useful for each section of Introductory Biology are included in the appendix to this article.

1. *Scientific Method.* Most introductory biology courses include a presentation of the modern conception of the scientific method. This provides an ideal opportunity for presenting a feminist critique of the methodology of science, which can then be tested when assessing the research and data presented in individual areas. In the feminist critique of the scientific method, the following issues need to be raised: To what extent are the scientific method and the theories derived from it biased by the particular social and historical context of the scientist? To what extent is the language of scientific theories reflective of a particular social and historical period and class? Is the scientific method really an androcentric approach to the world? Is this androcentric bias reflected in experimental design, male subjects and models used for experimentation, and the languge and conceptualization of scientific theories?

A means of making the students aware of how much previous experience and worldview may affect the "objective" reporting of data is to ask them to repeat an experiment that Thomas Kuhn recounts.[7] He showed a deck of cards with a red ace of spades in it to an observer, who reported he had seen a black ace, since that is what he anticipated. This experiment, particularly if it is reenacted by the students, provides a concrete example of how their hypotheses may influence their data collection. This activity can then lead into a discussion of androcentric and other socio-historical biases in data collection and theory formation. An example taken from the work in primate behavior by Jane Lancaster illustrates how the language used to define problems and describe findings is laden with masculine values. Changing the language actually changes our understanding of findings. In her primate studies, Jane Lancaster describes a single-male troop of animals as follows:

> For a female, males are a resource in her environment which she may use to further the survival of herself and her offspring. If environmental conditions are such that the male role can be minimal, a one-male group is likely. Only one male is necessary for a group of females if his only role is to impregnate them.[8]

Her work points out the androcentric bias of primate behavior theories that would describe the above group as a "harem" and consider dominance and subordination in the description of behavior. Researchers have begun to formulate theories based on different perceptions of relationships, which appear to be more scientifically accurate.

2. *The Cell.* A feminist critique has not yet produced theoretical changes in the area of cell biology. The integration of a feminist perspective in this area will probably have to be raised in terms of the language and terminology in which theories are expressed and the very few examples of female scientists who have worked in this area.

Building on the critique of language begun in the first part of the course, students might be asked to make a list of the terminology used to describe cells and their interaction. They should then determine which of those terms are correlated with aggression, war, competition, or other "masculine"-defined characteristics in our society. This activity can be used to lead students to speculate about how the language might transform the theories if more "feminine" characteristics were used to describe the cell interactions. Students might be encouraged to look at the work of the black embryologist E.E. Just in the 1930s, now further substantiated by other scientists, concerning the nature of the interaction of the cell surface with the surrounding environment. Standard theory holds that the cell is in a struggle with the environment; the newer theory, originally proposed by Just, suggests that cooperative processes at the cell surface may be more important.[9]

The career of Barbara McClintock could also serve as an example here. Her research was discounted at the time it was begun because her descriptions and interpretation were counter to the established context of genetic theory. (She has since been awarded the Nobel prize.) She presents an alternative to the view upheld by traditional molecular biology that describes a linear hierarchy giving DNA a central, controlling role. In contrast, she demonstrates DNA in interaction with the entire cellular environment.[10] McClintock's "feeling for the organism" analyzed by Keller in her book by that title presents a direct challenge to the androcentric language and assumptions of the scientific establishment.

3. *Genetics.* McClintock's career provides a good transition to the section on genetics. The study of genetics and DNA provides an excellent locus to raise the issues of the position of women in science and why women are not accepted as "good" scientists. Questions such as why most of the data collection and technical work in science are done by women, while most of the theorizing and decision-making are done by men, must be addressed. Why are hypotheses suggested by women not accepted?

The ideal activity to emphasize the difference between the positions of males and females in science is to ask the students to read *Rosalind Franklin and DNA* by Anne Sayre and *The Double Helix* by James Watson.[11] This pair of books demonstrates the difficulties encountered by women in science in being taken seriously and achieving the necessary research positions. Several excellent resources regarding careers and the position of women in science are now available.

4. *Development.* The area of developmental biology including, for purposes of an introductory course, endocrinology, provides opportunities to begin to raise the issues of how the male models, experimental subjects, and language used to describe those models are beginning to be transformed by a feminist critique.

The evidence from developmental biology that the initial groundplan for development in most species is female will surprise some students who are used to the androcentric Western view that the male is primary in all realms and that the female is derivative or secondary.[12]

The study of parthenogenesis reemphasizes the importance of the female. The student learns that it is the reacting biological system in which the developing egg is located that is important rather than what is applied to the egg (the sperm).[13]

The increasing evidence that most hormones operate on a cyclic rather than steady-state basis raises the question of why male rats and monkeys are used as experimental subjects, when females would obviously provide a more accurate model. With the exception of insulin and the hormones of the female reproductive cycle, traditional endocrinological theory predicted that most hormones are kept constant in level in both males and females. Thus, the male of the species, whether rodent or primate, was chosen as the experimental subject because of his noncyclicity. Yet new techniques of measuring blood hormone levels have demonstrated episodic, rather than steady, patterns of secretion of hormones in both males and females. As Hoffman points out, the rhythmic cycle of hormone secretion, as also portrayed in the cycling female rat, appears to be a more accurate model for the secretion of most hormones. The steady-state theory of hormone secretion developed from the model of the male rat appears to be less accurate for most hormones.[14]

Students can begin to see that the "cleaner" data derived from male models due to their assumed noncyclicity may lead scientists to oversimplified conclusions. Perhaps the "messier" data derived from female models is in fact more reflective of biological complexity.

An explanation of the subtle problems that occur with biochemical conversions of hormones within the body so that an injection of testosterone may be converted to estrogen or another derivative by the time it reaches the brain may lead students to ask questions about proper controls and extrapolating from biochemical to behavioral traits.[15] The effort to find a unique cause or a simple explanation for complex relationships between biochemistry and behavior may, in the name of traditional scientific method, lead to less than adequate science. The researcher may overlook complicated interrelationships and also fail to take into account the social context and interpretations of certain behaviors.

Reading Keller's *A Feeling for the Organism* about Barbara McClintock or Manning's *Black Apollo of Science* about E.E. Just would help a student understand the resistance to ideas outside the mainstream as defined by white, male developmental biologists.

5. *Evolution.* The field of evolution and its subdiscipline, animal behavior, provide ample opportunity for a feminist critique of the language, experimental subjects, data collection, and theoretical conclusions. One may begin by questioning the extent to which Darwin's theory of natural selection was biased by the Victorian social and historical context of its time. One should probably point out to students that Darwin's theoretical language (competition, struggle for existence, survival of the fittest) led to theories of biological determinism as a basis for origins of behavioral difference and abilities, which were used to explain differences of social and economic class during his time.[16] Then many of them will be able to understand the problems of some animal behavior research in which behavior in lower animals is observed in a search for "universal" behavior patterns in males of all species or in all males of a particular order or class, such as primates or mammals. The problems raised by then extrapolating these patterns to humans must be addressed. The claims of sociobiologists that behavior is genetically determined and that differences between males in role, status, and performance are biologically based[17] can then be refuted by explaining the alternative theories to the classical andro- and ethnocentric descriptions of animal behavior now provided by feminist scientists.[18]

Viewing a sociobiology film or videotape and reading a feminist critique of sociobiology should provide students with alternative approaches to the biologically deterministic theory. The Nova tape "Sociobiology" or the film "Sociobiology: Doing What Comes Naturally" are excellent pro-sociobiology visual representations. The article "Sociobiology and Biosociology: Can Science

Prove the Biological Basis of Sex Difference in Behavior?" provides a feminist critique of sociobiology.[19]

6. *Ecology.* Ecology is the one field within biology where the traditional scientific theory and approach are most in harmony with a feminist approach to the subject. Ecology emphasizes the interrelationships between organisms, including human beings, and the earth. Feminists have also focused on the position of human beings as a part of the environmental network. Both ecologists and feminists deplore the position that industrialized Western man has taken as a superior being who has dominion over and the right to exploit the earth and its other living beings, including women. The fusion of feminist and scientific theory in the field of ecology brings together the ultimate goal of the course: the integration of a feminist perspective into science. It is thus the ideal subject matter with which to end the course.

An activity designed to help students to understand the parallels between feminist and ecological theory is to ask them to make the following four lists: (a) the scientific terms they learned to describe ecological processes, (b) the scientific terms they learned to describe Darwin's theory of natural selection, (c) the terms associated with women and/or femininity in American culture, especially white, middle class culture, and (d) the terms associated with men and/or masculinity in white, American culture. Presumably terms such as "cooperation," "dependence," and "importance of relationships" will appear on lists a and c, whereas terms such as "competition," "dominant," and "independent" will appear on lists b and d.

In summary, the issues, activities for students, and readings for faculty in the different areas in biology vary in the extent to which a feminist perspective and scientific theory can be smoothly integrated. Taken together, it becomes evident that the inclusion of a feminist perspective leads to changes in models, experimental subjects, and interpretations of the data. These changes entail more inclusive, enriched theories compared to the traditional, restrictive, unicausal theories. These alternative, multidimensional theories generally provide a more accurate description of the realities of our complex biological world, and they should be integrated into the standard biology curriculum, particularly at the introductory level.

Notes

1. Thomas S. Kuhn, *The Structure of Scientific Revolutions* (Chicago: The University of Chicago Press, 1970).

2. Ruth Hubbard, "Have Only Men Evolved?" in Ruth Hubbard, Mary Sue Henifin, and Barbara Fried, eds., *Women Look at Biology Looking at Women* (Cambridge, Mass: Schenkman Publishing Co., 1979).

3. Evelyn Fox Keller, "Feminism and Science," *Signs: Journal of Women in Culture and Society* 7, no. 3 (1982): 589–602.

4. Elizabeth Fee, "Is Feminism a Threat to Scientific Objectivity?" *International Journal of Women's Studies* 4, no. 4 (1981): 213–33; Fee, "A Feminist Critique of Scientific Objectivity," *Science for the People* 14, no. 4 (1982): 8; Donna Haraway, "Animal Sociology and a Natural Economy of the Body Politic, Part I: A Political Physiology of Dominance" and "Animal Sociology and a Natural Economy of the Body Politic, Part II: The Past is the Contested Zone: Human Nature and Theories of Production and Reproduction in Primate Behavior Studies," *Signs: Journal of Women in Culture and Society* 4, no. 1 (1978): 21–60; Hilde Hein, "Women and Science, Fitting Men to Think About Nature," *International Journal of Women's Studies* 4, no. 4 (1981): 369–77; and Keller, "Feminism and Science."

5. Margaret W. Rossiter, *Women Scientists in America: Struggles and Strategies to 1940* (Baltimore: The Johns Hopkins University Press, 1982) p. xv.

6. Sue V. Rosser, "Teaching About Sexuality and Human Reproduction: Attempting to Include Multiple Perspectives," *Women's Studies Quarterly* 12, no. 4 (Winter 1984).

7. Kuhn, *The Structure of Scientific Revolutions*, pp. 62–63.

8. Jane Lancaster, *Primate Behavior and the Emergence of Human Culture* (New York: Holt, Rinehart and Winston, 1975), p. 34.

9. Kenneth R. Manning, *Black Apollo of Science* (Oxford: Oxford University Press, 1983).

10. Evelyn Fox Keller, *A Feeling for the Organism: The Life and Work of Barbara McClintock* (New York: W.H. Freeman and Co., 1983), and "Feminism and Science."

11. Anne Sayre, *Rosalind Franklin and DNA* (New York: W.W. Norton & Co., 1975); and James D. Watson, *The Double Helix* (New York: Atheneum, 1968; Mentor paperback, 1969).

12. Mary Jane Sherfey, *The Nature and Evolution of Female Sexuality* (New York: Random House, 1972).

13. Manning, *Black Apollo of Science*.

14. Joan C. Hoffman, "Biorhythms in Human Reproduction: The Not-So-Steady States," *Signs: Journal of Women in Culture and Society* 7, no. 4 (1982): 829–44.

15. Ruth Bleier, "Social and Political Bias in Science: An Examination of Animal Studies and Their Generalizations to Human Behavior and Evolution" in Ruth Hubbard and Marian Lowe, eds., *Genes and Gender II* (Staten Island, N.Y.: Gordian Press, 1979), pp. 49–70.

16. Sarah B. Hrdy, *The Woman That Never Evolved* (Cambridge: Harvard University Press, 1981).

17. E.O. Wilson, *Sociobiology: The New Synthesis* (Cambridge: Harvard University Press, 1975).

18. Lancaster, *Primate Behavior*.

19. Ruth Hubbard and Marian Lowe, "Sociobiology and Biosociology: Can Science Prove the Biological Basis of Sex Differences in Behavior?" in Hubbard and Lowe, eds., *Genes and Gender II* (Staten Island, N.Y.: Gordian Press, 1979).

Appendix A:
Additional Readings for Introductory Biology

GENERAL REFERENCES ON SCIENCE AND WOMEN

Bleier, Ruth. *Science and Gender: A Critique of Biology and Its Theories on Women.* See *Resources*: Biology I.
Brighton Women and Science Group. *Alice through the Microscope.* London: Virago, 1980.
Gersh, Eileen S., and Isadore Gersh. *Biology of Women.* Baltimore: University Park Press, 1981.
Hubbard, Ruth, Mary Sue Henifin, and Barbara Fried, eds. *Biological Women—The Convenient Myth: A Collection of Feminist Essays and a Comprehesive Bibliography.* See *Resources*: Biology II.
Lowe, Marian, and Ruth Hubbard, eds. *Woman's Nature: Rationalizations of Inequality.* See *Resources*: Science II.
Rose, Steven, ed. *Towards a Liberatory Biology.* New York: Allison and Busby, 1982.
Sayers, Janet. *Biological Politics: Feminist and Anti-feminist Perspectives.* See *Resources*: Biology I.
Sloane, Ethel. *Biology of Women.* See *Resources*: Biology I.
Special issues of journals devoted to women and science:
Signs: Journal of Women in Culture and Society 4, no. 1 (Autumn 1978).
International Journal of Women's Studies 4, no. 4 (1981).

FEMINIST CRITIQUE OF SCIENTIFIC METHODOLOGY AND HISTORY OF SCIENCE

Arditti, Rita. "Feminism and Science." In Arditti, Brenen, and Cavrak, eds., *Science and Liberation.* See *Resources*: Biology I, Science I.
Bleier, Ruth. "Comment on Haraway's 'In the Beginning Was the World: The Genesis of Biological Theory.'" *Signs: Journal of Women in Culture and Society* 7, no. 3 (1982): 725–27.
_____. "Myths of the Biological Inferiority of Women: An Exploration of the Sociology of Biological Research." Ann Arbor: University of Michigan Papers in Women's Studies, 1982.

Harding, Sandra, and Merill B. Hintikka, eds. *Discovering Reality: Feminist Perspectives on Epistemology, Metaphysics, Methodology, and Philosophy of Science.* See *Resources*: Philosophy I. *Methodology, and Philosophy of Science.* See *Resources*: Philosophy I.

Keller, Evelyn F. "Gender and Science." See *Resources*: Psychology and Education II.

————. "Feminism as an Analytic Tool for the Study of Science." *Academe Bulletin of the American Association of University Professors* 69, no. 5 (1983): 15–21.

Longino, Helen, and Ruth Doell. "Body, Bias, and Behavior: A Comparative Analysis of Reasoning in Two Areas of Biological Science." See *Resources*: Biology II.

Rose, Hilary. "Hand, Brain, and Heart: A Feminist Epistemology for the Natural Sciences." See *Resources*: Science II.

Tuana, Nancy. "Re-fusing Nature/Nurture." *Women's Studies International Forum* 6, no. 6 (1983): 621–32.

THE INFLUENCE OF LANGUAGE ON SCIENCE AND CELL BIOLOGY

Fried, Barbara, "Boys Will Be Boys Will Be Boys." In *Women Look at Biology Looking at Women.* See *Resources*: Science I.

Hogsett, A. Charlotte, and Sue V. Rosser. "Darwin and Sexism: Victorian Causes, Contemporary Effects." In *Women's Studies and the Curriculum*, edited by Marianne Triplette. Winston-Salem, N.C.: Salem College, 1983. Pp. 67–75.

Martyna, Wendy. "Beyond the 'He/Man' Approach: The Case of Non-sexist Language." In *Feminist Frontiers*, edited by Laurel Richardson and Verta Taylor. Reading, Mass.: Addison-Wesley Publishing Co., 1983.

Vetterling-Braggin, Mary, ed. *Sexist Language: A Modern Philosophical Analysis.* See *Resources*: Philosophy I.

THE POSITION OF WOMEN IN SCIENCE AND GENETICS

Goodfield, June. *An Imagined World.* See *Resources*: Science II.

Gornick, Vivian. *Women in Science: Portraits from a World in Transition.* See *Resources*: Science II.

Haber, Louis. *Women Pioneers of Science.* See *Resources*: Science II.

Hubbard, Ruth. "Reflections on the Story of the Double Helix." In *Feminist Frontiers*, edited by Laurel Richardson and Verta Taylor. Reading, Mass.: Addison-Wesley Publishing Co., 1983. Pp. 136–44.

Keller, Evelyn F. "The Anomaly of a Woman in Physics." In *Working It Out: 23 Women Writers, Scientists and Scholars Talk About Their Lives*. See *Resources*: Sociology I.

Malcom, Shirley Mahaley, Paula Quick Hall, and Janet Welsh Brown. *The Double Bind: The Price of Being a Minority Woman in Science*. Washington, D.C.: American Association for the Advancement of Science, 1975.

Martin, Ben R., and John Irvine. "Women in Science—The Astronomical Brain Drain." *Women's Studies International Forum* 5, no. 1 (1982): 41–68.

National Research Council. *Climbing the Academic Ladder: Doctoral Women Scientists in Academe*. Washington, D.C.: National Academy of Sciences, 1979.

Rossiter, Margaret W. *Women Scientists in America: Struggles and Strategies to 1940*. See *Resources*: Science I.

Vetter, Betty M. "Opportunities in Science and Engineering." Scientific Manpower Commission slide-tape presentation produced under NSF Grant No. SPI-7913025, 1980.

———. "Sex Discrimination in the Halls of Science." *Chemical and Engineering News*. March (1980): 37–38.

Weisstein, Naomi. "Adventures of a Woman in Science." In Hubbard, Henifin, and Fried, eds., *Women Look at Biology Looking at Women*. See *Resources*: Science I.

DEVELOPMENTAL BIOLOGY AND ENDOCRINOLOGY

Gordon, Susan. "What's New in Endocrinology? Target: Sex Hormones." *Genes and Gender IV*, edited by Myra Fooden, Susan Gordon, and Betty Hughley. Staten Island, N.Y.: Gordian Press, 1983.

Hoffman, Joan C. "Biorhythms in Human Reproduction: The Not-So-Steady States." *Signs: Journal of Women in Culture and Society* 7, no. 4 (1982): 829–44.

Star, Susan Leigh. "The Politics of Right and Left: Sex Differences in Hemispheric Brain Asymmetry." In Hubbard,

Henifin, and Fried, eds., *Women Look at Biology Looking at Women*. See *Resources*: Science I.

Villars, Trudy. "Sexual Dimorphisms in the Brain and Behavior: Reflections on the Concept." In *Women's Studies and the Curriculum*, edited by Marianne Triplette. Winston-Salem, N.C.: Salem College, 1983.

A FEMINIST VIEW OF EVOLUTION AND SOCIOBIOLOGY

Barash, David. *Sociobiology and Behavior*. New York: Elsevier, 1977.

Blackwell, Antoinette Brown. *The Sexes Throughout Nature*. [1875] Repr. Westport, Conn.: Hyperion Press, 1976.

Chasin, Barbara. "Sociobiology: A Sexist Synthesis." *Science for the People*. May/June 1977.

Dahlberg, Frances, ed. *Woman the Gatherer*. See *Resources*: Anthropology I.

Leavitt, R.R. *Peaceable Primates and Gentle People: Anthropological Approaches to Women's Studies*. New York: Harper & Row, 1975.

Lowe, Marian. "Sociobiology and Sex Differences." *Signs: Journal of Women in Culture and Society* 4, no. 1 (1978): 118–25.

Montagu, Ashley, ed. *Sociobiology Examined*. Oxford: Oxford University Press, 1980.

Reed, Evelyn. *Sexism and Science*. New York: Pathfinder Press, 1978.

Rosser, Sue V. "Androgyny and Sociobiology." *International Journal of Women's Studies* 5, no. 5 (1982): 435–44.

Tanner, Nancy M. *On Becoming Human*. See *Resources*: Anthropology II, Biology II.

FEMINISM AND ECOLOGY

Griffin, Susan. *Women and Nature*. New York: Harper & Row, 1978.

————. "Women and Nature." In *Made from This Earth: An Anthology of Writings*. New York: Harper & Row, 1983.

King, Ynestra. "Toward an Ecological Feminism and a Feminist Ecology." In *Machina Ex Dea: Feminist Perspectives on Technology*, edited by Jean Rothschild. New York: Pergamon Press, 1983.

McStay, Jan R., and Riley E. Dunlap. "Male-Female Differences in Concern for Environmental Quality." *International Journal of Women's Studies* 6, no. 4 (1983): 291–301.

Merchant, Carolyn. *The Death of Nature: Women, Ecology, and the Scientific Revolution.* New York: Harper & Row, 1979.

————. "Mining the Earth's Womb." In *Machina Ex Dea: Feminist Perspectives on Technology,* edited by Joan Rothschild, 1983.

Nelkin, D. "Nuclear Power as a Feminist Issue." *Environment* 23 (1981): 14–20, 38–39.

Pasino, E.M., and J.W. Lousbury. "Sex Differences in Opposition To and Support For Construction of a Proposed Nuclear Power Plant." In *The Behavioral Basis of Design, Book I,* edited by L.M. Ward, S. Coren, A. Gruft, and J.B. Collins. Stroudsburg, Pa.: Dowden, Hutchinson, and Ross, 1976.

Ruether, R.R. *New Woman, New Earth.* See *Resources*: Religion II.

Appendix B: Syllabus

Mary Baldwin College Instructor: Sue V. Rosser
Associate Professor of Biology

0401.110 CONTEMPORARY GENERAL BIOLOGY
Syllabus and Reading List
Fall, 1983

8/29   Introduction to the course and the scientific method.
8/31   In what sense is the scientific method "objective"? (1:1–
        19)
9/2   Discussion of Kuhn experiment done in lab. Atomk and
        molecules (3:36–42)
9/5   NO CLASS–LABOR DAY RECESS
9/7   Macromolecules (6:84–94; 16:284–285)
9/9   Cells (4D:50–70)
9/12   Cells
9/14   Cellular transport (5:71–73; 75–83)
9/16   Cellular communication. Discussion of terminology lists
        describing cells and their interaction generated in lab.
        (14:221–231)
9/19   Glycolysis and respiration (7:102–104)
9/21   Glycolysis and respiration
9/23   Gas exchange (16:292–297)
9/26   Photosynthesis (7:95–102)
9/28   Photosynthesis
9/30   Exam I (covers material up to 9/23)
10/3   Summary of energy transformations (7:115–118)
10/5   Mitosis and meiosis (8:120–140)
10/7   Mitosis and meiosis–LAST DAY TO DROP A CLASS
10/10   Biochemical genetics (10:165–178)
10/12   Biochemical genetics (11:179–185)
10/14   Biochemical genetics. Complete reading of *Rosalind
        Franklin and DNA*
10/17   Gene regulation (11:185–191)
10/19   Patterns of inheritance (9:141–147)
10/21   Patterns of inheritance (9:148–164). Complete reading of
        The Double Helix

10/24   Human genetics. Discussion of positions of women and men in science as portrayed in *Rosalind Franklin and DNA* and *The Double Helix*

10/26   Reproduction: Basic concepts

10/28   Reproduction and development in animals (18:321–350)

10/31   Exam II (covers material up to 10/24)

11/2   Reproduction and development in animals: The initial female groundplan

11/4   Reproduction and development in plants. (23:426–443)

11/7   Reproduction and development in plants. Discussion of *A Feeling for the Organism* (19:365–367)

11/9   Evolution: basic concepts (2:20–34)

11/11   Genetic variation. Videotape: "Sociobiology" (25:468–472)

11/14   The Hardy-Weinberg principle

11/16   Selection (25:472–477)

11/18   Adaptation. Discussion of the article, "Sociobiology and Biosociology: Can Science Prove the Biological Basis of Sex Differences in Behavior?"

11/21   Speciation (25:477–481)

11/23   Diversification (23:394–410)

11/25   NO CLASS—THANKSGIVING RECESS

11/28   Ecology (26:482–495)

11/30   Ecology: Inter-dependence of all organisms (28:510–534)

12/2   Ecology (29:535–538)

12/7   Discussion of lists describing ecological processes, Darwin's theory of natural selection, femininity, and masculinity, generated in lab.

12/9   Exam III (covers material up to 12/7)

12/12   Review and evaluation of course. Can science be taught from a feminist perspective?

12/15   FINAL EXAMINATION—8–10 A.M.

TEXTS: Starr, C. and R. Taggart. *Biology: The Unity and Diversity of Life*. Belmont, California: Wadsworth, 1981. Reading assignments in parentheses are from this text.

Keller, Evelyn F. *A Feeling for the Organism: The Life and Work of Barbara McClintock*. New York: W.H. Freeman and Company, 1983.

Lowe, Marian and Ruth Hubbard. "Sociobiology and Biosociology: Can Science Prove the Biological Basis of Sex Differences in Behavior?" *Genes and Gender II.* R. Hubbard and M. Lowe, eds. New York: Gordian Press, 1979.

Sayre, Anne. *Rosalind Franklin and DNA.* New York: W.W. Norton and Company, Inc. 1975.

Watson, James D. *The Double Helix.* New York: Atheneum, 1968, Mentor, 1969.

IV

Resources

Syllabus Redesign Guidelines

Marilyn R. Schuster and Susan R. Van Dyne

The first step toward transforming traditional courses is to look at the syllabi we now teach. The following guidelines to syllabus redesign for courses in the three major areas of the liberal arts (the humanities, social sciences, and science) propose questions that enable us to identify the conventions that underlie our courses. By asking questions about the four components of a syllabus (goal, content, organization, method) we can begin to identify transformative strategies.

By "syllabus" we mean not only the paper we hand to students at the beginning of the semester, but all the spoken and unspoken principles of selection and organization that govern course structure and content. The written document is, however, crucial. The more clearly we can articulate the goals and expectations we have for ourselves and our students (and that they have for us and the course), the less likely we are to be stalled by silent misperceptions.

Each guideline asks specific questions about each aspect of the syllabus, summarizes key issues for each field, and proposes essential bibliography to aid in finding answers to these questions. Often the conventions of one field can suggest transformative insights to another. These are intended, then, not as finished formulae, but as a stimulus to fresh thinking about the full range of courses that we teach.

Literature and the Arts

What would we learn about conventional syllabi if we asked these questions about their implicit design?

Two kinds of transformation are possible when women, minorities, class, and sexuality are raised as central to our understanding of meaning and art. First, the ways in which we read or see the conventional canon are enriched when women's and minority responses to the canon are heard. Second, our understanding and valuing of women's experience and forms of expression enlarges our sense of what the canon could be.

I. GOAL

Convention

- What is the goal of this course, to cover certain material? To acquaint students with the vocabulary and methods of literary or esthetic forms of inquiry and evaluation?
- How does the course fit in the departmental and liberal arts curriculum?
- Does the course teach students to read and write, observe, interpret and judge? develop informed taste?

Transformation

- What material is considered central to your discipline? What kinds of material are valued most? Who decides?
- How might the teaching of reading and writing, observation, and "taste" change if the gender, race, and class of readers, writers, and artists were explicitly taken into account?
- How might a change in this syllabus affect its relation to the rest of the curriculum?

II. CONTENT

Convention

- Who are the "great writers" or the "great artists" chosen for inclusion in mainstream courses?
- How is greatness defined? What are the most valued movements or periods? Why? How have these definitions changed over time?

• What is the cultural context in which the dominant "taste makers" or critics were formed? What is their gender, race, class? What social and ideological values are inherent in the aesthetic promoted by the canon? Is ideology highlighted or camouflaged by the dominant aesthetic norms?

Transformation

• How does incorporating women's and minorities' responses enrich our sense of the conventional canon and what it means?
• How does understanding women's experience and female forms of self-expression enlarge the canon?
• How might implied hierarchies of value shift if the writing and artistic production of women, minorities, and non-elite classes were valued? How might implied values shift, such as an epic is better than a short story, a novel is more literary than a journal, "finished" is better than informal, individual production is better than collective, public art is better than domestic?

III. ORGANIZATION

Convention

• What is the underlying principle of organization or selection in the syllabus? chronology? great works? genres? movements?
• What norms determine selection? Are these norms derived from a partial sample of literary forms?

Transformation

• Does the principle of organization or do the norms for selection obscure or distort women's experience? the experience of racial and ethnic minorities?
• What other organizing principles could be devised to include works that are now outside the conventional canon?
• Could groups of thematically related works be taught that cut across conventional boundaries of genre and gender? Could alternative responses to a topic (e.g., creation myth,

bildungsroman) by dominant and subordinate groups be paired more visibly on syllabus?

IV. METHOD

Convention

- What methodological assumptions underlie both the content and organization of the syllabus? of canon-formation in your field?
- What questions are asked about form, interpretation, or experience that is worthy of literary or artistic expression? What questions are not asked? are assumed?
- What are the criteria for judgment and where do they come from? What is considered "universal"? objective? significant? lasting?
- What assumptions are made about the creative process, especially with regard to the relationship between the individual and social context? Where do these assumptions come from?

Transformation

- What questions might be asked if gender, race, and class of the writer, artist, reader, and critic were taken into account?
- What surprises, baffles, perplexes us in women's texts? How might these problems lead to new questions and methods of interpretation?
- How do women writers and artists use and test the conventions available to them?
- How are our assumptions about universality and objectivity challenged when gender, race, and class become categories of analysis?

Conclusion

Examination and transformation of syllabi in literature and the arts raise fundamental questions about canon-formation. Further, this process leads to heightened consciousness of the role of context (social, economic, political, aesthetic) in both artistic production and critical interpretation.

Elaine Showalter (see reference below) has summed up the current state of feminist literary theory as providing two modes of inquiry. The first is ideological, concerned with the feminist reader and provides readings, interpretations of texts in and outside of the canon. The second she calls "gynocriticism" and it goes beyond revisionary readings to a close study of literature by women, attempting to define what the *difference* of women's writing is.

Similar modes of inquiry are available in nonverbal arts. By focusing on the specificity of the woman reader, writer, observer, or artist (and the racial or cultural distinctiveness of readers, writers, observers, and artists) conventional concepts about universality, objectivity, the integrity, or autonomy of the text, art object, or standards of judgment are called into serious question.

Essential Bibliography

Bell, Roseann P., Bettye J. Parker and Beverly Guy-Sheftall, eds. *Sturdy Black Bridges*. Garden City, N.Y.: Anchor Books, 1979.

Gilbert, Sandra, and Susan Gubar. "Toward a Feminist Poetics." Part I of *Madwoman in the Attic*. New Haven: Yale University Press, 1979.

Kolodny, Annette. "Dancing Through the Minefield: Some Observations on the Theory, Practice, and Politics of a Feminist Literary Criticism." *Feminist Studies* 6, no. 1 (Spring 1980): 1–25.

Lauter, Paul, ed. *Reconstructing American Literature: Courses, Syllabi, Issues*. Old Westbury, N.Y.: The Feminist Press, 1983.

Showalter, Elaine. "Feminist Criticism in the Wilderness." *Critical Inquiry* 8, no. 2 (Winter 1981): 179–205.

Smith, Barbara. "Toward a Black Feminist Criticism." *Conditions: Two* 1, no. 2 (October 1977): 25–52.

Broude, Norma, and Mary Garrard. *Feminism and Art History: Questioning the Litany*. New York: W.W. Norton, 1982.

Government and History

What would we learn about conventional syllabi if we asked these questions about their implicit design?

A critical analysis of conventional syllabi illustrates that it is not enough to "add" women as a discrete unit. The shape of the discipline comes into question. To transform the syllabus does not

mean sacrificing what we know, but enlarging and deepening
what we can know.

I. GOAL

Convention

- What is the goal of this course? What does it intend to
  accomplish within the department, the liberal arts curriculum?
- Does it inform students about a specific *body of data*?
- Does it enable them to use the *vocabulary* and *methods of a
  discipline's* habitual forms of inquiry?

Transformation

- How would this course change if part of the goal were explicitly to include the study of women's experience, and racial,
  ethnic, and class diversity?
- What bodies of data are privileged in your discipline? why?

II. CONTENT

Who are the *generators of knowledge* in the syllabus and *what
populations are they studying*?

Convention

- Are the generators male or female?
- What is their racial, ethnic, or class background?
- How do these recorders, theorists, generators of meaning
  define what is "historical," "political"?
- Do the value systems of the generators of knowledge in the
  conventional syllabus relegate women, minorities, non-elite
  classes to marginal or subordinate status?

Transformation

- Are the generators of these definitions, and this body of
  knowledge of the same sex, race, cultural or class background
  as the population studied? If not, what is their relationship to
  their subject? (power relationship, historical connection)

- What dominant generalizations emerge? Do they more often correspond to the values of the generators of knowledge or to the populations studied?
- Do the dominant generalizations that account for the experience of white men adequately explain the experience of women? of non-white, non-elite men?
- If women's experience were valued equally with men's, which of the generators of knowledge now on the syllabus would be able to do so? how?

III. ORGANIZATION

Convention

- What is the underlying *principle of organization* or *selection*? chronology? historical periodization? dominant "schools of thought," analytical perspectives? survey of "great thinkers"?

Transformation

- Would women's experience be visible within these categories or periods?
- Are periods, boundaries, landmark events predominantly derived from the experience of men?
- If women's experience were regarded as *central*, what groupings, periods, frames of reference emerge?
- If women's and men's experience are represented as equally valuable to the discipline's body of knowledge, what principle(s) of organization could account for both adequately?

IV. METHOD

What methodological assumptions underlie both the content and the organization of the syllabus?

Convention

- What questions are asked?
- What activity is documented, studied? (e.g., public or private? individual or group? elite or subordinate?)

• What is considered sound evidence?
• What are the criteria for evaluation and interpretation of evidence?

Transformation

• Are questions asked of every group that generalizations intend to represent?
• What questions are *not* asked? why?
• If the evidence of women's experience were documented, how would such data be gathered? judged?
• How would an awareness of gender, racial, and cultural diversity suggest other sources of evidence (oral history, diaries, letters)?

Conclusion

Carl Degler (see reference below), in analyzing the effect of the women's movement in American History, says that recognizing women in history leads to these changes: (a) the discovery of new subjects to be included in formal history, (b) a re-interpretation of old subjects, and (c) the devising of fresh methods for perceiving and analyzing the past.

In poltical science, feminist critiques have shown that essential paradigms (public and private sphere and the privileging of the public) need to be re-examined. At the same time other types of power relationships become important subjects to study (the family, the community).

Essential Bibliography

Degler, Carl. "What the Women's Movement Has Done to American History." *Soundings* 64, no. 4 (Winter 1981): 403–21.
Hull, Gloria T., Patricia Bell Scott, and Barbara Smith, eds. *But Some of Us Are Brave: Black Women's Studies*. Old Westbury, N.Y.: The Feminist Press, 1982.
McIntosh, Peggy. "The Study of Women: Implications for Reconstructing the Liberal Arts Disciplines." *Forum* 4, no. 1 (October 1981): 1–3.
Okin, Susan Moller. *Women in Western Political Thought*. Princeton: Princeton University Press, 1979.

Natural Sciences and Psychology

What would we learn about conventional syllabi if we asked these questions about their implicit design?

Feminist critiques of the natural sciences have brought to light the ways in which blindness about gender and culture have compromised some of the most cherished values in the sciences: objectivity, neutrality, universality of findings. Three areas are of particular interest to the teaching scientist/researcher: how gender and cultural context have determined the choice and definition of problems to be researched, how the language of description and observation is laden with gender and cultural bias, how bias about gender, race, and class is carried into the classroom and laboratory and informs the in eraction between teacher and students.

I. GOAL

Convention

- What is the goal of this course? What is its function in the departmental and liberal arts curriculum?
- Is the goal to expose the students to a body of data? to the language and research techniques of a specific area of scientific inquiry? to make students "science literate" and/or to train a new generation of scientists?

Transformation

- How would the goals of the course change if it were to include a critique of scientific method that included gender, race, and class as categories of analysis? If more conscious attention were paid to the choice of research problems, the uses to which the research is put, who is served by the research?

II. CONTENT

Convention

- What areas of research are privileged, considered most important in your discipline? Where do those values come from? Who benefits from that value system, and what areas or researchers are dismissed as less important?

- What groups are devalued or considered deviant or marginal by the normative descriptions or generalizations about human behavior or capability?

Transformation

- Are the descriptions of representative human behavior derived from a sample limited by gender, race, or class? How would these descriptions change if the samples studied were more inclusive?
- How would the discipline change if women's health issues were considered of primary importance to the majority of researchers in the sciences?
- Who is credited with making the most important discoveries in your field in the last decade? How could the collaborative nature of most research be more tangibly acknowledged and rewarded?

III. ORGANIZATION

Convention

- When is gender relevant in your field? In the design of your departmental curriculum and of individual courses?
- Is female behavior studied primarily in reference to male behavior? in interaction with males?

Transformation

- How could gender be taken into account beyond the study of reproduction or sex roles?
- What new courses or research questions become possible when the interests and needs of women are recognized (e.g., biology of gender, physiology of menstruation and menopause, psychology of women)?

IV. METHOD

Convention

- Are the gender, race, class, and sexuality of the researcher the same as the subject of study? If not, is this difference considered significant in the research design? analysis of findings?

- How often does the language or framework of reference for observing non-human subjects reflect the cultural values of the researcher (e.g., sexual division of labor or traits? focus on male of species as more significant or representative behavior)?
- What techniques are current in your field for ensuring social and cultural neutrality? "scientific objectivity"?

Transformation

- Is any research design ever free of social context? Should it be?
- What social and cultural biases and expectations are carried into the laboratory or into the field that affect the development of women, blacks, and other minorities as scientists differently from the development of white men? What pedagogical strategies could be devised to recognize and correct those social and cultural biases?

Conclusion

In the natural sciences and psychology, as in other fields, this sort of critical examination of syllabi raises questions about the shape of the discipline and more particularly about method. Psychologists are calling into question the polarity that underlies gender description in physiology, behavior, attributes, and capabilities. Evelyn Fox Keller (see reference below) has identified several levels in the critique of the sciences that asserts science is permeated by an androcentric bias:

1. The "liberal critique" charges unfair employment practices: almost all scientists are men.
2. Androcentric bias has distorted the choice and definition of problems, particularly in the health and behavioral sciences.
3. The design and interpretation of experiments is gender-biased. For example, male rats are taken to represent the species in animal-learning research. The androcentric bias of ordinary language shapes the interpretation of findings

and distorts theoretical formulations particularly in the socially oriented sciences.

4. A more radical critique locates androcentric bias even in the "hard" sciences by examining the development of scientific thought in its historical, social, ideological context.

Keller suggests that to the familiar methods of rational and empirical inquiry must be added critical self-reflection. One needs to become aware of the role of the observer in the gathering of data, formulation of theory, interpretation of results.

Essential Bibliography

Fausto-Sterling, Anne. "Course Closeup: The Biology of Gender." *Women's Studies Quarterly* 10, no. 2 (Summer 1982): 17–19.

Gilligan, Carol. *In a Different Voice.* Cambridge: Harvard University Press, 1982.

Hubbard, Ruth, Mary Sue Henifin, and Barbara Fried, eds. *Women Look at Biology Looking at Women.* G.K. Hall and Co., 1979.

Keller, Evelyn Fox. "Feminism and Science." *Signs* 7, no. 3 (Spring 1982): 589–602.

Selected Bibliography for Integrating Research on Women's Experience in the Liberal Arts Curriculum

Compiled by
Marilyn R. Schuster and Susan R. Van Dyne

This bibliography is made possible by contributions from faculty members at Smith College, especially the Advisory Committee on the Study of Women, as well as the participants in the Mellon seminar on the Humanities at the Wellesley Center for Research on Women (1982–83), and by numerous other scholars whose research on women has encouraged and enabled the transformation of the liberal arts curriculum, and by teachers who have tested these materials and perspectives in their classrooms. We are grateful for the careful assistance of Crane Willemse.

Contents

How to Use the Bibliography

The primary goal of the collection is to enable teachers to understand the significance of research on women and to incorporate these insights into every class they teach, whether women-focused or an integrated course.

Because much of the best research on women is interdisciplinary, many of the entries throughout the Bibliography provide crucial insights for a number of academic fields. Teachers should be certain to consult listings for fields related to their own in order to find the full range of relevant titles.

Citations are grouped according to two main categories:

I. *Classroom Use:* Books, anthologies and some essays that teachers have used successfully to present a balanced view of human experience with attention to sex, race, class, and culture, in introductory or intermediate courses in the liberal arts.

II. *Teacher Preparation:* More specialized works, landmark essays, review essays about scholarship on women in each discipline, and theoretical essays about the changing shape of knowledge as a result of this body of data.

Although the primary purpose of this bibliography is to enable faculty to understand the impact of scholarship about women throughout the traditional liberal arts curriculum and to design better integrated courses, we hope this bibliography will also be useful to teachers who want to do research on women. The landmark essays and review essays provide access to the essential bibliography for a research in each field.

Key Resources for Curriculum Transformation

Schmitz, Betty, ed. *Sourcebook for Integrating the Study of Women into the Curriculum.* 1984. $23.50. Prepared by the Northwest Women's Studies Association, with the support of FIPSE, this valuable sourcebook contains directories of resources, additional bibliographies, sample syllabi, and is available from Betty Schmitz, Letters and Science, Montana State University, Bozeman, MT 59717.

Spanier, Bonnie, Alexander Bloom, and Darlene Boroviak, eds. *Toward a Balanced Curriculum: A Sourcebook for Initiating Gender Integration Projects.* Cambridge: Schenkman, 1984. The proceedings of the dissemination conference of the FIPSE-funded Wheaton College project.

Selected working papers from the Wellesley College Center for Research on Women that analyze scholarship on women in particular fields are listed throughout the bibliography. A full listing of current titles is available from the Wellesley College Center for Research on Women, Wellesley, MA 02181.

Several collections of essays assess the impact of scholarship on women in specific academic disciplines:

Abel, Elizabeth, and E.K. Abel, eds. *The SIGNS Reader: Women, Gender and Scholarship*. Chicago: University of Chicago Press, 1983.
Langland, Elizabeth, and Walter Gove, eds. *A Feminist Perspective in the Academy: The Difference It Makes*. University of Chicago Press, 1983.
Sherman, Julia A., and Evelyn Torton Beck, eds. *The Prism of Sex: Essays in the Sociology of Knowledge*. Madison: The University of Wisconsin Press, 1979.
Spender, Dale, ed. *Men's Studies Modified: The Impact of Feminism on the Academic Disciplines*. New York: Pergamon Press Ltd., 1981.

Selected Periodicals About Scholarship on Women's Experience

Multidisciplinary, for a general audience

Chrysalis: A Magazine of Women's Culture. Quarterly, 1976–. Kirsten Grimstad, Managing Editor. The Women's Building, 1729 N. Spring St., Los Angeles, Calif. 90012. $10/yr. ind., $15/yr. inst.
Feminist Studies. 3/year, 1972–. Claire G. Moses, Managing Editor. c/o Women's Studies Program, University of Maryland, College Park, Md. 20742. $15/yr. ind., $30/yr. inst.
Feminist Review. 3/year, 1979–. 11 Carleton Gardens, Brechnock Road, London, N19 5AQ, England. $18/yr. ind., $50/yr. inst.
Frontiers: A Journal of Women Studies. 3/year, 1975–. c/o Women's Studies Program, University of Colorado, Boulder, Colo. 80309. $12/yr. ind., $24/yr. inst. Each issue focuses on a theme.
Quest: A Feminist Quarterly. Quarterly, 1974–. P.O. Box 8843, Washington, D.C. 20003. $9/yr. ind., $25/yr. inst.
SIGNS: Journal of Women in Culture and Society. Quarterly, 1975–. Barbara C. Gelpi, *Signs*, Center for Research on Women, Serra House, Serra St., Stanford University, Stanford, Calif. 94305. $27.50/yr. ind., $55/yr. inst.
The Women's Review of Books. Monthly, 1983–. Linda Gardiner, Editor. c/o Wellesley College Center for Research on Women, Wellesley, Mass. 02181. $12/yr. ind., $25/yr. inst.
Women's Studies International Forum. Bimonthly, 1978–. Dale Spender, Pergamon Press, Inc., Maxwell House, Fairview Park, Elmsford, N.Y. 10523. $30/yr. ind., $95/yr. inst.
Women's Studies Quarterly. quarterly, 1972–. Florence Howe, The Feminist Press, P.O. Box 334, Old Westbury, N.Y. 11568. $18/yr. ind., $25/yr. inst.

Specialized/Disciplinary Journals

Camera Obscura: A Journal of Feminism and Film Theory. 3/year, 1976–. P.O. Box 25899, Los Angeles, Calif. 90025. $10.50/yr. ind., $21/yr. inst.

Concerns: Newsletter of the Women's Caucus of the Modern Language Association. Quarterly, 1971–. Mary Wyer and Annis Pratt, c/o Women's Studies, 209 N. Brooks St., University of Wisconsin, Madison, WI 53706.

Conditions. Semiannual, 1976–, focus on women's writing. P.O. Box 56, Van Brunt Station, Brooklyn, N.Y. 11215. 3 issues: $15/ind., $25/inst.

Harvard Women's Law Journal. Annual, 1978–. Hastings Hall, Harvard Law School, Cambridge, Mass. 02138. $7.

Healthsharing: A Canadian Women's Health Quarterly. Quarterly, 1979–. P.O. Box 230, Station M, Toronto, Ontario M6S 4T3, Canada. $9.50/yr. ind., $16.50/yr. inst.

Heresies: A Feminist Publication on Art & Politics. Quarterly, 1977–. P.O. Box 766, Canal Street Station, New York, N.Y. 11013. $15/yr. ind., $24/yr. inst.

Hypatia: A Journal of Feminist Philosophy. 1983–. Azizah al-Hibri, Editor. c/o Department of Philosophy, Logan Hall CN, University of Pennsylvania, Philadelphia, Pa. 19104. Inaugural issue published by *Women's Studies International Forum* 6, no. 6 (1983).

Jump Cut: A Review of Contemporary Cinema. Quarterly, 1974–. P.O. Box 865, Berkeley, Calif. 94701. $6/four issues.

Psychology of Women Quarterly. Quarterly, 1976–. Human Sciences Press, 72 Fifth Ave., New York, N.Y. 10011. $54/yr. inst., ind. rates available on request.

Sinister Wisdom. Quarterly, 1976–. Literature and art, focus on lesbians. P.O. Box 1023, Rockland, Me. $10/yr. ind., $15/yr. inst.

Tulsa Studies in Women's Literature. 2/yr., 1982–. The University of Tulsa, Tulsa, Okla. 74104. $8/yr. ind., $9/yr. inst.

Woman's Art Journal. Semiannual, 1980–. 7008 Sherwood Dr., Knoxville, Tenn. 37919. $9/yr. ind., $13/yr. inst.

Women and Health. Quarterly, 1976–. The Haworth Press, Inc., 28 E. 22nd St., New York, N.Y. 10010. $32/yr. ind., $60/yr. inst.

Women and Literature. Semiannual, 1973–. Janet M. Todd, Editor. Department of English, Douglass College, Rutgers University, New Brunswick, N.J. 08903. $7/yr.

Women & Politics. Quarterly, 1980–. The Haworth Press, Inc., 28 E. 22nd St., New York, N.Y. 10010. $28/yr. ind., $48/yr. inst.

Women's Rights Law Reporter. Quarterly, 1971–. Rutgers Law School, 15 Washington St., Newark, N.J. 07102. $18/yr. ind., $32/yr. inst.

Women's Studies in Communications. 2/year, 1977–. Janice Schuetz, Department of Speech Communication, University of New Mexico, Albuquerque, N.M. 87131. $12/yr. ind., $15/yr. inst.

For a more complete listing and regularly updated information, see:

Feminist Periodicals. Quarterly, 1980–. Susan E. Searing, Women's Studies Librarian-at-Large, University of Wisconsin System, 112A Memorial Library, 728 State Street, Madison, Wis. 53706. $12/yr ind., $24/yr. inst.

Academic Fields

ANTHROPOLOGY

I. Classroom Use:

Ardener, Shirley, ed. *Perceiving Women*. New York: Halsted Press, 1975.

Dahlberg, Frances, ed. *Woman the Gatherer*. New Haven: Yale University Press, 1981.

Friedl, Ernestine. *Women and Men: An Anthropologist's View*. New York: Holt, Rinehart and Winston, 1975.

Leacock, Eleanor Burke. *Myths of Male Dominance. Collected Articles on Women Cross-Culturally*. New York: Monthly Review Press, 1981.

Lloyd, Barbara, and John Archer, eds. *Exploring Sex Differences*. New York: Academic Press, 1976.

MacCormack, Carol, and Marilyn Strathern, eds. *Nature, Culture and Gender*. New York: Cambridge University Press, 1980.

Ortner, Sherry B. and Harriet Whitehead, eds. *Sexual Meanings: The Cultural Construction of Gender and Sexuality*. New York: Cambridge University Press, 1981.

Reiter, Rayna R., ed. *Toward an Anthropology of Women*. New York: Monthly Review Press, 1975.

Rohrlich-Leavitt, Ruby, ed. *Women Cross-Culturally: Change and Challenge*. Hawthorne, N.Y.: Aldine, 1975.

Rosaldo, Michelle Z. "The Use and Abuse of Anthropology: Reflections on Feminism and Cross-Cultural Understanding." *Signs* 5, no. 3 (1980): 389–417.

Rosaldo, Michelle, and Louise Lamphere, eds. *Woman, Culture, and Society*. Stanford, Calif.: Stanford University Press, 1974.

Sanday, Peggy. *Female Power and Male Dominance: On the Origins of Sexual Inequality*. New York: Cambridge University Press, 1981.

II. Teacher Preparation:

Ardener, Shirley. *Women and Space: Ground Rules and Social Maps*. New York: St. Martin's Press, 1981.

Atkinson, Jane. "Anthropology." *Signs* 8, no. 2 (Winter 1982): 236–58.

Dwyer, Daisy H. "Ideologies of Sexual Inequality and Strategies for Change in Male-Female Relations." *American Ethnologist* 5, no. 2 (1978): 227–40.

Etienne, Mona, and Eleanor Leacock, eds. *Women and Colonization: Anthropological Perspectives*. New York: Praeger, 1980.

Lamphere, Louise. "Review Essay: Anthropology." *Signs* 2, no. 3 (1977): 612–27.

Murphy, Yolanda, and Robert Francis Murphy. *Women of the Forest*. New York: Columbia University Press, 1974.

Nash, June, and Helen Safa, eds. *Sex and Class in Latin America*. New York: Praeger, 1976.

Ortner, Sherry B. "Is Female to Male as Nature Is to Culture?" In *Woman, Culture, and Society*, edited by M.Z. Rosaldo and L. Lamphere. Stanford, Calif.: Stanford University Press, 1974.

Rogers, Susan. "Women's Place: A Critical Review of Anthropological Theory." *Comparative Studies in Society and History* 20, no. 1 (1978): 123–62.

Shapiro, Judith. "Anthropology and the Study of Gender." *Soundings* 64, no. 4 (1981): 446–65. Reprinted in *A Feminist Perspective in the Academy*, edited by E. Langland and W. Gove. Chicago: University of Chicago Press, 1983.

Tanner, Nancy M. *On Becoming Human*. New York: Cambridge University Press, 1981.

Tiffany, Sharon. "Models and the Social Anthropology of Women: A Preliminary Assessment." *Man* 13, no. 1 (1978): 34–51.

Weiner, Annette B. *Women of Value, Men of Reknown*. Austin: University of Texas Press, 1976.

ART

I. Classroom Use:

Broude, Norma, and Mary Garrard, eds. *Feminism and Art History: Questioning the Litany*. New York: Harper & Row, 1982.

Callen, Anthea. *Women Artists of the Arts and Crafts Movement. 1870–1914*. New York: Pantheon Books, 1974.

Fine, Elsa H. *Women and Art: A History of Women Painters and Sculptors from the Renaissance to the Twentieth Century*. Montclair, N.J.: Allanheld & Schram, 1978.

Harris, Ann S., and Linda Nochlin. *Women Artists: 1550–1950*. Los Angeles, Calif.: Los Angeles County Museum of Art, 1976.

Hayden, Dolores. *The Grand Domestic Revolution: A History of Feminist Designs for American Homes, Neighborhoods, and Cities*. Cambridge: M.I.T. Press, 1981.

Hess, Thomas, and Elizabeth Baker, eds. *Art and Sexual Politics*. New York: Macmillan, 1973.

Lippard, Lucy R. *From the Center: Feminist Essays on Women's Art*. New York: E.P. Dutton, 1976.

Nemser, Cindy. *Art Talk*. New York: Charles Scribner's Sons, 1975.

Nochlin, Linda, and Thomas B. Hess, eds. *Art News Annual: Woman as Sex Object*. New York: Newsweek Books, 1972.

Petersen, Karen, and J.J. Wilson. *Women Artists: Recognition and Reappraisal from the Early Middle Ages to the Twentieth Century*. New York: Harper & Row, 1976.

Pollock, Griselda, and Rozsica Parker. *Old Mistresses: Women, Art, and Ideology*. New York: Pantheon Books, 1981.

Rubinstein, Charlotte S. *American Women Artists From Early Indian Times to the Present*. Boston: G.K. Hall, 1982.

Sherman, Claire R., and Adele Holcomb, eds. *Women as Interpreters of the Visual Arts, 1820–1979*. Westport, Conn.: Greenwood Press, 1981.

Torre, Susana, ed. *Women in American Architecture: A Historic and Contemporary Perspective*. New York: Watson-Guptill, 1977.

Tufts, Eleanor. *Our Hidden Heritage: Five Centuries of Women Artists*. New York: Paddington Press, 1974.

Wright, Gwendolyn. *Moralism and the Model Home: Domestic Architecture and Cultural Conflict in Chicago, 1873–1913*. Chicago: University of Chicago Press, 1980.

II. Teacher Preparation:

Alpers, Svetlana. "Is Art History?" *Daedalus* 106, no. 3 (1977): 1–13.

Bachman, Donna, and Sherry Pilard. *Women Artists: An Historical, Contemporary and Feminist Bibliography.* Metuchen, N.J.: Scarecrow Press, 1978.
Bonfante, Larissa. "Etruscan Women: A Question of Interpretation." *Archaeology* 26 (October 1973): 242–49.
Carr, A.W. "Woman Artists in the Middle Ages." *Feminist Art Journal* 5, no. 1 (1976): 5–9, 26.
Chiarmonte, Paula. *Art Documentation* 1, no. 5 (October 1982). Issue on "Women Artists: A Resource and Research Guide."
Comini, Alessandra. "State of the Field 1980: The Women Artists of German Expressionism." *Arts Magazine*, November 1980, pp. 47–53.
Duncan, Carol. "The Esthetics of Power in Modern Erotic Art." *Heresies* I (1977): 46–50.
Garrard, Mary. "Artemisia Gentileschi's Self-Portrait as the Allegory of Painting." *Art Bulletin* 62 (1980): 97–112.
Havelock, Christine. "Mourners on Greek Vases: Remarks on the Social History of Women." In Broude and Garrard, *Feminism and Art History: Questioning the Litany.*
Hayden, Dolores, and Gwendolyn Wright. "Review Essay: Architecture and Urban Planning." *Signs* 1, no. 4 (1976): 923–33.
Heresies II 3, no. 3 (1981), Issue on "Making Room: Women and Architecture."
Kahr, M.M. "Danae: Virtuous, Voluptuous, Venal Woman." *Art Bulletin* 60 (1978): 43–55.
Kampen, Natalie. "Hellenistic Artists: Female." *Archeologia* 27 (1975): 9–17.
———. *Image and Status: Representations of Roman Working Women in Ostia.* Berlin: Gebr. Mann, 1981.
Kampen, Natalie, and Elizabeth G. Grossman. "Feminism and Methodology: Dynamics of Change in the History of Art and Architecture." Working paper no. 122, Wellesley College Center for Research on Women, 1983.
McNally, Sheila. "The Maenad in Early Greek Art." *Arethusa* 11, nos. 1 and 2 (1978): 101–35.
Orenstein, Gloria. "Review Essay: Art History." *Signs* 1, no. 2 (1975): 505–25.
Prather-Moses, Alice. *The International Dictionary of Women Workers in the Decorative Arts, A Historical Survey from the Distant Past to the Early Decades of the Twentieth Century.* Metuchen, N.J.: Scarecrow Press, 1981.
Russell, H. Diane. "Review Essay: Art History." *Signs* 5, no. 3 (1980): 468–81.
Signs 5, no. 3 (1980). Issue on Women and the American City.
Swerdlow, Amy. "The Greek Citizen Woman in Attic Vase Painting: New Views and New Questions." *Women's Studies* 5 (1978): 267–84.
Tufts, Eleanor. "Beyond Gardner, Gombrich, and Janson: Towards a Total History of Art." *Arts Magazine* 55, no. 8 (1981): 150–54.
Vogel, Lisa. "Fine Arts and Feminism." *Feminist Studies* 2, no. 1 (1974): 3–37.
Will, Elizabeth. "Women in Pompeii." *Archeology* 32 (September–October 1979): 34–43.
Williams, Ora. *American Black Women in the Arts and Social Sciences: A Bibliographic Survey.* Rev. ed. Metuchen, N.J.: Scarecrow Press, 1978.
Wright, Gwendolyn. "On the Fringe of the Profession: Women in American Architecture." In *The Architect*, edited by S. Kostof. New York: Oxford University Press, 1977. Pp. 280–308.
Yeldham, Charlotte. *Women Artists in Nineteenth Century France and England: Their Art Education, Exhibition Opportunities, and Membership, Assessment of*

the Subject Matter of Their Work, and Summary Biographies. New York: Garland Publications, 1983.
Zinserling, Vera. *Women in Greece and Rome.* New York: Abner Schram/Universe Books, 1973.

BIOLOGY

I. Classroom Use:

Arditti, Rita, Patricia Brennan, and Steve Cavrak, eds. *Science and Liberation.* Boston: South End Press, 1980.
Bleier, Ruth. *Science and Gender: A Critique of Biology and Its Theories on Women.* New York: Pergamon Press, 1984.
Dreifus, Claudia, ed. *Seizing Our Bodies: The Politics of Women's Health.* New York: Random House/Vintage, 1978.
Hubbard, Ruth M., Mary Sue Henifin, and Barbara Fried, eds. *Women Look at Biology Looking at Women.* Boston: G.K. Hall & Co., 1979.
Richardson, Laura, and Verta Taylor. *Feminist Frontiers: Rethinking Sex, Gender and Society.* Reading, Mass.: Addison-Wesley, 1983.
Rose, Hilary, and Steven Rose, eds. *Ideology of/in the Natural Sciences.* Boston: G.K. Hall Co., 1980.
Sayers, Janet. *Biological Politics: Feminist and Anti-feminist Perspectives.* New York: Methuen/Tavistock Publications, 1982.
Sloane, Ethel. *Biology of Women.* New York: John Wiley, 1980.
Walsh, Mary Roth. *Doctors Wanted, No Women Need Apply: Sexual Barriers in the Medical Profession, 1835–1975.* New Haven: Yale University Press, 1977.

II. Teacher Preparation:

Ann Arbor Science for the People Collective, ed. *Biology as a Social Weapon.* Minneapolis: Burgess Publishing Co., 1977.
Baker, Susan. "Review Essay: Biological Influences on Human Sex and Gender." *Signs* 6, no. 1 (1980): 80–96.
Caplan, A.L., ed. *The Sociobiology Debate: Readings on Ethical and Scientific Issues.* New York: Harper & Row, 1979.
Chaff, Sandra, Carol Fenichel, Ruth Haimbach, and Nina B. Woodside, eds. *Women in Medicine: A Bibliography of the Literature on Women Physicians.* Metuchen, N.J.: Scarecrow Press, 1977.
Ehrenreich, Barbara, and Deirdre English, eds. *For Her Own Good: 150 Years of the Experts' Advice to Women.* New York: Anchor Press/Doubleday, 1978.
Fausto-Sterling, Anne. "Women's Studies and Science." *Women's Studies Quarterly* 8, no. 1 (Winter 1980): 4–7.
———. "Course Closeup: The Biology of Gender." *Women's Studies Quarterly* 10, no. 2 (Summer 1982): 17–19.
Friedman, Richard, Stephen Hunt, Michael Arnoff, and John Clarkin. "Behavior and the Menstrual Cycle." *Signs* 5, no. 4 (Summer 1980): 719–38.
Goodman, Madeleine. "Toward a Biology of Menopause." *Signs* 5, no. 4 (Summer 1980): 739–53.
Hall, D.L. and D. Long. "The Social Implications of the Scientific Study of Sex." *The Scholar and the Feminist IV.* New York: Barnard College Women's Center, 1977. Pp. 11–21. (?)

Haraway, Donna. "In the Beginning Was the Word: The Genesis of Biological Theory." *Signs* 6, no. 3 (1981): 469–82.

Hubbard, Ruth, Mary Sue Henifin, and Barbara Fried, eds. *Biological Woman: The Convenient Myth.* Cambridge: Schenckman, 1982.

Hubbard, Ruth, and Marian Lowe, eds. *Genes and Gender II: Pitfalls in Research on Sex and Gender.* Staten Island, N.Y.: Gordian Press, 1979.

Keller, Evelyn Fox. "Feminism and Science." *Signs* 7, no. 3 (1982): 589–602.

Lancaster, Jane. *Primate Behavior and the Emergence of Human Culture.* New York: Holt, Rinehart and Winston, 1975.

Leeson, Joyce, and Judith Gray. *Women and Medicine.* New York: Methuen/ Tavistock Publications, 1978.

Leifer, Myra. "Pregnancy." *Signs* 5, no. 4 (Summer 1980): 754–65.

Levin, Beatrice. *Women and Medicine.* Metuchen, N.J.: Scarecrow Press, 1980.

Longino, Helen, and Ruth Doell. "Body, Bias, and Behavior: A Comparative Analysis of Reasoning in Two Areas of Biological Science." *Signs* 9, no. 2 (Winter 1983): 206–27.

Markell Morantz, Regina, Cynthia Pomerleau, and Carol Fenichel, eds. *In Her Own Words: Oral Histories of Women Physicians.* Westport, Conn.: Greenwood Press, 1982.

Miller, Patricia, and Martha Fowlkes. "Social and Behavioral Constructions of Female Sexuality." *Signs* 5, no. 4 (Summer 1980): 783–800.

Roberts, Joan L., ed. *Beyond Intellectual Sexism.* New York: David McKay Co., 1976.

Rose, Steven, ed. *Against Biological Determinism.* New York: Allison and Busby, 1982.

Sayre, Anne. *Rosalind Franklin and DNA.* New York: W.W. Norton, 1975.

Schrom Dye, Naomi. "History of Childbirth in America." *Signs* 6, no. 1 (1980): 97–108.

Tanner, Nancy M. *On Becoming Human.* New York: Cambridge University Press, 1981.

Tobach, Ethel, and Betty Rosoff, eds. *Genes and Gender I.* Staten Island, N.Y.: Gordian Press, 1979.

Weisskopf, Susan Contratto. "Maternal Sexuality and Asexual Motherhood." *Signs* 5, no. 4 (Summer 1980): 766–82.

CLASSICS

I. Classroom Use:

Bridenthal, Renate, and Claudia Koonz, eds. *Becoming Visible: Women in European History.* Boston: Houghton-Mifflin, 1977.

Carroll, Berenice A., ed. *Liberating Women's History: Theoretical and Critical Essays.* Champaign: University of Illinois Press, 1976.

Dover, Kenneth J. *Greek Homosexuality.* New York: Random House, 1980.

Foley, Helene P., ed. *Reflections of Women in Antiquity.* New York: Gordon and Breach Science Publishers, 1981.

Friedl, Ernestine. *Women and Men: An Anthropologist's View.* New York: Holt, Rinehart and Winston, 1975.

Lacey, W.K. *The Family in Classical Greece.* Ithaca: Cornell University Press, 1968.

Lefkowitz, Mary. *Heroines and Hysterics.* New York: St. Martin's Press, 1981.
Lefkowitz, Mary, and M.B. Fant. *Women in Greece and Rome.* Sarasota, Fla.: Samuel-Stevens, 1977.
Peradotto, John, and John Sullivan, eds. *Women in the Ancient World: The Arethusa Papers.* Albany: State University of New York Press, 1983.
Pomeroy, Sarah. *Goddesses, Whores, Wives and Slaves: Women in Classical Antiquity.* New York: Schocken, 1976.
Seltman, Charles. *Women in Antiquity.* [1956] Repr. Westport, Conn.: Hyperion Press, 1981.
Slater, Phillip. *The Glory of Hera: Greek Mythology and the Greek Family.* Boston: Beacon Press, 1971.

II. Teacher Preparation:

Arethusa 6, no. 1 (1973). Issue on Women in Antiquity.
Arethusa 11, no. 1–2 (1978). Issue on Women in the Ancient World.
Arthur, Marilyn. "Classics." *Signs* 2, no. 2 (1976): 382–403.
Bacon, Helen. "Women's Two Faces: Sophocles' View of the Tragedy of Oedipus and His Family." *Science and Psychoanalysis*, 1966, pp. 10–24.
Beard, Mary. "The Sexual Status of Vestal Virgins." *Journal of Roman Studies* 70 (1980): 12–27.
Cartledge, Paul. "Spartan Wives: Liberation or License?" *Classical Quarterly* 75, no. 31 (1981): 84–105.
Dickinson, Sheila K. "Women in Antiquity: A Review Article." *Helios* 4 (1976): 59–69.
Finley, Moses I. "The Silent Women of Rome." In Finley, ed., *Aspects of Antiquity.* New York: Penguin Books, 1977. Pp. 129–40.
Goodwater, Leanna. *Women in Antiquity: An Annotated Bibliography.* Metuchen, N.J.: Scarecrow Press, 1975.
Gould, John. "Law, Custom and Myth: Aspects of the Social Position of Women in Classical Athens." *Journal of Hellenic Studies* 100 (1980): 38–59.
Hallett, Judith P. "Sappho and Her Social Context: Sense and Sensuality." *Signs* 4, no. 3 (1979): 447–64.
Hyeob, Sharon, *The Cult of Isis Among Women in the Graeco-Roman World.* London: E.J. Brill, 1975.
Hunter, Virginia J. "Review of *Women in Greece and Rome*, by Lefkowitz, M.R., and M.B. Fant." *Helios* 7, no. 1 (1979–1980): 82–95.
Lefkowitz, Mary. "Critical Stereotypes and the Poetry of Sappho." *Greek, Roman and Byzantine Studies* 14 (1973): 113–23.
MacMullen, Ramsey. "Women in Public in the Roman Empire." *Historia* 29 (1980): 209–18.
Phillips, J.E. "Roman Mothers and the Lives of Their Adult Daughters." *Helios* 6, no. 1 (1978): 1–8.
Pomeroy, Sarah. "Technai kai mousai." *American Journal of Ancient History* 2 (1977): 51–68.
Richter, D.J. "The Position of Women in Classical Athens." *Classical Journal* 67 (1971): 1–8.
Slater, Philip. "The Greek Family in History and Myth." *Arethusa* 7, no. 1 (1974): 9–44.
Thomas, C.G. "Matriarchy in Early Greece: The Bronze and Dark Ages." *Arethusa* 6, no. 2 (1973): 173–95.

Treggiari, Susan. "Jobs in the Houshold of Livia." *Papers of the British School at Rome* 43 (1975): 48–77.
_____. "Jobs for Women." *American Journal of Ancient History* 1 (1976): 75–104.
Women's Studies 8, no. 1–2 (1981). Issue on Women in Antiquity.
Zeitlin, Froma I. "The Dynamics of Misogyny: Myth and Mythmaking in the Oresteia." *Arethusa* 11, no. 1 (1978): 149–84.

ECONOMICS

I. Classroom Use:

Amsden, Alice H. *The Economics of Women and Work*. New York: St. Martin's Press, 1980.
Roserup, Ester. *Women's Role in Economic Development*. New York: St. Martin's Press, 1974.
Brownlee, W. Elliot, and Mary M. Brownlee, eds. *Women in the American Economy: A Documentary History, 1675–1929*. New Haven: Yale University Press, 1976.
Ginzberg, Eli, ed. *Jobs for Americans*. Englewood Cliffs, N.J.: Prentice-Hall, 1976.
Harris, Alice K. *Women Have Always Worked*. Old Westbury, N.Y.: The Feminist Press, 1981.
Iglehart, A.P. *Married Women and Work: 1957 and 1976*. Lexington, Mass.: D.C. Heath, Lexington Books, 1979.
Kreps, Juanita, ed. *Women and the American Economy: A Look to the 1980's*. Englewood Cliffs, N.J.: Prentice-Hall, 1976.
Lloyd, Cynthia B., ed. *Women in the Labor Market*. New York: Columbia University Press, 1979.
Lloyd, Cynthia B., and Beth Niemi. *The Economics of Sex Differentials*. New York: Columbia Univesity Press, 1979.
Smith, Ralph, ed. *The Subtle Revolution: Women at Work*. Washington, D.C.: The Urban Institute Press, 1979.
Stromberg, Ann H., and Shirley Harkess, eds. *Women Working: Theories and Facts in Perspective*. Palo Alto, Calif.: Mayfield, 1978.
Tilly, Louise A., and Joan W. Scott. *Women, Work, and Family*. New York: Holt, Rinehart and Winston, 1978.

II. Teacher Preparation:

Barrett, Nancy S. "Women in the Job Market." In R. Smith, *The Subtle Revolution*.
Bianchi, S.M. *Household Composition and Racial Inequality*. New Brunswick, N.J.: Rutgers University Press, 1981.
Blaxall, Martha, and Barbara Reagan, eds. *Women and the Workplace: The Implications of Occupational Segregation*. Chicago: University of Chicago Press, 1976.
Ferber, Marianne. "Women and Work: Issues of the 1980's." *Signs* 8, no. 2 (Winter 1982): 273–95.
Foner, Phillip. *Women and the American Labor Movement: From Colonial Times to the Eve of WWI*. New York: Free Press, 1979.
McFeely, Mary, *Women's Work in Britain and America from the Nineties to World War I: An Annotated Bibliography*. Boston: G.K. Hall, 1982.
Schiller, Bernard R. *The Economics of Poverty and Discrimination*. Englewood Cliffs, N.J.: Prentice-Hall, 1980.

Schreiber, C.T. *Changing Places: Men and Women in Transitional Occupations.* Cambridge: M.I.T. Press, 1979.

Signs 3, no. 1 (1977). Special issue on Women and National Development: The Complexities of Change.

Tentler, Leslie. *Wage Earning Women: Industrial Work and Family Life in the United States, 1900–1930.* New York: Oxford University Press, 1982.

Treiman, Donald J., and Heidi I. Hartmann, eds. *Women, Work and Wages: Equal Pay for Jobs of Equal Value.* Washington, D.C.: National Academy Press, 1981.

Wallace, Phyllis. *Black Women in the Labor Force.* Cambridge: M.I.T. Press, 1980.

Youssef, Nadia. *Women and Work in Developing Societies.* Westport, Conn.: Greenwood Press, 1975.

GOVERNMENT

I. Classroom Use:

Amundsen, Kristen. *A New Look at the Silenced Majority: Women and American Democracy.* Englewood Cliffs, N.J.: Prentice-Hall, 1977.

Beck, Lois, and Nikki Keddie, eds. *Women in the Muslim World.* Cambridge: Harvard University Press, 1978.

Bourque, Susan C., and Kay B. Warren. *Women of the Andes.* Ann Arbor: University of Michigan Press, 1981.

Caplan, Paula, and Jane M. Bujra, eds. *Women United, Women Divided: Comparative Studies of Ten Contemporary Cultures.* Bloomington: Indiana University Press, 1979.

Chafe, William H. *Women and Equality: Changing Patterns in American Culture.* New York: Oxford University Press, 1977.

Diamond, Irene, ed. *Families, Politics and Public Policy: A Feminist Dialogue on Women and the State.* New York: Longman, 1983.

Eisenstein, Zillah R., ed. *Capitalist Patriarchy and the Case for Socialist Feminism.* New York: Monthly Review Press, 1978.

————. *The Radical Future of Liberal Feminism.* New York: Longman, 1981.

Epstein, Cynthia F., and Rose Laub Coser, eds. *Access to Power: Cross-National Studies of Women and Elites.* Winchester, Mass.: Allen & Unwin, 1980.

Feinstein, Karen, ed. *Working Women and Families.* Beverly Hills, Calif.: Sage, 1979.

Fernea, Eliabeth, and Basima Bezirgan, eds. *Middle Eastern Women Speak.* Austin: University of Texas Press, 1977.

Green, Philip. *The Pursuit of Inequality.* New York: Pantheon, 1981.

————. *Retrieving Democracy: In Search of Civic Equality.* Totowa, N.J.: Rowman & Allanheld, 1985.

Hartsock, Nancy. *Money, Sex and Power: An Essay on Domination and Community.* Feminist Theory Series. New York: Longman, 1981.

Jordan, Winthrop. *White Over Black: American Attitudes Toward the Negro, 1550–1812.* Chapel Hill: University of North Carolina Press, 1968.

Millman, Marcia, and Rosabeth M. Kanter, eds. *Another Voice: Feminist Perspectives on Social Life and Social Science.* New York: Octagon Books, 1975.

Okin, Susan M. *Women in Western Political Thought.* Princeton: Princeton University Press, 1979.

Randall, Vicky. *Women and Politics.* New York: St. Martin's Press, 1982.

Rosenberg, Rosalind. *Beyond Separate Spheres: Intellectual Roots of Modern Feminism.* New Haven: Yale University Press, 1982.

Rowbotham, Sheila. *Women, Resistance, and Revolution.* New York: Pantheon Books, 1972.
Rubin, Lillian B. *Worlds of Pain: Life in the Working Class Family.* New York: Basic Books, 1977.
Tilly, Louise A., and Joan W. Scott. *Women, Work and Family.* New York: Holt, Rinehart and Winston, 1978.
Tinker, Irene, Michelle Bramsen, and Mayra Buvinic, eds. *Women and World Development.* New York: Praeger Press, 1976.
Wekerle, Gerda, Rebecca Peterson, and David Morely, eds. *New Space for Women.* Boulder, Colo.: Westview Press, 1980.

II. Teacher Preparation:

Abadan-Unat, Nermin. *Women in Turkish Society.* London: E.J. Brill, 1982.
Allman, James, ed. *Women's Status and Fertility in the Muslim World.* New York: Praeger Press, 1978.
American Politics Quarterly 5, no. 3 (1977). Issue on Women and Politics.
Blumberg, R.L. "Fairy Tales and Facts: Economy, Family, Fertility and the Female." In Tinker, Bramson, and Buvinic, *Women and World Development.* Pp. 12–21.
Boneparth, Ellen. "Integrating Materials on Women: American Government." *News for Teachers of Political Science* 26 (1980): 1–7.
_____. *Women, Power and Policy.* New York: Pergamon, 1982.
Bourque, Susan C., and Jean Grossholtz. "Politics as Unnatural Practice–Political Science Looks at Female Participation." *Politics and Society* 4, no. 2 (1974): 225–66.
Carroll, Berenice. "Review Essay: Political Science, Part I: American Politics and Political Behavior." *Signs* 5, no. 2 (1979): 289–306.
_____. "Review Essay: Political Science, Part II: International Politics, Comparative Politics, and Feminist Radicals." *Signs* 5, no. 3 (1980): 449–58.
Chafe, William. *The American Woman: Her Changing Social, Economic and Political Roles, 1920–1970.* New York: Oxford University Press, 1974.
Evans, Judith. "Attitudes to Women in American Political Science." *Government and Opposition* 15, no. 1 (1980): 101–14.
Flora, C.B. "The Passive Female and Social Change." In *Female and Male in Latin America: Essays,* edited by A. Pescatello. Pittsburgh: University of Pittsburgh Press, 1979. Pp. 59–86.
Giraldo, Z.I. *Public Policy and the Family.* Lexington, Mass.: D.C. Heath, 1980.
Harris, Barbara. *Beyond Her Sphere: Women and the Professions in American History.* Westport, Conn.: Greenwood Press, 1978.
Hayden, Dolores. *The Grand Domestic Revolution: A History of Feminist Designs for American Homes, Neighborhoods & Cities.* Cambridge: M.I.T. Press, 1981.
Halimi, Gisèle. *The Right to Choose.* St. Lucia: University of Queensland Press, 1977.
Iglitzin, Lynne B. "A Case Study in Patriarchal Politics: Women on Welfare." *American Behavioral Scientist* 17 (March 1974): 487–506.
Jackson, Larry. "Welfare Mothers and Black Liberation." *The Black Scholar* 1, no. 6 (April 1970): 31–37.
Jaggar, Alison M. *Feminist Politics and Human Nature.* Totowa, N.J.: Rowman & Allanheld, 1983.
Journal of Politics 41, no. 2 (1979). Special issue on women and politics.
Kerber, Linda. *Women of the Republic: Intellect and Ideology in Revolutionary America.* Chapel Hill: University of North Carolina Press, 1980.

Lansing, Marjorie, and Sandra Baxter. *Women and Politics: The Invisible Majority.* Ann Arbor: University of Michigan Press, 1981.

Maher, Vanessa. *Women and Property in Morocco: Their Changing Relation to the Process of Social Stratification in the Middle Atlas.* New York: Cambridge University Press, 1974.

Mayo, Marjorie, ed. *Women in the Community.* Boston: Routledge & Kegan Paul, 1977.

Pateman, Carolyn. *The Problem of Political Obligation: A Critical Analysis of Liberal Theory.* New York: John Wiley, 1979.

————. "Women and Consent." *Political Theory* 8, no. 2 (1980): 149–68.

Rohrlich-Levitt, Ruby, ed. *Women Cross-Culturally: Change and Challenge.* Hawthorne, N.Y.: Beresford Book Service, 1975. Distributed by Aldine.

Shanley, Mary L. "Invisible Woman: Thoughts on Teaching Political Philosophy." *News for Teachers of Political Science* no. 24 (1980): 2–4.

Signs 5, no. 3 (1980). Special issue on Women and the American City.

Stewart, Debra, ed. *Women in Local Politics.* Metuchen, N.J.: Scarecrow Press, 1980.

Tinker, Irene. "The Adverse Impact of Development on Women." In Tinker, Bramson, and Buvinic, *Women and World Development.* Pp. 22–34.

HISTORY

I. Classroom Use:

Aptheker, Bettina. *Woman's Legacy: Essays on Race, Sex and Class in American History.* Amherst: University of Massachusetts Press, 1982.

Bell, S.G. *Women: From the Greeks to the French Revolution.* Stanford, Calif.: Stanford University Press, 1980.

Bridenthal, Renate, and Claudia Koonz, eds. *Becoming Visible: Women in European History.* Boston: Houghton-Mifflin, 1977.

Carroll, Berenice, ed. *Liberating Women's History: Theoretical and Critical Essays.* Champaign: University of Illinois Press, 1976.

Chafe, William H. *The American Woman: Her Changing Social, Economic, and Political Roles, 1920–1970.* New York: Oxford University Press, 1974.

Clark, Elizabeth, and Herbert Richardson, eds. *Women and Religion: Readings in the Western Tradition from Aeschylus to Mary Daly.* New York: Harper & Row, 1977.

Cott, Nancy F. *The Bonds of Womanhood: "Woman's Sphere" in New England 1780–1835.* New Haven: Yale University Press, 1978.

Davis, Natalie. *Society and Culture in Early Modern France.* Stanford, Calif.: Stanford University Press, 1975.

Degler, Carl N. *At Odds: Women and the Family in America from the Revolution to the Present.* New York: Oxford University Press, 1980.

Flexner, Eleanor. *Century of Struggle: The Woman's Rights Movement in the United States.* Rev. ed. Cambridge: Harvard University Press, 1975.

Friedman, Jean E., and William G. Shade, eds. *Our American Sisters: Women in American Life and Thought.* 2nd ed. Lexington, Mass.: D.C. Heath, 1982.

Gadol, Joan Kelly. "Did Women Have a Renaissance?" In Bridenthal and Koonz, *Becoming Visible: Women in European History.* Pp. 137–64.

Gordon, Linda. *Woman's Body, Woman's Rights: A Social History of Birth Control in America.* New York: Viking Press, 1976.

Hartman, M.S., and Lois W. Banner, eds. *Clio's Consciousness Raised.* New York: Harper Torchbooks, 1974.

Hellerstein, Erna, Leslie Hume, and Karen Offen, eds. *Victorian Women: A Documentary Account of Women's Lives*. Stanford, Calif.: Stanford University Press, 1980.
Kerber, Linda K. *Women of the Republic: Intellect and Ideology in Revolutionary America*. Chapel Hill: University of North Carolina Press, 1980.
Kerber, Linda K., and J. D. Mathews, eds. *Women's America: Refocusing the Past*. New York: Oxford University Press, 1982.
Labalme, Patricia L., ed. *Beyond Their Sex: Learned Women of the European Past*. New York: N.Y.U. Press, 1980.
Lerner, Gerda, ed. *Black Women in White America: A Documentary History*. New York: Pantheon, 1972.
_____. ed. *The Female Experience: An American Documentary*. Indianapolis: Bobbs-Merrill, 1977.
_____. *The Majority Finds Its Past: Placing Women in History*. New York: Oxford University Press, 1979.
Norton, Mary B. *Liberty's Daughters: The Revolutionary Experience of American Women, 1750–1800*. Boston: Little, Brown, 1980.
O'Faolain, Julia, and Lauro Martines, eds. *Not in God's Image: A History of Women in Europe from the Greeks to the Nineteenth Century*. New York: Harper & Row, 1973.
Pomeroy, Sarah. *Goddesses, Whores, Wives, and Slaves: Women in Classical Antiquity*. New York: Schocken, 1976.
Power, Elaine. "The Position of Women." In *Legacy of the Middle Ages*, edited by C.G. Crump and E.F. Jacob. New York: Oxford University Press, 1926. Pp. 401–33.
Ruether, Rosemary R., ed. *Religion and Sexism: The Image of Women in the Jewish and Christian Traditions*. New York: Simon & Schuster, 1974.
Stuard, Susan M., ed. *Women in Medieval Society*. Philadelphia: University of Pennsylvania Press, 1976.
Vicinus, Martha, ed. *Suffer and Be Still: Women in the Victorian Age*. Bloomington: Indiana University Press, 1972.

II. Teacher Preparation:

Abram, A. "Women Traders in Medieval London." *Economic Journal* 26 (1916): 276–85.
Baker, Derek, ed. *Medieval Women*. New York: Oxford University Press, 1978.
Conway, Jill Ker. *The Female Experience in Eighteenth and Nineteenth Century America: A Guide to the History of Women*. New York: Garland, 1982.
de Mause, Lloyd, ed. *The History of Childhood*. New York: Harper & Row, 1974.
Degler, Carl N. "What the Women's Movement Has Done to American History." *Soundings* 64, no. 4 (1981): 403–21. Repr. in *A Feminist Perspective in the Academy*, edited by E. Langland and W. Gove. Chicago: University of Chicago Press, 1983.
Dubois, Ellen. "The Radicalism of the Women Suffrage Movement: Notes toward the Reconstruction of Nineteenth Century Feminism." *Feminist Studies* 3 (1975): 63–71.
_____. *Feminism and Suffrage; The Emergence of an Independent Women's Movement in America*. Ithaca: Cornell University Press, 1978.
Duby, Georges. *Medieval Marriage: Two Models from Twelfth Century France*. Translated by E. Forster. Baltimore: Johns Hopkins University Press, 1978.
Erikson, Carolly, and Kathleen Casey. "Women in the Middle Ages: A Working Bibliography." *Medieval Studies* 37 (1975): 340–59.

Fairbanks, Carol, and S. Brooks Sundberg. *Farm Women on the Prairie Frontier: A Sourcebook for Canada and the United States.* Metuchen, N.J.: Scarecrow Press, 1983.
Frei, Linda, Marcia Frei, and Joanne Schneider, eds. *Women in Western European History: A Select Chronological, Geographical, and Topical Bibliography from Antiquity to the French Revolution.* Westport, Conn.: Greenwood Press, 1982.
Frontiers, A Journal of Women's Studies 2, no. 2 (1977). Special issue on women's oral history.
Gadol, Joan Kelly. "The Social Relations of the Sexes: Methodological Implications of Women's History." *Signs* 1, no. 4 (1976): 809–23.
Gordon, Linda, Persis Hunt, Elizabeth Pleck, Rochelle Goldberg Ruthchild, and Marcia Scott. "Historians' Phallacies: Sexism in American Historical Writing." In B. Carroll, *Liberating Women's History.* Pp. 55–74.
Harris, Bertha. *Beyond Her Sphere: Women and the Professions in American History.* Westport, Conn.: Greenwood Press, 1978.
Hinding, Andrea, and Clark Chambers, eds. *Women's History Sources; A Guide to Archives and Manuscript Collections in the U.S.* New York: R.R. Bowker, 1979.
James, Edward, Janet Wilson James, and Paul S. Boyer, eds. *Notable American Women 1607–1950: A Bibliographic Dictionary.* Cambridge: Belknap Press of Harvard University Press, 1971.
Jeffrey, J.R. *Frontier Women: The Trans-Mississippi West, 1840–1880.* New York: Hill and Wang, 1979.
Kelly, Joan. *Bibliography in the History of European Women.* 5th ed. Bronxville, N.Y.: Sarah Lawrence College Women's Studies Publication, 1982.
Klink, A.L. "Anglo-Saxon Women and the Law." *Journal of Medieval History* 8 (1982): 107–21.
Litoff, J.B. *American Midwives: 1860 to the Present.* Westport, Conn.: Greenwood Press, 1978.
McDonnell, Ernest. *The Beguines and Beghards in Medieval Culture.* New Brunswick: Rutgers University Press, 1954.
McGaw, Judith. "Women and the History of American Technology." *Signs* 7, no. 4 (1982): 798–828.
Sicherman, Barbara, and Carol Hurd Green, eds. *Notable American Women, The Modern Period: A Bibliographic Dictionary.* Cambridge: Belknap Press of Harvard University Press, 1980.
Sklar, Kathryn K. "American Female Historians in Context, 1770–1930." *Feminist Studies* 3 (1975): 171–84.
Smith-Rosenberg, Carol. "The New Woman and the New History." *Feminist Studies* 3 (1975): 185–98.
Tilly, Louise, and Joan W. Scott. *Women, Work and Family.* New York: Holt, Rinehart & Winston, 1978.
Treggiari, Susan. "Jobs in the Household of Livia." *Papers of the British School at Rome* 43 (1975): 48–77.
————. "Jobs for Women." *American Journal of Ancient History* 1 (1976): 76–104.
Viator 4 (1973). Section on marriage in the Middle Ages.
Vicinus, Martha, ed. *A Widening Sphere: Changing Roles of Victorian Women.* Bloomington: Indiana University Press, 1977.
Wemple, Suzanne. *Women in Frankish Society: Marriage and the Cloister 500 to 900.* Philadelphia: University of Pennsylvania Press, 1981.
Wertheimer, Barbara. *We Were There: The Story of Working Women in America.* New York: Pantheon, 1977.

LITERATURE: ENGLISH AND AMERICAN

I. Classroom Use:

Beaty, Jerome, ed. *The Norton Introduction to Literature: Short Novel.* New York: W.W. Norton, 1981.

Bell, Roseann, Bettye Parker, and Beverley Guy-Sheftall. *Sturdy Black Bridges: Visions of Black Women in Literature.* New York: Anchor Press/Doubleday, 1979.

Bernikow, Louise, ed. *The World Split Open: Four Centuries of Women Poets in England and America, 1552–1950.* New York: Random House, 1974.

Brooks, Cleanth, R. W. B. Lewis, and Robert Penn Warren, eds. *American Literature: The Makers and the Making.* New York: St. Martin's Press, 1973.

Cade, Toni, ed. *The Black Woman: An Anthology.* New York: New American Library, 1974.

Cahill, Susan, ed. *Women and Fiction: Short Stories By and About Women.* New York: New American Library. Vol. 1, 1975. Vol. 2, 1978.

Christian, Barbara. *Black Women Novelists: The Development of a Tradition, 1892–1976.* Westport, Conn.: Greenwood Press, 1980.

Diamond, Arlyn, and Lee R. Edwards, eds. *The Authority of Experience: Essays in Feminist Criticism.* Amherst: University of Massachusetts Press, 1977.

Evans, Mari, ed. *Black Women Writers (1950–1980): A Critical Evaluation.* Garden City, N.Y.: Anchor Press/Doubleday, 1984.

Ferguson, Mary Ann. *Images of Women in Literature.* 3rd ed. Boston: Houghton Mifflin, 1981.

Fisher, Dexter, ed. *The Third Woman: Minority Writers of the United States.* Boston: Houghton Mifflin, 1980.

Howe, Florence, and Ellen Bass, eds. *No More Masks!* New York: Doubleday, 1973.

Katz, Jane, ed. *I Am the Fire of Time: The Voices of Native American Women.* New York: E.P. Dutton, 1977.

Kolodny, Annette. "Dancing through the Minefield: Some Observations on the Theory, Practice and Politics of Feminist Literary Criticism." *Feminist Studies* 6, no. 1 (1980): 1–25.

Mason, Mary G., and Carol Hurd Green, eds. *Journeys: Autobiographical Writings by Women.* Boston: G.K. Hall, 1979.

Moraga, Cherrie, and Gloria Anzaldua, eds. *This Bridge Called My Back: Writings by Radical Women of Color.* New York: Kitchen Table Press, 1981.

Solomon, Barbara, ed. *The Experience of American Women: Thirty Stories.* New York: New American Library, 1978.

Washington, Mary Helen, ed. *Black-Eyed Susans: Classic Stories By and About Black Women.* New York: Anchor/Doubleday, 1975.

————, ed. *Midnight Birds: Stories of Contemporary Black Women Writers.* New York: Anchor/Doubleday, 1980.

II. Teacher Preparation:

Addis, Patricia. *Through a Woman's I: An Annotated Bibliography of American Women's Autobiographical Writings, 1946–1976.* Metuchen, N.J.: Scarecrow Press, 1983.

Auerbach, Nina. *Woman and the Demon: The Life of a Victorian Myth.* Cambridge: Harvard University Press, 1982.

Baym, Nina. *Woman's Fiction: A Guide to Novels by and about Women in America, 1820–1870.* Ithaca: Cornell University Press, 1978.

Bethel, Lorraine, and Barbara Smith, eds. *Conditions: Five* (1979). "The Black Woman's Issue."

Bogle, Donald. *Toms, Coons, Mulattos, Mammys and Bucks.* New York: Viking Press, 1973.

Chown, Linda. "American Critics and Spanish Women Novelists, 1942–1980." *Signs* 9, no. 1 (Autumn 1983): 91–107.

Cole, Phyllis, and Deborah Lambert. "Gender and Race Proposal for Two New Courses." Working Paper no. 115, Wellesley College Center for Research on Women, 1983.

Conklin, Nancy, Brenda McCallum, and Marcia Wade, eds. *The Culture of Southern Black Women, Approaches and Materials.* Archive of American Minority and Women's Studies Program. University: University of Alabama Press, 1983.

Critical Inquiry 8, no. 2 (1981). Special issue on "Writing and Sexual Difference."

Culler, Jonathan. "On Reading as a Woman." *On Deconstruction: Theory and Criticism after Structuralism.* Ithaca: Cornell University Press, 1982. Pp. 43–64.

Davis, Arthur P. *From the Dark Tower: Afro-American Authors, 1900–1960.* Washington, D.C.: Howard University Press, 1974.

Donovan, Josephine, ed. *Feminist Literary Criticism.* Lexington: University Press of Kentucky, 1975.

Duke, Maurice, Jackson R. Bryer, and M. Thomas Inge, eds. *American Women Writers: Biographial Essays.* Westport, Conn.: Greenwood Press, 1983.

Eisenstein, Hester, and Alice Jardine, eds. *The Future of Difference.* Boston: G.K. Hall, 1980.

Fairbanks, Carol. *More Women in Literature: Criticism of the Seventies.* Metuchen, N.J.: Scarecrow Press, 1979.

Fairbanks Myers, Carol. *Women in Literautre: Criticism of the Seventies.* Metuchen, N.J.: Scarecrow Press, 1976.

Felman, Shoshana, ed. *Literature and Psychoanalysis: The Question of Reading Otherwise.* Baltimore: Johns Hopkins University Press, 1982.

Gilbert, Sandra, and Susan Gubar. *The Madwoman in the Attic: The Woman Writer and the Nineteenth Century Imagination.* New Haven: Yale University Press, 1979.

————, eds. *Shakespeare's Sisters: Feminist Essays on Women Poets.* Bloomington: Indiana University Press, 1979.

Green, Rayna. *Native American Women: A Contextual Bibliography.* Bloomington: Indiana University Press, 1983.

Heilbrun, Carolyn, and Catharine Stimpson. "Theories of Feminist Literary Criticism: A Diologue." In Donovan, *Feminist Literary Criticism.*

Hoffman, Lenore, and Deborah Rosenfeld, eds. *Teaching Women's Literature from a Regional Perspective.* New York: Modern Language Association, 1982.

Homans, Margaret. *Women Writers and Poetic Identity.* Princeton: Princeton University Press, 1980.

Howe, Florence. "Feminism and Literature." In *Images of Women in Fiction: Feminist Perspectives*, edited by S. Cornillon. Bowling Green, Ohio: Bowling Green University Popular Press, 1977. Pp. 253–77.

Jacobson, Angeline. *Contemporary Native American Literature: A Selected and Partially Annotated Bibliography.* Metuchen, N.J.: Scarecrow Press, 1977.

Jacobus, Mary, ed. *Women Writing and Writing About Women.* Totowa, N.J.: Barnes and Noble, 1979.

Jehlen, Myra. "Archimedes and the Paradox of Feminist Criticism." *Signs* 6, no. 4 (1981): 575–601.

Jelineck, Estelle, ed. *Women's Autobiography: Essays in Criticism.* Bloomington: Indiana University Press, 1980.

Juhasz, Suzanne. *Naked and Fiery Forms: Modern American Poetry by Women, a New Tradition.* New York: Harper Colophon Books, 1976.

Kent, George. *Blackness and the Adventure of Western Culture.* Chicago: Third World Press, 1972.

_____. "Maya Angelou's *I Know Why the Caged Bird Sings* and Black Autobiographical Tradition." *Kansas Quarterly* 7, no. 3 (1975): 72–78.

Lauter, Paul. "Race and Gender in the Shaping of the American Literary Canon: A Case Study from the Twenties." *Feminist Studies* 9, no. 3 (Fall 1983): 435–63.

_____, ed. *Reconstructing American Literature: Courses, Syllabi, Issues.* Old Westbury, N.Y.: The Feminist Press, 1983.

Loewenberg, Bert J., and Ruth Bogin, eds. *Black Women in the Nineteenth Century: Their Words, Their Thoughts, Their Feelings.* University Park: Pennsylvania State University Press, 1976.

Mainiero, Lina, ed. *American Women Writers: A Critical Reference Guide from Colonial Times to the Present.* New York: Frederick Ungar, 1979–1982.

Mason, Mary, and Martha Chew. "Two Studies: A Feminist Approach to Teaching Non-Traditional Students." Working Paper No. 123, Wellesley College Center for Research on Women, 1983.

Moers, Ellen. *Literary Women.* New York: Doubleday, 1976.

Mora, Gabriela, and Karen S. Van Hooff, eds. *Theory and Practice of Feminist Literary Criticism.* Seattle, Wash.: Bilingual Books, 1982.

Poovey, Mary. *The Proper Lady and The Victorian Writer: Ideology as Style in Mary Wollstonecraft, Mary Shelley, Jane Austen.* Chicago: University of Chicago Press, 1984.

Reardon, Joan, and Kristine Thorsen. *Poetry by American Women, 1900–1975: A Bibliography.* Metuchen, N.J.: Scarecrow Press, 1979.

Rich, Adrienne. *On Lies, Secrets, and Silence: Selected Prose, 1966–1978.* New York: W.W. Norton, 1979.

Register, Cheri. "Literary Criticism." *Signs* 6, no. 2 (1980): 268–82.

Rushing, Andrea B. "Images of Black Women in Afro-American Poetry." *Black World* 24 (September 1975): 18–30.

Showalter, Elaine, "Women and the Literary Curriculum." *College English* 32 (1971): 855–62.

_____. "Literary Criticism." *Signs* 1, no. 2 (1975): 435–60.

_____. *A Literature of Their Own: English Women Novelists from Bronte to Lessing.* Princeton: Princeton University Press, 1977.

Smith, Barbara. "Toward a Black Feminist Criticism." *Conditions: Two* (1977): 25–52.

Spacks, Patricia M. *The Female Imagination.* New York: Alfred A. Knopf, 1975.

_____. "The Difference It Makes." *Soundings* 64, no. 4 (1981): 343–60. Repr. in *A Feminist Perspective*, edited by E. Langland and W. Gove. Chicago: University of Chicago Press, 1983.

Walker, Cheryl. *The Nightingale's Burden: Women Poets and American Culture before 1900.* Bloomington: Indiana University Press, 1982.

Washington, Mary Helen. "Black Women Image Makers." *Black World* 23 (August 1974): 10–18.

Westbrook, Arlen, and Perry Westbrook, eds. *The Writing Women of New England, 1630–1900: An Anthology.* Metuchen, N.J.: Scarecrow Press, 1982.

White, B.A. *American Women Writers: An Annotated Bibliography of Criticism.* New York: Garland, 1977.

LITERATURE: FOREIGN

I. Classroom Use:

Ferre, Rosario. *Sitio a Eros*. Mexico City: Joaquin Mortiz Press, 1980.

Fox-Lockert, Lucia. *Women Novelists in Spain and Spanish America*. Metuchen, N.J.: Scarecrow Press, 1979.

Katz, Naomi, and Nancy Milton, eds. *Fragment from a Lost Diary and Other Stories: Women of Asia, Africa, and Latin America*. New York: Pantheon Books, 1973.

Hermann, E.R., and E.H. Spitz, eds. *German Women Writers of the Twentieth Century*. New York: Pergamon Press, 1978.

Marks, Elaine, and Isabelle de Courtivron, eds. *New French Feminisms*. Amherst: University of Massachusetts Press, 1980; New York: Schocken Books, 1981.

Meyer, Doris, and Margarite Fernandez-Olmos, eds. *Contemporary Women Authors of Latin America*. Brooklyn: Brooklyn College Press, 1983.

Miller, Beth, ed. *Women in Hispanic Literature*. Berkeley: University of California Press, 1983.

Miller, Yvette E., and Charles M. Tatum, eds. *Latin American Women Writers: Yesterday and Today*. Latin American Literary Review. Pittsburgh: University of Pittsburgh Press, 1977.

II. Teacher Preparation:

Albistur, Maite, and Armogathe Daniel. *Histoire du féminisme français du Moyen Age à nos jours*. Paris: des Femmes, 1977.

Beauvoir, Simone de, ed. *Les Femmes s'entêtent*. Paris: Editions Gallimard, 1975.

Burke, Carolyn G. "Report from Paris: Women's Writing and the Women's Movement." *Signs* 3, no. 4 (1978): 843–55.

Chown, Linda. "American Critics and Spanish Women Novelists, 1942–1980." *Signs* 9, no. 1 (1983): 91–107.

Diacritics 5, no. 4 (1975). Special issue on "Textual Politics."

Eisenstein, Hester, and Alice Jardine, eds. *The Future of Difference*. Boston: G.K. Hall, 1980.

Fairbanks, Carol. *More Women in Literature: Criticism of the Seventies*. Metuchen, N.J.: Scarecrow Press, 1979.

Fairbanks Myers, Carol. *Women in Literature: Criticism of the Seventies*. Metuchen, N.J.: Scarecrow Press, 1976.

Feminist Studies 7, no. 2 (1981). Special section "The French Connection."

Gonzáles, Patricia Elena, and Eliana Ortega, eds. *La Sartén por el mango: encuentro de escritoras latinoamericanas*. Río Piedras, P.R.: Ediciones Huracán, 1984.

Guerra-Cunningham, Lucia. "Algunas reflexiones teóricas sobre la novela femenina." *Hispamérica* 10, no. 28 (1981): 29–39.

Jacquette, J.S. "Literary Archetypes and Female Role Alternatives: The Woman and the Novel in Latin America." In *Female and Male in Latin America*, edited by A. Pescatello. Pittsburgh: University of Pittsburgh Press, 1979.

Johnson, Julie Greer. *Women in Colonial Spanish American Literature: Literary Images*. Westport, Conn.: Greenwood Press, 1983.

Kamenszian, Tamara. "Género femenino y género poético." *Revista de la Universidad de Mexico* 40, no. 39 (1984): 11–14.

Lindstrom, Naomi. "Feminist Criticism of Latin American Literature: Bibliographic Notes." *Latin American Research Review* 15, no. 1 (1980): 151–59.

Marks, Elaine. "Women and Literature in France." *Signs* 3, no. 4 (1978): 832–42.
────── . "Lesbian Intertextuality." In *Homosexuality and French Literature*, edited by E. Marks and G. Stambolian. Ithaca: Cornell University Press, 1979.
Mora, Gabriela. "Narradoras hispanoamericanas: vieja y nueva problemática en renovadoras elaboraciones." In *Theory and Practice of Feminist Literary Criticism*, edited by G. Mora and K.S. Van Hooff. Seattle, Wash.: Bilingual Books, 1982.
Revue des Sciences Humaines 168 (1977). Special issue on "Ecriture, Féminité, Féminisme."
Rupp, Leila. "Mothers of the Volk: The Image of Women in Nazi Ideology." *Signs* 3, no. 2 (1977): 362–79.
Signs 7, no. 1 (1981). Issue on "French Feminist Theory."
Weitz, M.C. "An Annotated Bibliography of Recent French Studies on Women." *Contemporary French Civilization*, 3, no. 1 (1979).
Yale French Studies 62 (1981). Special issue: "Feminist Readings: French Texts, American Contexts."

MUSIC

I. Classroom Use:

Ammer, Christine. *Unsung: A History of Women in American Music*. Westport, Conn.: Greenwood Press, 1980.
Block, Adrienne, and Carol Neuls-Bates, eds. *Women in American Music: A Bibliography of Music and Literature*. Westport, Conn.: Greenwood Press, 1979.
Bogin, Meg. *The Women Troubadours*. New York: Paddington Press, 1976.
Bonaventura, Arnaldo. "Le Donne italiane e la musica." *Revista Musicale Italiana* 23 (1925): 519–34.
Borroff, Edith. "Women Composers: Reminescence and History." *College Music Symposium* 15 (1975): 26–33.
Bowers, Jane, and Judith Tick, eds. *Women Making Music: Studies in the Social History of Women Musicians and Composers*. Berkeley: University of California Press, 1982.
Drinker, Sophie. *Women and Music: The Story of Women and Their Relation to Music*. New York: Coward-McCann, 1948.
Krille, Annemarie. *Beitrage zur Geschicte der Musikerziehung und Musikubung der deutschen Frau (von 1750 bis 1820)*. Berlin: Triltsche & Huther, 1938.
Neuls-Bates, Carol. "Five Women Composers, 1587–1875." *Feminist Art Journal* 5 (1976): 32–35.
────── , ed. *Women in Music: An Anthology of Source Readings from the Middle Ages to the Present*. New York: Harper & Row, 1982.
Quasten, Johannes. "The Liturgical Singing of Women in Christian Antiquity." *Catholic Historical Review* 27 (1947): 149–65.
Rokseth, Yvonne. "Les Femmes Musiciennes du XIIe au XIVe Siècle." *Romania* 61 (1935): 464–80.
Rosen, Judith, and Grace Rubin-Rabson. "Why Haven't Women Become Great Composers?" *High Fidelity* 23 (1973): 46–52.

II. Teacher Preparation:

Bowers, Jane. "Teaching about the History of Women in Western Music." *Women's Studies Newsletter* 5, no. 3 (Summer 1977): 11–15.

Claghorn, Gene. *Women Composers and Hymnists: A Concise Biographical Dictionary*. Netuchen, N.J.: Scarecrow Press, 1984.
Cohen, Aaron I., ed. *International Encyclopedia of Women Composers*. New York: R.R. Bowker, 1981.
Handy, D. Antoinette. *Black Women in American Bands and Orchestras*. Metuchen, N.J.: Scarecrow Press, 1981.
Heresies 10. Special issue on Women and Music.
Hixon, Don, and Don Hennessee. *Women in Music: A Bibliography*. Metuchen, N.J.: Scarecrow Press, 1975.
Neuls-Bates, Carol. "Sources and Resources for Women's Studies in American Music." *Notes* 35 (1978): 269–83.
Plummer, J.F., ed. *Vox Feminae: Studies in Medieval Woman's Songs*. Kalamazoo, Mich.: Medieval Institute Publishers, Western Michigan University, 1981.
Pool, Jeannie G. *Women Composers of Classical Music: A Research Guide*. Boston: G.K. Hall, 1982.
Skowronski, JoAnn. *Women in American Music: A Bibliography*. Metuchen, N.J.: Scarecrow Press, 1978.
Stern, Susan. *Women Composers: A Handbook*. Metuchen, N.J.: Scarecrow Press, 1978.
Tick, Judith. "Women as Professional Musicians in the United States, 1870–1900." *Yearbook for International Musical Research*. Vol. 9. Austin: University of Texas, 1973. Pp. 95–133.
_____. "Why Have There Been No Great Women Composers?" *International Musicians* 79 (July 1975): 6, 22.
Weiner Lepage, Jane. *Women Composers, Conductors and Musicians of the Twentieth Century: Selected Biographies – Volumes I and II*. Metuchen, N.J.: Scarecrow Press, 1980 and 1983.
Wood, Elizabeth. "Women in Music." *Signs* 6, no. 2 (1980): 283–97.
Williams, Ora. *American Black Women in the Arts and Social Sciences: A Bibliographic Survey*. Rev. ed. Metuchen, N.J.: Scarecrow Press, 1978.
Zaimont, Judith L., and Karen Famera, eds. *Contemporary Concert Music by Women: A Directory of the Composers and Their Works*. Westport, Conn.: Greenwood Press, 1981.

PHILOSOPHY

I. Classroom Use:

Agonito, Rosemary, ed. *History of Ideas on Woman: A Sourcebook*. New York: G.P. Putnam & Sons, 1977.
Baker, Robert, and Frederick Elliston, eds. *Philosophy and Sex*. Buffalo, N.Y.: Prometheus, 1975.
Bishop, Sharon, and Marjorie Weinzweig, eds. *Philosophy and Women*. Belmont, Calif.: Wadsworth, 1979.
Beauvoir, Simone de. *The Second Sex*. New York: Alfred A. Knopf, 1953.
Bunch, Charlotte, and *Quest* staff, eds. *Building Feminist Theory*. New York: Longman, 1981.
Clark, Lorene, and Lydia Lange, eds. *The Sexism of Social and Political Theory: Women and Reproduction from Plato to Neitzche*. Toronto: University of Toronto Press, 1979.
English, Jane, ed. *Sex Equality*. Englewood Cliffs, N.J.: Prentice-Hall, 1977.

Gould, Carol, ed. *Beyond Domination: New Perspectives on Women and Philosophy.* Totowa, N.J.: Rowman & Allanheld, 1983.
Gould, Carol, and Marx Wartofsky, eds. *Women and Philosophy.* New York: G.P. Putnam & Sons, 1976.
Harding, Sandra, and Merrill Hintikka, eds. *Discovering Reality: Feminist Perspectives on Epistemology, Metaphysics, Methodology and Philosophy of Science.* Boston: D. Reidel, Synthese Library, 1983.
Jaggar, Alison, and Paula R. Struhl, eds. *Feminist Frameworks: Alternative Theoretical Accounts of the Relations Between Women and Men.* New York: McGraw-Hill, 1978.
Koedt, Anne, Ellen Levine, and Anita Rapone, eds. *Radical Feminism.* New York: Time Books, 1973.
Mahowald, Mary, ed. *Philosophy of Woman: Classical to Current Concepts.* Indianapolis: Hackett, 1977.
Ochs, Carol. *Women and Spirituality.* Totowa, N.J.: Rowman & Allanheld, 1983.
Osborne, Martha L., ed. *Women in Western Thought.* New York: Random House, 1978.
Pierce, Christine. "Philosophy." *Signs* 1, no. 2 (1975): 487–503.
Sherman, Julia, and Evelyn Torton Beck, eds. *The Prism of Sex.* Madison: University of Wisconsin Press, 1979.
Soble, Alan, ed. *Philosophy of Sex.* Totowa, N.J.: Rowman and Littlefield, 1980.
Tong, Rosemarie. *Women, Sex, and the Law.* Totowa, N.J.: Rowman & Allanheld, 1983.
Trebilcot, Joyce, ed. *Mothering: Essays in Feminist Theory.* Totowa, N.J.: Rowman & Allanheld, 1983.
Vetterling-Braggin, Mary. ed. *Sexist Language: A Modern Philosophical Analysis.* Totowa, N.J.: Rowman and Littlefield, 1981.
_____, ed. *"Femininity," "Masculinity," "Androgyny": A Modern Philosophical Analysis.* Totowa, N.J.: Rowman and Littlefield, 1977.
Vetterling-Braggin, Mary, Frederick Elliston, and Jane English, eds. *Feminism and Philosophy.* Totowa, N.J.: Rowman and Littlefield, 1977.
Wolgast, Elizabeth. *The Equality of Women.* Ithaca: Cornell University Press, 1980.

II. Teacher Preparation:

Balbus, Isaac. *Marxism and Domination.* Princeton: Princeton University Press, 1982.
Bazin, N. T. "The Concept of Androgyny: A Working Bibliography." *Women's Studies* 2, no. 2 (1974): 217–36.
English, Jane. "Philosophy." *Signs* 3, no. 4 (1978): 823–31.
Freeman, Eugene, ed. *The Monist* 57, no. 1 (1973). Special issue on "Women's Liberation: Ethical, social and political issues."
Gardiner, Linda. "Can This Discipline Be Saved? Feminist Theory Challenges Mainstream Philosophy." Working Paper No. 118, Wellesley College Center for Research on Women, 1983.
Jaggar, Alison M. *Feminist Politics and Human Nature.* Totowa, N.J.: Rowman & Allanheld, 1983.
Key, M.R. *Male/Female Language: With a Comprehensive Bibliography.* Metuchen, N.J.: Scarecrow Press, 1975.
Lakoff, Robin. *Language and Woman's Place.* New York: Harper & Row, 1975.

Longino. Helen E. "Scientific Objectivity and Feminist Theorizing." *Liberal Education* 67 (Fall 1981): 187–95.
McConnell-Ginet, Sally, Ruth Borker, and Nelly Furman, eds. *Women and Language in Literature and Society*. New York: Praeger, 1980.
Moulton, Janice. "Philosophy." *Signs* 2, no. 2 (1976): 422–33.
Osborne, Martha L. *Genuine Risk*. Indianapolis: Hackett. 1981.
Thorne, Barrie, and Nancy Henley, eds. *Language and Sex: Difference and Dominance*. Rowley, Mass.: Newbury House, 1975.
Warren, Mary Ann, ed. *The Nature of Woman: An Encyclopedia*. Point Reyes, Calif.: Edgepress, 1980.

PSYCHOLOGY AND EDUCATION

I. Classroom Use:

Berman, Phyllis, and Estelle Ramey. *Women: A Developmental Perspective*. Bethesda, Md.: U.S. Department of Health and Human Services, Public Health Service, National Institutes of Health Publication No. 82-2298. 1982.
Frieze, Irene, and Esther Sales, eds. *Women and Sex Roles: A Social Psychological Perspective*. New York: W.W. Norton, 1978.
Gilligan, Carol. *In a Different Voice: Psychological Theory and Women's Development*. Cambridge: Harvard University Press, 1982.
Henley, Nancy M. *Body Politics: Power, Sex and Nonverbal Communication*. Englewood Cliffs, N.J.: Prentice-Hall, 1977.
Hyde, Janet, and B.G. Rosenberg, *Half the Human Experience*. 2nd ed. Lexington, Mass.: D.C. Heath, 1980.
Katchadourian, H.A., ed. *Human Sexuality, A Comparative and Developmental Perspective*. Berkeley: University of California Press, 1979.
Kaufman, Deborah, and Barbara Richardson, eds. *Achievement and Woman: Challenging the Assumptions*. New York: The Free Press, 1982.
Kessler, Suzanne, and Wendy McKenna. *Gender, An Ethnomethodological Approach*. New York: Wiley Interscience, 1978.
Kopp, C.B. *Becoming Female: Perspectives on Development*. New York: Plenum Press, 1979.
Laws, J.L., and Pepper Schwartz. *Sexual Scripts*. Lanham, Md.: University Press of America, 1982.
Lloyd, Barbara, and John Archer, eds. *Exploring Sex Differences*. New York: Academic Press, 1976.
May, Robert. *Sex and Fantasy: Patterns of Male and Female Development*. New York: W.W. Norton, 1980.
Miller, Jean Baker. *Toward a New Psychology of Women*. Boston: Beacon Press, 1976.
O'Leary, Virginia. *Toward Understanding Women*. Belmont, Calif.: Wadsworth, 1977.
Pleck, Joseph H., and Jack Sawyer, eds. *Men and Masculinity*. Englewood Cliffs. N.J.: Prentice-Hall, 1974.
Rohrbaugh, Joanna. *Women: Psychology's Puzzle*. New York: Basic Books, 1979.
Sherfey, Mary Jane. *The Nature and Evolution of Female Sexuality*. New York: Random House, 1972; Vintage, 1973.
Sherman, J.A., and F.L. Denmark, eds. *The Psychology of Women: Future Directions of Research*. New York: Psychological Dimensions, 1978.

Tavris, Carol, and Carole Offir. *The Longest War: Sex Differences in Perspective.* New York: Harcourt Brace Jovanovich, 1977.

II. Teacher Preparation:

Bem, Sandra. "Gender Schema Theory and its Implications for Child Development: Raising Aschematic Children in a Gender-Schematic Society." *Signs* 8, no. 4 (1983): 598–617.

Best, Raphaela. *We've All Got Scars: What Boys and Girls Learn in Elementary School.* Bloomington: Indiana University Press, 1983.

Breines, Winifred, and Linda Gordon. "The New Scholarship on Family Violence." *Signs* 8, no. 3 (1983): 490–531.

Brenzel, Barbara. "History of Nineteenth Century Women's Education: A Plea for Inclusion of Class, Race and Ethnicity." Working Paper No. 114, Wellesley College Center for Research on Women, 1983.

Broverman, Inge K., Susan R. Vogel, Paul S. Rosenkrantz, Donald M. Broverman, and Frank E. Clarkson. "Sex Role Stereotypes and Clinical Judgments of Mental Health." *Journal of Consulting Psychology* 34 (1970): 11–17.

Chodorow, Nancy. *The Reproduction of Mothering: Psychoanalysis and the Sociology of Gender.* Berkeley: University of California Press, 1978.

Ferguson, Marilyn. *The Aquarian Conspiracy: Personal and Social Transformation in the 80's.* Los Angeles: J.P. Tarcher, 1980. (New York: distributed by St. Martin's Press).

Giele, Janet. "Adulthood as Transcendence of Age and Sex." In *Themes of Work and Love in Adulthood,* edited by N. Smelser and E. Erikson. Cambridge: Harvard University Press, 1982.

Harvard Educational Review 49, no. 4 (1979) and 50, no. 1 (1980). Issues on Women and Education.

Kegan, Robert. *The Evolving Self: Problem and Process in Human Development.* Cambridge: Harvard University Press, 1982.

Keller, Evelyn Fox. "Gender and Science." *Psychoanalysis and Contemporary Science* 1 (1978): 409–33.

Lewis, Judith Herman. *Father-Daughter Incest.* Cambridge: Harvard University Press, 1982.

McGuigan, D.G., ed. *Women's Lives: New Theory, Research and Policy.* Ann Arbor: University of Michigan, Center for Continuing Education of Women, 1980.

Mednick, Martha. "Psychology of Women: Research Issues and Trends." *New York Academy of Science Annals* 309 (1978): 77–92.

Miller, Patricia, and Martha Fowlkes. "Social and Behavioral Constructions of Female Sexuality." *Signs* 5, no. 4 (1980): 783–800.

Parlee, Mary B. "Psychology." *Signs* 1, no. 1 (1975): 119–38.

Reinharz, Shulamit, Marti Bombyk, and Jan Wright. *Feminist Research Methodology in Sociology and Psychology: A Topical and Chronological Selected Bibliography with Introductory Essays.* Ann Arbor: University of Michigan Press, 1982.

Russo, Nancy F., and Natalie J. Malovich. *Assessing the Introductory Psychology Course.* Washington, D.C.: American Psychological Association, 1982.

Schmuck, Patricia, W.W. Charters, and Richard O. Carlson, eds. *Educational Policy and Management: Sex Differentials.* New York: Academic Press, 1981.

Sherif, Carolyn. "What Every Intelligent Person Should Know About Psychology and Women." In *The Study of Women: Enlarging Perspectives of Social Reality,* edited by E. Snyder. New York: Harper & Row, 1979.

Sherman, Julia. *Sex-related Cognitive Differences: An Essay on Theory and Evidence*. Springfield, Ill.: Charles C. Thomas, 1978.
Speizer, Jean. "Role Models, Mentors and Sponsors: The Elusive Concepts." *Signs* 6, no. 4 (Summer 1981): 692–712.
Stimpson, Catharine, and Ethel Person, eds. *Signs* 5, no. 4, and 6, no. 1 (1981). Special issues on "Women, Sex and Sexuality."
Tyack, David, and Elizabeth Hansot. *Managers of Virtue: Public School Leadership in America, 1820–1980*. New York: Basic Books, 1982.
Vaughter, Reese M. "Psychology." *Signs* 2, no. 1 (1976): 121–33.
Walker, L.E. *The Battered Woman*. New York: Harper & Row, 1979.
Warner, Richard. "Racial and Sexual Bias in Psychiatric Diagnosis, Psychiatrists, and Other Mental Health Professionals Compared By Race and Sex and Discipline." *Journal of Nervous and Mental Disease* 167 (1979): 303–10.

RELIGION

I. Classroom Use:

Bell, Susan G., ed. *Women: From the Greeks to the French Revolution*. Stanford, Calif.: Stanford University Press, 1973.
Clark, Elizabeth, and Herbert Richardson, eds. *Women and Religion: A Feminist Sourcebook of Christian Thought*. New York: Harper & Row, 1977.
Falk, N.A., and Rita M. Gross, eds. *Unspoken Worlds: Women's Religious Lives in Non-Western Cultures*. New York: Harper & Row, 1980.
O'Faolain, Janet, and Lauro Martines, eds. *Not in God's Image: Women in History from the Greeks to the Victorians*. New York: Harper & Row, 1973.
Ruether, Rosemary R., ed. *Religion and Sexism: The Image of Women in the Jewish and Christian Traditions*. New York: Simon & Schuster, 1974.
Ruether, Rosemary R., and R.S. Keller, eds. *Women and Religion in America. Vol. I: The Nineteenth Century. A Documentary History*. New York: Harper & Row, 1981.

II. Teacher Preparation:

Baum, Charlotte, Paula Hyman, and Sonya Michel, eds. *The Jewish Woman in America*. New York: Dial, 1976.
Crumbine, Nancy. "Religion and the Feminist Critique of Culture." Working Paper No. 116, Wellesley College Center for Research on Women, 1983.
Daly, Mary. *The Church and the Second Sex*. New York: Harper & Row, 1968.
———. *Beyond God the Father: Toward a Philosophy of Women's Liberation*. Boston: Beacon Press, 1973.
———. *Gyn/Ecology: The Metaethics of Radical Feminism*. Boston: Beacon Press, 1978.
Engelsman, Joan. *The Feminine Dimension of the Divine*. Philadelphia: Westminster, 1979.
Goldenberg, Naomi. *Changing of the Gods: Feminism and the End of Traditional Religions*. Boston: Beacon Press, 1979.
Heschel, Susannah, ed. *On Being a Jewish Feminist: A Reader*. New York: Schocken, 1983.
Heyob, Sharon. *The Cult of Isis Among Women in the Graeco-Roman World*. London: E.J. Brill, 1975.

Koltun, Elizabeth, ed. *The Jewish Woman: New Perspectives.* New York: Schocken, 1976.

Kraemer, Ross. "Ecstasy and Possession: The Attraction of Women to the Cult of Dionysus." *Harvard Theological Review* 72 (1979): 55–80.

Lefkowitz, Mary. "The Motivations for St. Perpetua's Martyrdom." *Journal of the American Academy of Religion* 44 (September 1976): 417–21.

Ochs, Carol. *Behind the Sex of God.* Boston: Beacon Press, 1977.

Pagels, Elaine. "What Became of God the Mother? Conflicting Images of God in Early Christianity." *Signs* 2, no. 2 (1976): 293–303.

Porterfield, Ann. *Feminine Spirituality in America: From Sarah Edwards to Martha Graham.* Philadelphia: Temple University Press, 1980.

Ruether, Rosemary R. *Faith and Fratricide: The Image of Jews in Early Christianity.* New York: Seabury Press, 1974.

———. *The New Woman/New Earth: Sexist Ideologies and Human Liberation.* New York: Seabury Press, 1975.

———. *Mary: The Feminine Face of the Church.* Philadelphia: Westminster, 1977.

———. *Sexism and God-Talk: Toward a Feminist Theology.* Boston: Beacon Press, 1983.

Ruether, Rosemary R., and Eugene Blanchi, eds. *From Machismo to Mutuality: Essays of Sexism and Woman-Man Liberation.* Ramsey, N.J.: Paulist Press, 1975.

Ruether, Rosemary R., and Eleanor McLaughlin, eds. *Women of Spirit: Female Leadership in the Jewish and Christian Traditions.* New York: Simon & Schuster, 1979.

Trible, Phyllis. *God and the Rhetoric of Sexuality.* Philadelphia: Fortress Press, 1978.

Wilson-Kastner, Patricia, Rosemary Rader, G. Ronald Kastner, Ann Millin, and Jeremiah Reedy, eds. *A Lost Tradition: Women Writers of the Early Church.* Lanham, Md.: University Press of America, 1981.

SCIENCE

I. Classroom Use:

Arditti, Rita, Pat Brennan, and Steve Cavrak, eds. *Science and Liberation.* Boston: South End Press, 1980.

Cole, Stephen, and Jonathan Cole. *Social Stratification in Science.* Chicago: University of Chicago Press, 1973.

Hubbard, Ruth, Mary Sue Henifin and Barbara Fried, eds. *Women Look at Biology Looking at Women.* Cambridge: Schenkman, 1979.

Keller, Evelyn Fox. "Feminism and Science." *Signs* 7, no. 3 (1982): 589–602.

Merchant, Carolyn. *The Death of Nature: Women, Ecology, and the Scientific Revolution.* New York: Harper & Row, 1980.

Perl, Terri. *Math Equals.* Reading, Mass.: Addison-Wesley Publishing Co., 1978.

Roberts, J.L., ed. *Beyond Intellectual Sexism.* New York: David McKay Co., 1976.

Rose, Hilary, and Steven Rose, eds. *Ideology of/in The Natural Sciences.* Boston: G.K. Hall Co., 1980.

Rossiter, Margaret W. *Women Scientists in America: Struggles and Strategies to 1940.* Baltimore: Johns Hopkins University Press, 1982.

Walsh, Mary Roth. *Doctors Wanted; No Women Need Apply: Sexual Barriers in the Medical Profession, 1835–1975.* New Haven: Yale University Press, 1977.

II. Teacher Preparation:

Aldrich, Michele L. "Review Essay: Women in Science." *Signs* 4, no. 1 (1978): 126–35.

Chinn, Phyllis Zweig. *Women in Science and Mathematics: Bibliography.* Distributed by American Association for the Advancement of Science, 1979.

Ehrenreich, Barbara, and Deirdre English, eds. *For Her Own Good: 150 Years of the Experts' Advice to Women.* New York: Anchor Press, 1978.

Fee, Elizabeth. "Is Feminism a Threat to Scientific Objectivity?" *International Journal of Women's Studies* 4, no. 4 (1981): 213–33.

————. "A Feminist Critique of Scientific Objectivity." *Science for the People* 14, no. 4 (July–August 1982): 5–8, 30–33.

Fitzpatrick, M. Louise. "Nursing." *Signs* 2, no. 4 (1977): 818–34.

Fox, Lynn. *The Problem of Women and Mathematics: A Report to the Ford Foundation.* New York: Ford Foundation, 1981.

Fox. Lynn H., Linda Brody, and Dianne Tobin. *Women and the Mathematical Mystique.* Baltimore: Johns Hopkins University Press, 1980.

Frankenstein, Marilyn. "Teaching Radical Math." *Science for the People* 15, no. 1 (1983): 12–17.

Goodfield, June. *An Imagined World.* New York: Harper & Row, 1980.

Gornick, Vivian. *Women in Science: Recovering the Life Within.* New York: Simon & Schuster, 1983.

Haber, Louis. *Women Pioneers in Science.* New York: Harcourt Brace Jovanovich, 1979.

Heresies 13 (1981). Special issue on Feminism and Ecology.

Humphreys, S.M., ed. *Women and Minorities in Science: Strategies for Increasing Participation.* Boulder, Colo.: Westview, 1982.

Jacobs, Judith, ed. *Perspectives on Women and Mathematics.* Reston, Va.: National Council of Teachers of Mathematics, 1978.

Keller, Evelyn Fox. *A Feeling for the Organism: The Life and Work of Barbara McClintock.* New York: W.H. Freeman, 1983.

Kenschaft, Patricia C. "Women in Mathematics around 1900." *Signs* 7, no. 4 (1982): 906–9.

Lantz, Alma. "Strategies to Increase the Number of Women in Science." *Signs* 5, no. 1 (1979): 186–88.

Longino, Helen E. "Scientific Objectivity and Feminist Theorizing." *Liberal Education* 67 (Fall 1981): 187–95.

Lowe, Marian, and Ruth Hubbard, eds. *Woman's Nature: Rationalizations of Inequality.* New York: Pergamon Press, 1983.

Markell Morantz, Regina, Cynthia Pomerleau, and Carol Fenichel, eds. *In Her Own Words: Oral Histories of Women Physicians.* Westport, Conn.: Greenwood Press, 1982.

McGaw, Judith. "Women and the History of American Technology." *Signs* 7, no. 4 (1982): 798–828.

Mozans, H.J. *Women in Science.* Cambridge: M.I.T. Press, 1974.

Rose, Hilary. "Hand, Brain, and Heart: A Feminist Epistemology for the Natural Sciences." *Signs* 9, no. 1 (Autumn 1983): 73–90.

Sayre, Anne. *Rosalind Franklin and DNA.* New York: W.W. Norton, 1975.

Signs 4, no. 1 (1978). Issue on "Women, Science, and Society."

Verbrugge, Martha M. "Women and Science in Nineteenth Century America." *Signs* 1, no. 4 (1976): 957–72.

Vetter, Betty M. "Women in the Natural Sciences." *Signs* 1, no. 3 (1976): part 1, 713–20.

SOCIOLOGY
I. Classroom Use:

Andersen, Margaret. *Thinking About Women: Sociological and Feminist Perspectives.* New York: Macmillan, 1983.

Bernard, Jessica. *The Female World.* New York: Free Press, 1981.

Bowker, Lee, ed. *Women and Crime in America.* New York: Macmillan, 1981.

Davis, Angela. *Women, Race and Class.* New York: Random House, 1981.

Freeman, Jo. *Women: A Feminist Perspective.* 3rd. ed. Palo Alto, Calif.: Mayfield, 1983.

Hess, Elizabeth, Elizabeth Markson, and Peter Stein, eds. *Sociology.* New York: Macmillan, 1982.

Hooks, Bell. *Ain't I a Woman? Black Women and Feminism.* Boston: South End Press, 1981.

Janeway, Elizabeth. *Powers of the Weak.* New York: Alfred A. Knopf, 1980.

Kahn-Hut, Rachel, Arlene K. Daniels, and Richard Colvard, eds. *Women and Work: Problems and Perspectives.* New York: Oxford University Press, 1982.

Kanter, Rosabeth M. *Men and Women of the Corporation.* New York: Basic Books, 1977.

La Rodgers-Rose, Frances, ed. *The Black Woman.* Beverly Hills, Calif.: Sage Publishers, 1980.

Lerner, Gerda, ed. *Black Women in White America.* New York: Vintage Books, 1973.

Melville, Margarita. *Twice a Minority: Mexican-American Women.* St. Louis, Mo.: C.V. Mosby, 1980.

Mora, Magdalena, and Adelaida del Castillo, eds. *Mexican Women in the United States: Struggles Past and Present.* Los Angeles: University of California Chicano Studies Research Center Pubs., 1980.

Richardson, Laura W. *The Dynamics of Sex and Gender.* Boston: Houghton-Mifflin, 1981.

Richardson, Laura, and Verta Taylor. *Feminist Frontiers: Rethinking Sex, Gender and Society.* Reading, Mass.: Addison-Wesley, 1983.

Ruddick, Sara, and Pamela Daniels, eds. *Working It Out: 23 Women Writers, Artists, Scientists and Scholars Talk about Their Lives and Work.* New York: Pantheon Books, 1977.

Signs 5, no. 3 (1980). Issue on Women and the American City.

Stack, Carolyn. *All Our Kin: Strategies for Survival in a Black Community.* New York: Harper & Row, 1975.

Snyder, Eloise, ed. *The Study of Women: Enlarging Perspectives of Social Reality.* New York: Harper & Row, 1979.

Thorne, Barrie, and Marilyn Yalom, eds. *Rethinking the Family: Some Feminist Questions.* New York: Longman, 1982.

II. Teacher Preparation:

Andersen, Margaret. "Thinking About Women and Rethinking Sociology." Working Paper No. 113, Wellesley College Center for Research on Women, 1983.

Baca Zinn, Maxine. "Mexican-American Women in the Social Sciences." *Signs* 8, no. 2 (1982): 259–72.

Breines, Winifred, and Linda Gordon. "The New Scholarship on Family Violence." *Signs* 8, no. 3 (1983): 490–531.

Conklin, Nancy, Brenda McCallum, and Marcia Wade, eds. *The Culture of Southern Black Women, Approaches and Materials.* Archive of American Minority and Women's Studies Program. University: University of Alabama Press, 1983.

English, Jane, ed. *Sex Equality.* Englewood Cliffs, N.J.: Prentice-Hall, 1977.
Epstein, Cynthia F. "Women in Sociological Analysis: New Scholarship Versus
  Old Paradigms." *Soundings* 4 (1981): 485–98. Repr. in *A Feminist Perspective in
  the Academy,* edited by E. Langland and W. Gove. Chicago: University of Chi-
  cago Press, 1983.
Epstein, Cynthia F., and Rose Coser, eds. *Access to Power: Cross-National Studies
  on Women and Elites.* Winchester, Mass.: George Allen and Unwin, 1981.
Gordon, Francine E., and Myra H. Strober, eds. *Bringing Women into Manage-
  ment.* New York: McGraw-Hill, 1975.
Gould, Meredith. "The New Sociology." *Signs* 5, no. 3 (1980): 459–67.
Krieger, Susan. "Lesbian Identity and Community: Recent Social Science Litera-
  ture." *Signs* 8, no. 1 (1982): 91–108.
Millman, Marcia, and Rosabeth Kanter, eds. *Another Voice.* New York: Double-
  day, 1975.
Roberts, Helen. "Some of the Boys Won't Play Anymore: The Impact of Femin-
  ism on Sociology." In *Men's Studies Modified,* edited by D. Spender. New York:
  Pergamon Press, 1981.
Rossi, Alice, ed. *Essays on Sex Equality.* Chicago: University of Chicago Press,
  1970.
Scott, Patricia Bell. "Debunking Sapphire: Toward a Non-Racist and Non-Sexist
  Social Science." In *All the Women Are White, All the Blacks Are Men, But Some
  of Us Are Brave: Black Women's Studies,* edited by G. Hull, P.B. Scott and B.
  Smith. Old Westbury, N.Y.: The Feminist Press, 1983. Pp. 85–92.
Smith, Dorothy. "Women's Perspective as a Radical Critique of Sociology."
  Sociology Inquiry 44 (1974): 7–13.
———. "A Sociology for Women." In *The Prism of Sex: Essays in the Sociology
  of Knowledge,* edited by J. Sherman and E. Beck. Madison: The University of
  Wisconsin Press, 1979. Pp. 135–87.
Wekerle, Gerda. "Women in the Urban Environment." *Signs* 5, no. 3 (1980):
  S188–S214 (Supplement).
Westkott, Marcia. "Feminist Criticism of the Social Sciences." *Harvard Educa-
  tional Review* 49 (1979): 422–30.

THEATER

I. Classroom Use:

Barlow, Joel, ed. *Plays by American Women: The Early Years.* New York: Avon/
  Bard, 1981.
Bogle, Donald. *Brown Sugar: Eighty Years of America's Black Female Superstars.*
  New York: Harmony Books, 1980.
Chinoy, Helen K., and Linda W. Jenkins, eds. *Women in American Theatre.* New
  York: Crown, 1981.
Cohen, Robert. *The Theatre.* Palo Alto, Calif.: Mayfield, 1981.
France, Rachel, ed. *A Century of Plays By American Women.* New York: Richards
  Rosen Press, 1979.
Kriegel, Harriet, ed. *Women in Drama: An Anthology.* New York: New American
  Library: Mentor Books, 1975.
Malpede, Karen, ed. *Women in Theatre: Compassion and Hope.* New York:
  Drama Book Publishers, 1983.
Moore, Honor, ed. *The New Women's Theatre: Ten Plays by Contemporary Ameri-
  can Women.* New York: Vintage Press, 1977.

Sampson, Henry, ed. *Blacks in Blackface: A Sourcebook on Early Black Musical Shows.* Metuchen, N.J.: Scarecrow Press, 1980.
Sullivan, Victoria, and James Hatch, eds. *Plays by and about Women: An Anthology.* New York: Random House, 1974.
Wandor, Michelene. *Plays by Women*, Vol. 1. New York: Eyre Methuen Press, 1982.

II. Teacher Preparation:

Brown, Janet. *Feminist Drama: Definition and Critical Analysis.* Metuchen, N.J.: Scarecrow Press, 1979.
Coven, Brenda. *American Women Dramatists of the Twentieth Century: A Bibliography.* Metuchen, N.J.: Scarecrow Press, 1982.
Diamond, Arlyn, and Lee R. Edwards, eds. *The Authority of Experience: Essays in Feminist Criticism.* Amherst: University of Massachusetts Press, 1977.
French, Marilyn. *Shakespeare's Division of Experience.* New York: Summit Books, 1981.
Gilder, Rosamond. *Enter the Actress: The First Women in the Theatre.* New York: Theatre Arts Books, 1960.
Heck-Rabi, Louise. *Women Filmmakers: A Critical Reception.* Metuchen, N.J.: Scarecrow Press, 1984.
Hollander, Anne. *Seeing Through Clothes.* New York: Viking Press, 1975.
Pitt, Angela. *Shakespeare's Women.* Totowa, N.J.: Barnes & Noble, 1981.
Sullivan, Kaye. *Films for, by and about Women.* Metuchen, N.J.: Scarecrow Press, 1980.
Tuchman, Gaye, Arlene Daniels, and James Benet, eds. *Hearth and Home: Images of Women in Mass Media.* New York: Oxford University Press, 1978.

THIRD WORLD

I. Classroom Use:

Bell, Roseanne, Bettye Parker, and Beverley Guy-Sheftall, eds. *Sturdy Black Bridges: Visions of Black Women in Literature.* New York: Anchor Press/Doubleday, 1979.
Bogle, Donald. *Brown Sugar: Eighty Years of America's Black Female Superstars.* New York: Harmony Books, 1980.
Cade, Toni, ed. *The Black Woman.* New York: Doubleday, 1971.
Caplan, Patricia, and Janet M. Burge, eds. *Women United, Women Divided: Comparative Studies of Ten Contemporary Cultures.* Bloomington: Indiana University Press, 1979.
Christian, Barbara. *Black Women Novelists: The Development of a Tradition, 1892–1976.* Westport, Conn.: Greenwood Press, 1980.
Davis, Angela. *Women, Race and Class.* New York: Random House, 1981.
de Jesus, C.M. *Child of the Dark.* New York: E.P. Dutton, 1962.
Evans, Mari, ed. *Black Women Writers (1950–1980): A Critical Evaluation.* Garden City, N.Y.: Anchor Press/Doubleday, 1984.
Evans, Sara. *Personal Politics: The Roots of Women's Liberation in the Civil Rights Movement and the New Left.* New York: Alfred A. Knopf, 1978; Random House, 1979.
Fisher, Dexter, ed. *The Third Woman: Minority Writers of the United States.* Boston: Houghton Mifflin, 1980.

Hooks, Bell. *Ain't I a Woman? Black Women and Feminism.* Boston: South End Press, 1981.

Hull, Gloria, Patricia B. Scott, and Barbara Smith, eds. *All the Women Are White, All the Blacks Are Men, but Some of Us Are Brave: Black Women's Studies.* New York: Feminist Press, 1982.

Joseph, Gloria I., and Jill Lewis. *Common Differences.* New York: Anchor Press, 1981.

Katz, Jane, ed. *I Am the Fire of Time: The Voices of Native American Women.* New York: E.P. Dutton, 1977.

Katz, Naomi, and Nancy Milton, eds. *Fragment From a Lost Diary and Other Stories: Women of Asia, Africa, and Latin America.* New York: Pantheon Books, 1973.

La Rodgers-Rose, Frances, ed. *The Black Woman.* Beverly Hills, Calif.: Sage Publishers, 1980.

Leacock, Eleanor B., ed. *Myths of Male Dominance: Collected Articles on Women Cross-Culturally.* New York: Monthly Review Press, 1981.

Leghorn, Lisa, and Katherine Parker. *Women's Worth: Sexual Economics and the World of Women.* Boston: Routledge & Kegan Paul, 1981.

Lerner, Gerda, ed. *Black Women in White America.* 2nd ed. New York: Random House, 1973.

Melville, Margarita. *Twice a Minority: Mexican-American Women.* St. Louis, Mo.: C.V. Mosby, 1980.

Meyer, Doris, and Margarite Fernandez-Olmos, eds. *Contemporary Women Authors of Latin America.* Brooklyn: Brooklyn College Press, 1983.

Miller, Beth, ed. *Women in Hispanic Literature.* Berkeley: University of California Press, 1983.

Miller, Yvette E., and Charles M. Tatum, eds. *Latin American Women Writers Yesterday and Today.* Latin American Literary Review, Pittsburgh: University of Pittsburgh Press, 1977.

Mirande, Alfredo, and Evangelina Enriquez. *La Chicana.* Chicago: University of Chicago Press, 1979.

Moraga, Cherrie, and Gloria Anzaldua, eds. *This Bridge Called My Back: Writings by Radical Women of Color.* Watertown, Mass.: Persephone Press, 1981.

Sampson, Henry, ed. *Blacks in Blackface; A Sourcebook on Early Black Musical Shows.* Metuchen, N.J.: Scarecrow Press, 1980.

Stack, Carolyn. *All Our Kin: Strategies for Survival in a Black Community.* New York: Harper & Row, 1975.

Steady, Filomena C., ed. *The Black Woman Cross-Culturally.* Cambridge: Schenkman Publishing Co., 1981.

Washington, Mary Helen, ed. *Black-Eyed Susans: Classic Stories By and About Black Women.* New York: Anchor/Doubleday, 1975.

_____, ed. *Midnight Birds: Stories of Contemporary Black Women Writers.* New York: Anchor/Doubleday, 1980.

II. Teacher Preparation:

Abadan-Unat, Nermin. *Women in Turkish Society.* London: E.J. Brill, 1982.

Acosta Belen, Etna. *La mujer en la sociedad puertorriqueña.* Rio Piédras, P.R.: Ediciones Huracán, 1980.

Allman, James, ed. *Women's Status and Fertility in the Muslim World.* New York: Praeger, 1978.

Amerasia 4, no. 1 (1977). Special issue on women.

Baca Zinn, Maxine. "Mexican-American Women in the Social Sciences." *Signs* 8, no. 2 (Winter 1982): 259–72.
Bethel, Lorraine, and Barbara Smith, eds. *Conditions: Five (1979).* "The Black Women's Issue."
Bianchi, S.M. *Household Composition and Racial Inequality.* New Brunswick: Rutgers University Press, 1981.
Blicksilver, Edith. *The Ethnic American Woman: Problems, Protests, Lifestyles.* Dubuque, Iowa: Kendall Hunt Publishers, 1979.
Bogle, Donald. *Toms, Coons, Mulattos, Mammys and Bucks.* New York: Viking Press, 1973.
Buvinic, Mayra. *Women and World Development,* Vol. 2. Washington, D.C.: Overseas Development Council, 1976.
Cabello-Argandona, Roberto, Juan Gomez-Quinones, and Patricia Herrera Duran. *The Chicana: A Comprehensive Bibliographic Study.* Los Angeles: University of California Chicano Studies Center, 1975.
Candelaria, Cordelia. "Six Reference Works on Mexican-American Women: A Review Essay." *Frontiers* 5, no. 2 (1980): 75–80.
Chafe, William. *Women and Equality.* New York: Oxford University Press, 1977.
Conklin, Nancy, Brenda McCallum, and Marcia Wade, eds. *The Culture of Southern Black Women, Approaches and Materials.* Archive of American Minority and Women's Studies Program. University: University of Alabama Press, 1983.
Croll, E.J. *Feminism and Socialism in China.* Boston: Routledge & Kegan Paul, 1978.
Davis, Arthur P. *From the Dark Tower: Afro-American Authors, 1900–1960.* Washington, D.C.: Howard University Press, 1974.
Davis, L.G. *The Black Woman in American Society: A Selected Annotated Bibliography.* Boston: G.K. Hall, 1975.
Fernea, Elizabeth, and Basima Beziergan, eds. *Middle Eastern Women Speak.* Austin: University of Texas Press, 1977.
Flora, C.B. "The Passive Female and Social Change." In *Female and Male in Latin America: Essays,* edited by A. Pescatello. Pittsburgh: University of Pittsburgh Press, 1979. Pp. 59–86.
Frontiers, A Journal of Women's Studies 5, no. 2 (1980). Special issue: "Chicanas in the National Landscape."
Gonzáles, Patricia Elena, and Eliana Ortega, eds. *La Sartén por el mango: Encuentro de escritoras latinoamericanas.* Río Piedras, P.R.: Ediciones Huracán, 1984.
Green, Rayna. "Native American Women." *Signs* 6, no. 2 (Winter 1980): 248–67.
———. *Native American Women: A Contextual Bibliography.* Bloomington: Indiana University Press, 1983.
Hafkin, N.H., and E.G. Bay, eds. *Women in Africa: Studies in Social and Economic Change.* Stanford, Calif.: Stanford University Press, 1976.
Heresies 2, no. 4 (1979). Special issue: Third World Women in the U.S.: The Politics of Being Other.
Jackson, Larry. "Welfare Mothers and Black Liberation." *The Black Scholar* 1 (April 1970): 31–37.
Jacobson, Angeline. *Contemporary Native American Literature: A Selected and Partially Annotated Bibliography.* Metuchen, N.J.: Scarecrow Press, 1977.
Johnson, J.G. *Women in Colonial Spanish American Literature: Literary Images.* Westport, Conn.: Greenwood Press, 1983.
Kent, George. *Blackness and the Adventure of Western Culture.* Chicago: Third World Press, 1972.

————. "Maya Angelou's *I Know Why the Caged Bird Signs* and Black Autobiographical Tradition." *Kansas Quarterly* 7, no. 3 (1975): 72–78.

Knaster, Meri. *Women in Spanish America: An Annotated Bibliography from Preconquest to Contemporary Times*. Boston: G.K. Hall, 1977.

La Luz 6, no. 11 (1977). Special issue on Hispanic Women in America.

Lavrin, Asuncion, ed. *Latin American Women: Historical Perspectives*. Westport, Conn.: Greenwood Press, 1978.

Lerner, Gerda. *The Majority Finds Its Past: Placing Women in History*. New York: Oxford University Press, 1979.

Loeb, Catherine. "La Chicana: A Bibliographic Survey." *Frontiers* 5, no. 2 (1980): 59–74.

Lowenberg, B.J., and Ruth Bogin, eds. *Black Women in the Nineteenth Century: Their Words, Their Thoughts, Their Feelings*. University Park: Pennsylvania State University Press, 1976.

Maher, Vanessa. *Women and Property in Morocco: Their Changing Relation to the Process of Social Stratification in the Middle Atlas*. Cambridge: Cambridge University Press, 1974.

Meghdessian, S.R. *The Status of the Arab Woman: A Select Bibliography*. Westport, Conn.: Greenwood Press, 1980.

Mora, Magdalina, and Adelaida R. Del Castillo, eds. *Mexican Women in the United States: Struggles Past and Present*. Los Angeles: University of California, Chicano Studies Research Center Pubs., 1980.

Navarro, Marysa. "Review Essay: Research on Latin American Women." *Signs* 5, no. 1 (1979): 111–20.

Off Our Backs 9, no. 10 (1979). Special issue on racism.

Off Our Backs 9, no. 13 (1979). Special issue: "The Varied Voices of Black Women."

Rushing, Andrea B. "Images of Black Women in Afro-American Poetry." *Black World* 24 (September 1975): 18–30.

Safa, Helen, and June Nash. *Sex and Class in Latin America: Women's Perspectives on Economics, Politics, and the Family in the Third World*. Rev. ed. South Hadley, Mass.: Bergin Press, 1980.

Sakala, Carol. *Women of South Asia: A Guide to Resources*. Millwood, N.Y.: Kraus-Thomson, 1980.

Sanchez, Rosauro, and Rosa M. Cruz, eds. *Essays on La Mujer*. Berkeley: University of California, 1977.

Saulniers, Suzanne S., and Cathy A. Rakowski. *Women in the Development Process: A Select Bibliography on Women in Sub-Saharan Africa, and Latin America*. Austin: University of Texas Press, 1978.

Scott, Patricia Bell. "Debunking Sapphire: Toward a Non-Racist and Non-Sexist Social Science." In Hull, Scott, and Smith, *All the Women Are White, All the Blacks Are Men, But Some of Us Are Brave*, pp. 85–92.

Sims, Janet. *The Progress of Afro-American Women: A Selected Bibliography and Resource Guide*. Westport, Conn.: Greenwood Press, 1980.

Smith, Barbara, ed. *Home Girls: A Black Feminist Anthology*. New York: Kitchen Table: Women of Color Press, 1983.

Strobel, Myra. "Review Essay: African Women." *Signs* 8, no. 1 (1982): 109–31.

Wallace, Phyllis. *Black Women in the Labor Force*. Cambridge: M.I.T. Press, 1980.

Warner, Richard. "Racial and Sexual Bias in Psychiatric Diagnosis, Psychiatrists, and Other Mental Health Professionals Compared By Race and Sex and Discipline." *Journal of Nervous and Mental Disease* 169 (1979): 303–10.

Washington, Mary Helen. "Black Women Image Makers." *Black World* 23 (August 1974): 10–18.

Williams, Ora. *American Black Women in The Arts And Social Sciences: A Bibliographical Survey.* Rev. ed. Metuchen, N.J.: Scarecrow Press, 1978.

Notes on Contributors

Marilyn R. Schuster, co-editor, is Associate Professor of French and Comparative Literature at Smith College, where she also served for two years as an academic dean. With Susan Van Dyne she coordinated the original Smith College Curriculum Transformation Project, and they have participated in the Advisory Committee on the Study of Women since its founding. Smith College is the largest privately endowed college for women in the United States and is part of the Five College Consortium that also includes Amherst, Hampshire, and Mount Holyoke colleges, and the University of Massachusetts at Amherst.

Susan R. Van Dyne, co-editor, is Associate Professor of English at Smith College, where she also served for four years as an academic dean. She and Marilyn Schuster designed and coordinated the original Smith College Curriculum Transformation Project and founded the Smith College Advisory Committee on the Study of Women. They have consulted nationally on curriculum transformation with support from the Wellesley College Center for Research on Women.

Margaret L. Andersen is Associate Professor of Sociology and Director of the Women's Studies Interdisciplinary Program at the University of Delaware. She has lectured and published on black studies, women's studies, and the connections between them. She has served as a fellow at the Wellesley College Center for Research on Women and has consulted nationally on feminist transformation of the curriculum.

Judith Anderson is Professor of Speech Communication at the University of Rhode Island. With Stephen Grubman, she has worked in the area of women's studies and lectured on course transformation and the pedagogy of team-teaching, particularly as a man and woman teaching from a feminist perspective in a coeducational setting.

Elizabeth Arch is a lecturer in the Education Department at Lewis and Clark College. With Jane Monnig Atkinson and Susan Kirschner, she has written and lectured about the Lewis and Clark curriculum project. Lewis and Clark is a four-year coeducational college with a strong commitment to the liberal arts, in Portland, Oregon.

Jane Monnig Atkinson, an anthropologist, is Assistant Professor of Sociology at Lewis and Clark College. With Elizabeth Arch and Susan Kirschner, she has written and lectured about the Lewis and Clark curriculum project.

Johnnella E. Butler is Chair of the Afro-American Studies Department at Smith College and Co-Director of the FIPSE-funded project, Black Studies/Women's Studies: An Overdue Partnership. The project was the first of its kind, bringing together teachers in black studies and women's studies, and was situated in the Five College Consortium that includes Smith, Amherst, Hampshire, and Mount

Holyoke colleges, and the University of Massachusetts at Amherst. She has lectured nationally on black studies, women's studies, and curriculum transformation.

Barbara Caruso is Associate Professor of English and Coordinator of Women's Studies at Earlham College and Director of the 1983 Great Lakes Colleges Association National Summer Institute in Women's Studies (originally funded by the Lilly Endowment).

Myra Dinnerstein is chairperson of Women's Studies and Director of the Southwest Institute for Research on Women (SIROW) at the University of Arizona. She directed a major curriculum integration project at Arizona funded by the National Endowment for the Humanities and is now Co-Director of the Western States Project on Women in the Curriculum, funded by the Ford Foundation. She has lectured and consulted nationally on integrating feminist scholarship into the curriculum and organized the first national conference for curriculum integration projects, in 1981.

Jeanine Elliot is Associate Director of the School of Liberal and Professional Studies at Stephens College and coordinates an on-going, multi-faceted project to integrate women's studies into the curriculum, originally funded by the National Endowment for the Humanities. She is currently Director of the Women's Studies Senior Colloquium Curriculum Project at Stephens. Stephens College, in Columbia, Missouri, originally a two-year privately endowed college for women, became a four-year liberal arts college for women in the mid-sixties. Their curriculum integration project is part of their commitment to a strong liberal arts and pre-professional curriculum for women.

Stephen Grubman is Associate Professor of Communication Disorders at the University of Rhode Island. With Judith Anderson he has worked in the area of women's studies and lectured on course transformation and the pedagogy of team-teaching, particularly as a man and a woman teaching from a feminist perspective in a coeducational setting.

Susan Kirschner is a lecturer in the English Department at Lewis and Clark College. She served as coordinator of a Faculty Development Seminar on Women's Studies, funded by the National Endowment for the Humanities. The purpose of the seminar was to help faculty members teaching in the core general studies program prepare and incorporate materials and perspectives on women in their courses.

Helen E. Longino is Associate Professor of Philosophy and Coordinator of Women's Studies at Mills College. She has lectured and written about a feminist transformation of philosophy and particularly the philosophy of science. Mills College is a privately endowed college for women in Oakland, California.

Katherine Loring is Women's Studies Coordinator for the Great Lakes Colleges Association. Located in Ann Arbor, Michigan, the G.L.C.A. is a consortium of twelve colleges and universities: Albion, Antioch, Denison, Depauw, Earlham, Hope, Kalamazoo, Kenyon, Oberlin, Ohio Wesleyan, Wabash and Wooster.

Nancy Mairs, a poet and essayist, is the Assistant Director for the Ford Foundation-funded Western States Project on Women in the Curriculum in the Southwest Institute for Research on Women.

Elaine Marks is the director of the Women's Research Center and a Professor in the Department of French and Italian at University of Wisconsin in Madison. She has written and lectured widely on French feminist theory, French women writers, and the connections between French feminism(s) and American women's studies.

Sue V. Rosser is Associate Professor of Biology and Coordinator of Women's Studies at Mary Baldwin College. she has presented papers and consulted nationally on feminist transformation in the teaching of the sciences. Mary Baldwin College is a privately endowed college for women in Staunton, Virginia.

Greta Salem is Associate Professor of Political Science at Alverno College. With Stephen Sharkey she developed interdisciplinary courses in the social sciences as part of a curriculum project sponsored by the Public Leadership Education Network, funded by Carnegie. Alverno College is a Catholic women's college in Milwaukee, Wisconsin, with a long-standing commitment to participatory learning and with a substantial number of older, returning students.

John Schilb, formerly Assistant Professor of English at the University of North Carolina at Wilmington, is currently vice president of the Associated Colleges of the Midwest. He participated in the M.L.A./N.E.H. Institute on Women's Nontraditional Literature and the G.L.C.A. Summer Institute in Women's Studies and has written and lectured about transforming the curriculum by paying attention to differences of race, gender, and class.

Betty Schmitz is an assistant dean in the College of Letters and Science at Montana State University in Bozeman and co-directs the Western States Project on Women in the Curriculum. She directed two major curriculum change projects at Montana State University, an internal faculty development program funded by the Women's Educational Equity Act Program, 1979–81, and a regional program funded by the Fund for the Improvement of Postsecondary Education, 1981–83.

Stephen Sharkey is Associate Professor of Sociology at Alverno College. With Greta Salem he developed interdisciplinary courses in the social sciences as part of a curriculum transformation project sponsored by the Public Leadership Education Network, funded by Carnegie.

Bonnie B. Spanier, formerly Assistant Professor of Biology, was the Director of the three-year FIPSE-funded project to "gender-balance" the curriculum at Wheaton College. She is now the Director and Assistant Professor of Women's Studies at the State University of New York at Albany. Wheaton College is a privately endowed college for women in Norton, Massachusetts.